LEADERSHIP AND MANAGEMENT IN THE 21ST CENTURY

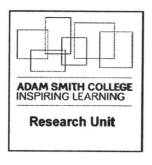

ADAM SMITH COLLEGE
INSPIRING LEARNING

Research Unit

LEADERSHIP AND MANAGEMENT IN THE 21ˢᵀ CENTURY

BUSINESS CHALLENGES OF THE FUTURE

Edited by
CARY L. COOPER

OXFORD
UNIVERSITY PRESS

OXFORD

UNIVERSITY PRESS

Great Clarendon Street, Oxford OX2 6DP

Oxford University Press is a department of the University of Oxford.
It furthers the University's objective of excellence in research, scholarship,
and education by publishing worldwide in

Oxford New York

Auckland Cape Town Dar es Salaam Hong Kong Karachi
Kuala Lumpur Madrid Melbourne Mexico City Nairobi
New Delhi Shanghai Taipei Toronto

With offices in

Argentina Austria Brazil Chile Czech Republic France Greece
Guatemala Hungary Italy Japan South Korea Poland Portugal
Singapore Switzerland Thailand Turkey Ukraine Vietnam

Oxford is a registered trade mark of Oxford University Press
in the UK and in certain other countries

Published in the United States
by Oxford University Press Inc., New York

© Gary L. Cooper 2005

First published 2005
Reprinted 2006

British Library Cataloguing in Publication Data
Data available

Library of Congress Cataloging in Publication Data
Data available

ISBN 0–19–926336–1

3 5 7 9 10 8 6 4 2

Typeset by Kolam Information Services Pvt. Ltd, Pondicherry, India
Printed in Great Britain
on acid-free paper by
Biddles Ltd., King's Lynn, Norfolk

Contents

List of Figures

List of Tables

Contributors

CARY L. COOPER, CBE Editor, Professor of Organizational Psychology and Health, Lancaster University Management School, UK and Pro Vice Chancellor, Lancaster University, UK

CHRIS ARGYRIS Professor of Educational and Organizational Behavior, Harvard Business School, USA

GEOFF ARMSTRONG Director General, Chartered Institute of Personnel and Development, UK

SIR MICHAEL BICHARD Director, The London Institute, UK

SUE COX Dean, Lancaster University Management School, UK

SIR HOWARD DAVIES Formerly CEO, The Financial Services Authority, Director of LSE, UK

FRED E. FIEDLER Professor Emeritus of Psychology and Management and Organization, University of Washington, USA

STEVE FOX Director of Research, Centre for Excellence in Leadership, Lancaster University Management School, UK

JOSEPH E. GARCIA Director, Center for Excellence in Management Education, Western Washington University, USA

VAL GOODING, CBE CEO, BUPA, UK

KEITH GRINT Professor, Lancaster University Management School, UK

PRABHU GUPTARA Executive Director, Wolfsberg (a subsidiary of UBS), Evmatingen, Switzerland

ANNE SIGISMUND HUFF Formerly Director, Advanced Management Institute, UK

NADA KAKABADSE Professor of Management and Business Research, University College Northampton, UK

ANDREW KAKABADSE Deputy Director, Cranfield School of Management, UK

GARY P. LATHAM Secretary of State Professor of Organizational Behaviour, University of Toronto, Canada

CYNTHIA D. MCCAULEY Center for Creative Leadership, University of Toronto

HAMISH MCRAE Associate Editor, *The Independent*, UK

KATHRIN MOESLEIN Research Associate, Advanced Management Institute, UK

DAVID RHIND, CBE Vice Chancellor, City University London, UK

CHRISTOPHER RODRIGUES CEO, Bradford & Bingley plc, UK

WILLIAM H. STARBUCK The Stern School, New York University, USA

KEN STARKEY Professor of Management and Organizational Learning, Nottingham University Business School, UK

SUE TEMPEST Nottingham University Business School, UK

Introduction

Cary L. Cooper

The Changing Nature of Work

The 1980s was described as the decade of the 'enterprise culture', with people working longer and harder to achieve individual success and material rewards. Globalization, privatization, process re-engineering, mergers and acquisitions, strategic alliances, joint ventures, and the like, all combine to transform workplaces into hot-house, free-market environments (Cooper, 1999).

By the end of the 1980s and into the early 1990s, a major restructuring of work, as we have never known it since the industrial revolution, was beginning to take place. The early years of the decade were dominated by the effects of the recession and efforts to get out of it. Organizations throughout the Western world, and even further afield, dramatically 'downsized', 'delayered', 'flattened', or 'rightsized'. Whatever euphemism you care to use, the hard reality experienced by many was job loss and wrenching change. Now, many organizations are smaller, with fewer people doing more and feeling much less secure. New technology, rather than being our saviour, has added the burden of information overload, as well as accelerating the pace of work at a greater speed of response (e.g. e-mails). And, at the same time, as more and more companies adopt a global perspective, organizations and the individuals they employ are finding that success in the global arena requires fundamental changes in organizational structures as well as individual competencies.

As Burke and Cooper (2003) suggest in their book *Lending in Turbulent Times*

some of the dramatic changes affecting work and organizations include increased global competition, the impact of information technology, the re-engineering of business processes, smaller companies that employ fewer people, the shift from making a product to providing a service, and the increasing disappearance of the job as a fixed collection of tasks. These forces have produced wrenching changes in all industrialized economies.

Just as organizations are redesigning to be more flexible and adaptive, individuals are expected to be open to continual change and life-long learning. Workers will be expected to diagnose their abilities, know where to get appropriate training in deficient skills, know how to network, be able to market themselves to organizations professionally, and tolerate ambiguity and insecurity.

As more organizations experiment with 'outsourcing', 'market testing', 'interim management', and the like, many more of us will be selling our services to organizations on a freelance or short-term contract basis. We are creating a corporate culture of blue-collar, white-collar, managerial, and professional temps—in a phrase, a 'contingent workforce'.

In predicting the nature of future organizations, Cooper and Jackson (1999) argue in their book *Creating Tomorrow's Organiza-*

tions that 'most organizations will have only a small core of full-time, permanent employees, working from a conventional office. They will buy most of the skills they need on a contract basis, either from individuals working at home and linked to the company by computers and modems (teleworking), or by hiring people on short-term contracts to do specific jobs or carry out specific projects'. In this way, companies will be able to maintain the flexibility they need to cope with a rapidly changing world (Handy, 1994; Makin *et al.*, 1996), or as Burke and Cooper (2003) suggest 'management has become more informational, based on knowledge workers, knowledge management, and learning organization concepts. Organizational structures have also changed dramatically from hierarchical command and control structured to flatter, network structures. Organizations are increasingly becoming flexible, more people centred, and fluid.'

In addition, as Burke and Cooper (2003) highlight:

the new world of work is also characterized by increasing diversity among employees. Dimensions among which employees may differ include gender, age, marital status, parental status, race ethnicity, education, sexual orientation, job tenure and experience, and physical disability. There is a sense that diversity has both potential benefits as well as disadvantages. The benefits include a more inclusive and representative workforce and services, and more innovation as a consequence of the existence of multiple perspectives. Disadvantages are thought to include heightened tensions between various subgroups and more flexibility in meeting these needs.

This means managing enormous change, as well as widening diversity. So what does the Twenty-First Century require in terms of management style and leadership?

Management Style and Leadership

Bertrand Russell (1962: 11) divided work into two kinds:

first, altering the position of matter at or near to the earth's surface relatively to other such matter; second, telling other people to do so. The first is unpleasant and ill paid; the second is pleasant and highly paid. The second kind is capable of indefinite extension; there are not only those who give orders but those who give advice as to what orders should be given.

Few managers would accept Russell's analysis concerning pleasure and pay, but many will have suffered from the extension of advice. It is interesting to note, however, that the piece was originally written in 1932, at a time when the emphasis in industry was still on 'power'; for example, using steam or electricity to power large machines. Since the Second World War, however, the emphasis has shifted from 'power' to 'control'; what has become known as the 'cybernetic revolution' and 'information technology' (Cooper and Makin, 1981; Makin, et al., 1996).

During this period, we have seen the rise of 'the manager' and recognition of the manager's role as a control mechanism. Within this role are, of course, aspects that require particular specialist knowledge; but of equal, and some might argue, greater importance, is a manager's skill at managing people. We would have no trouble finding definitions of the role of managers or management from among the best-sellers of Drucker or other leadership gurus, but the approach that appeals is to try to categorize the different types of managers by acknowledging the reality that individual managers behave in quite different ways.

Charles Handy wrote in 1976 that 'the last quarter century has seen the emergence of "the manager" as a recognized occupational role in society'. He then went on to suggest that managers seem to be increasingly playing two primary sets of roles: the manager as a *person* or the manager as a General Practitioner (GP). The manager as a person alludes to the increasing professionalization of managers, so that managers are acquiring a set of skills which are, and arguably should be, independent of any organization for whom he/she does, or could, work. Since organizations seem to have cared less for the home/work interface concerns of their managers than previously (Cooper and Lewis, 1998), it is in their interest to make sure they continue to make themselves marketable by further education and career-management. The manager as a GP concept, on the other hand, is based on the premise that the manager is the 'first recipient of problems' which require solutions or decisions. It is the role of the manager in this context to carry out four basic activities at work: (i) identify the symptoms in the situation; (ii) diagnose the cause of trouble; (iii) decide how to deal with it; and (iv) start the treatment or make the decision to create the action plans. Handy argued that all too often the symptoms were treated like diseases in the 'industrial wards' of the country, and that managers who did not follow the medical model above in dealing with issues and problems, but stopped at stage one, found that the illness or sources of grievance return in the same form or in disguise. Frequently, we find managers who can diagnose the symptoms, such as poor morale or bad communications, but then provide solutions without knowing the cause: for example, poor communications—start in-house journal; late arrivals to work—introduce time-clocks, etc. In order to identify adequately and accurately problems or situations, it is absolutely essential to understand the needs of individual workers, be they other managers or unskilled labourers. Diagnosis not only involves understanding individual behaviour but also the dynamics of groups developed sense of social skills and timing, but little else. He is the entrepreneur in its most extreme form.

The next managerial prototype is the *Agent*. He/she acts on behalf of others, takes no decisions hisself or herself and has historical roots in the commercial world of nineteenth-century England. His/her contemporary counterpart is the 'middle manager' of today, who feels, not by choice, that his power and ability to influence decisions is declining (due to globalization, mergers and acquisitions, the short-term contract culture, and so on).

The *Scientific Manager* is another breed of executive who is seen in organizational jungles from time to time. He or she tends to make decisions based on what appear to be rational and appropriate data, but frequently ignore the 'people problems' that result from these decisions or are created by them. In contrast to the factual manager, is the *Managerial Quisling*, or as Mant puts it, 'the manager in the role of the pal'. This stems from the human relations school of management of the 1940s, 1950s, and 1960s. This prototypic manager is one who is supposed to be concerned with the quality of worklife and the well-being of workers. This species of manager comes in different varieties. First, there is the *Genuine Quisling*, who really is concerned about the worker's health and well-being. Incidentally, this type of manager is usually so naive about the politic of his organization that he or she fails to achieve objectives, or achieves them at the expense of other people. Second, there is the *Entrepreneurial Quisling*, who 'appears to care' but is really using the 'flavour of the month' managerial style to achieve recognition, or enhance their own image, or accomplish some political manoeuvre. He is the classic Milo Minder-binder in Heller's Catch-22; 'it's all in the syndicate and everybody has a share'.

Another managerial prototype is the *Manager as a Technocrat*. This type of manager handles all issues as if they were technical problems capable of stress analysis, critical path analysis, and so on. His/her concern for the 'people component' is once again a mere 'given' in the decision-making process.

And finally, there is the *Manager as a Constitutionalist*. This style of management is not unlike the early Tavistock approach to applied problems in industry, in that it relies heavily on contractual arrangements. That is to say, they believe fundamentally that psychological contracts between individuals or representatives of groups are essentially for harmonious relationships at work. Managers are effective, according to this strategy, if they work with their subordinates and colleagues in designing contractual arrangements on most issues of importance. This reduces ambiguity and heightens the boundaries on tasks, roles, and organizational units.

What Mant (1977) did in trying to identify managerial types is to suggest implicitly that each of the caricatures of prototypic executives is ineffective, but in different ways. And although some managers utilize (consistently) one or more of these styles than others, the well-rounded and Twenty-First-Century manager will require a behavioural repertoire that encompasses nearly the whole range, but used flexibly and appropriately.

Makin *et al.*, (1996) later defined a number of leadership types that seemed to be emerging in the 1990s. They were 'the bureaucrat', 'the autocrat', 'the wheeler-dealer', 'the *laissez-faire*', 'the reluctant' and 'the open manager'.

The Bureaucrat. The bureaucrat will tend to be authoritarian, but will stay within the rules, and his or her limits of authority. They will tend to use the powers provided by the organization when dealing with subordinates. These are generally those of *position power*, based on their position within the organization, and *resource power*, based on their control of rewards. When dealing with superiors they will generally be compliant, but if they believe that rules are being broken they may use their control of information as a source of power. This may be used either positively, for example by the 'leaking' of information damaging to the superior, or negatively, by holding back information that would allow the system to take corrective action.

The Autocrat. Like the bureaucrat, the autocrat will use those sanctions that his or her position in the organization provides. These are position power and resource power. If the organization allows, they may also use coercive power. The 'benevolent' autocrat is likely to use resource power quite effectively, giving infrequent unpredictable, but large rewards (variable-ratio reinforcement).

The Wheeler-Dealer. The wheeler-dealer is often a senior manager who spends much of his or her time negotiating with other departments over the allocation of resources. Staff are not given much guidance and are often left to 'sink or swim' but initiatives by staff are usually well supported. Non-performance tends to be ignored. There is a general feeling of dynamism in the department, but also a certain amount of chaos.

The wheeler-dealer's style may range from the consultative, through participative to *laissez-faire.* They often delegate quite considerably but sometimes, especially at times of stress, they may show a flash of authoritarianism. Often they will regret this when things cool down, and smooth the feathers they have ruffled. They often use personal power—people work hard for them because they admire them. Approval is withdrawn from those not performing up to the mark.

The Laissez-faire Manager. This is often the style of a manager who has been promoted on the basis of his or her high level of technical competence. They are not, however, interested in managing. They are very energetic, enthusiastic, creative, and give strong verbal support to initiatives. In some respects they are very similar to the wheeler-dealer, but their interests are on the technical aspects of the job rather than managerial.

The Reluctant Manager. The reluctant manager has, like the *laissez-faire* manager, been promoted on the grounds of technical competence. The main difference between them is their behaviour towards their subordinates. They generally leave their department to run itself but, unlike the *laissez-faire* manager, they do not encourage their staff in any way. If a technical problem arises then they will offer help, if asked, and this help will be highly effective. The management of the department both internally and externally, is ignored. The management style is so *laissez-faire* as to be almost non-existent. Sanctions are rarely used.

The Open Manager. This manager has a very firm belief in the value of participation and getting everyone involved. He or she holds regular meetings to review progress and decide on future actions, as well as *ad hoc* gatherings of subgroups, or the department as a whole, to deal with issues as they arise. Most people appreciate this, but there is the feeling that on occasions too much time is spent ensuring that all involved are committed, when this commitment is not really necessary. Highly participative with 'position' and 'resource' power used only if and when required. They may also have some 'personal' power and are admired by their subordinates.

There have been many theories about what a good manager or leader should be throughout the decades, culminating in an article by Gosling and Mintzberg in 2003 on the 'five minds of a manager' in a recent *Harvard Business Review* article. They contend that there are five managerial mindsets: 'the reflective', 'the analytical', 'the worldly', 'the collaborative', and 'the action' mindsets. Organizations of the future they contend, need leaders or managers who can, from time to time, stop and reflect on their experiences and where they are going, which they term reflective managers. They also need those who can understand at a deeper level what is going on in the organization—'good analysis provides a language for organizing; it allows people to share an understanding of what is driving their effects; it provides measure of performance'. This also requires a more worldly mindset, in our globalized world. We need managers who can understand other cultures and subcultures so they can better plan their own future strategies, markets, etc. Given that there is now a more diverse and dispersed workforce means that managing people and collaborations between people is another critical mindset. This means an engaging but also listening management style. And finally, the authors suggest that 'an action mindset, especially at senior levels, is not about whipping the horses into a frenzy, careering hitherto and yon. It is about developing a sensitive awareness of the terrain and of what the team is capable of doing in it, and thereby helping to set and maintain direction, coaxing everyone along'. It is not only managing change but understanding that 'change has no meaning without continuity'.

The Book

What we need is a systematic exploration of the changing trends in organizations and what this might mean for the managers and leaders in the Twenty-First Century. This book draws on top management academics and practitioners alike to help us define the business trends that will inform us in developing the twenty-first-century manager and business leader of the future.

There is no magic formula that one can derive for designing the prototypic managers for the next decade or two, but there are a range of interesting ideas, given different organizational contexts and developments, about the kind of skills and characteristics that may be needed to manage our institutions in the future. The first two parts of the book are comprised of some of our leading international management scholars exploring the trends and changes needed for managers and business leaders in the future. The third part includes the views of a range of practitioners about their perceptions of the future of work and the role of managers/business leaders—a view from the coalface.

Part I Challenges of the Business Environment

Part I of the book comprises four chapters which explore the context of the business environment and organization and their impact on leadership.

Bill Starbuck begins by exploring the four great conflicts over the next decades: the affluent v. the poor, companies v. nations, top managers and other stakeholders and the short-run v. long-run. He feels that these conflicts can be helpful in stimulating new ideas if managed properly. The chapter identifies issues that managers should consider as they choose actions for themselves and their organizations. The role of the manager in the near future is to 'strongly influence humans' ability to see opportunities in turbulence and take advantage of them'.

Andrew Kakabadse and Nada Kakabadse take a similar view to Latham and McCauley by highlighting that leadership thinking has to encompass the concept of 'cadre' or shared leadership. They emphasize the need to harness the views and behaviours of multiple leaders, through what they term 'polylogues' or multiple dialogues between multiple stakeholders.

Prabhu Guptara feels, on the other hand, that technology itself will create the next generation of business leaders. The role of the manager will be determined by technology, and he highlights a number of 'technological and managerial givens': (1) technology can automate existing processes, (2) technology can build bridges between parts of the corporation, (3) technology can cancel traditional divisions and create entirely new ways of organizing companies, (4) technology can destroy the walls between an organization's internal divisions, and (5) technology can eliminate the boundaries between industries.

Ken Starkey and Sue Tempest take a different tack by suggesting that 'social capital' will be the key focus for the Twenty-First-Century manager and that the future of organizational life increasingly depends on relationships based upon trust, loyalty, connectivity, and communications. Social relationships, if they are to be effective in the long run they contend, depends upon 'cooperation' more than 'competition'.

Part II The Academics' View

The second part of the book looks specifically at leadership and managerial behaviours required over the next couple of decades, from the academics viewpoint.

Chris Argyris highlights the two mindsets that dominate the world of managerial action: 'productive' and 'defensive' reasoning. *Productive reasoning* is used in the service of producing valid knowledge, creating informed choices and emphasizing personal responsibility for the effectiveness of action. This involves (1) understandings the concepts and actions that are necessary to be effective; (2) the causal connections between ideas and actions; and (3) the effective monitoring of the implementation. Anything that promotes productive as opposed to less proactive or ineffective behaviour, or what the author terms defensive reasoning, is what leaders need to implement.

Fred Fiedler and Joseph Garcia emphasize the 'non-linear world' we now live in. They contend that the Twentieth Century was about hierarchy and predictability, based on mass production, standardization, and efficiency. The twenty-first century is moving away from the industrial model, given advances in technology and telecommunication, and moves from mechanistic to organic structures. Leaders are more likely to find themselves working in 'self-managed teams', that rely upon an informal mechanism of communication and co-ordination.

Gary Latham and Cynthia McCauley explore global trends that they feel will change both organizations and how they are managed. First, in terms of selecting and developing leaders for global organization, they feel we have moved from diversity issues *within* a country (eg, race, sex) to diversity *between* countries. Tomorrow's organizational leaders will have to face differences among countries regarding employee ethnicity, religions, national origins, and political ideology. Second, 'the complexity of decision making in global companies will demand a cross discipline perspective, making a functional approach of most business education necessary but not sufficient', therefore, the need for integrated decision making. Third, because of the complexity of organizational life in the Twenty-First Century, there will need to be a movement away from a 'participative management style' to smarter and more adaptable managers—a movement they call 'shared responsibility and accountability'. Fourth, leaders will not need dependent followers but people who can ask constant and changing questions of all organizational activities. That means leaders will be facilitators of shared work. And finally, leadership needs to be a collective as opposed to individual activity.

Keith Grint follows this line of argument, suggesting that since organizations are less hierarchical, with more sophisticated technologies making virtual organizations viable, and a more educated workforce, leaders need to reflect these changes. Traditional modes of leadership therefore are irrelevant to the new order. Drawing on historical precedent, he emphasizes the 'contingent' nature of leadership.

And finally, we conclude the second part of the book by Anne Huff and Kathrin Moeslein who highlight an agenda for understanding individual leadership in corporate leadership systems. They feel that a bridge needs to be created between the needs of individual leaders and the practices of large corporates. They recommend a six-step agenda for future leadership research which focuses on leadership systems within organizations.

Part III The Practitioners' View

In the third part of the book, we ask practitioners what they see as trends and issues that will forge the skills and characteristics of the Twenty-First-Century manager and business leader. We start with Hamish McRae, Associate Editor of *The Independent* and distinguished journalist and author, who suggests that the global economy will mean that managing human capital will be fundamental to the success of global businesses. Managing people from diverse cultures, managing diversified groups of people such as the self-employed, part-timers, the semi-retired, etc., and making the best use of the human capital within organizations will be the real challenges.

Sir Howard Davies, formerly CBI Chairman, CEO of the Financial Services Authority and currently Director of the London School of Economics, describes five trends that will have an impact on managerial behaviour: diverse workforce, short-term contracts, flattened organizational hierarchies, market-based approach to career planning, and issues concerning when people decide to retire.

Geoff Armstrong, who is the Director General of the UK's Chartered Institute of Personnel and Development, suggests that the key to the future success of management is 'managing performance through people'. With globalization and increased competition, the issue of 'managing enhanced performance but humanely' is the answer. In fact, a measure of the success of an organization is the effective management of people, their trust in management and willingness and motivation to want to deliver for the organization,

Sir Michael Bichard, who is Director of the London Institute and former Permanent Secretary to the DfES, talks about managers', whether in the public or private sector, need to be creative and innovative and not administrative. They need the energy to drive people enthusiastically, 'joining up policy and delivery'.

David Rhind CBE, Vice Chancellor of City University, highlights the importance of universities in providing management training but highlights the twenty-first-century management style needed by universities if they are to serve as training providers for others.

Professors Sue Cox (Dean) and Steve Fox, from a world-class management school perspective, explore the challenges for business schools of developing the managers and leaders of the future. They contend that management education in the past has concentrated on training managers and business leaders in the technical skills and in the specifics of their function, rather than in the interpersonal, human, social, cultural, political, and ethical issues and skills that are in today's world the fundamental armoury of leaders.

Val Gooding CBE, from a Chief Executive's (BUPA) perspective, sets the scene for looking at the role of managers and leaders in the management of change. She highlights the importance of work–life balance, communication, personalization, incentives, and meaning at work.

In conclusion, we seem to be moving towards a new leadership model with the bells and whistles of new technology. Trice and Beyer (1991) suggest that there were differences between old leaders and new leaders:

Old leadership	New leadership
Non-charismatic	Charismatic
Transactional	Transformational
Management	Leaders
Non-visionary	Visionary
Non-magical	Magical

In addition, the new leadership paradigm had different emphases:

Less emphasis on	More emphasis on
Planning	Vision
Routine	Change
Compliance	Commitment
Contract	Extra effort
Reaction	Proaction

Put these new leader behaviours together with the changing nature of work and new technology, and we have the beginnings of a new millennial model of leadership. Perhaps George Bernard Shaw described these individuals in *Mrs Warren's Profession*: 'People are always blaming their circumstances for what they are. I don't believe in circumstances. The people who get on in this world are the people who get up and look for the circumstances they want, and if they can't find them, make them.'

References

Burke, R. and Cooper, C. L. (2003). *Leading in Turbulent Times*. Oxford: Blackwell.

Cooper, C. L. (1999). 'The Changing Psychological Contract at Work.' *European Business Journal*, 1999, 115–18.

—— and Jackson, S. (1999). *Creating Tomorrow's Organizations*. New York and Chichester: John Wiley & Sons.

—— and Lewis, S. (1998). *Balancing your Career, Family and Life*. London: Kogan Page.

—— and Makin, P. (1981). *Psychology for Managers*. London: Macmillan and BPS.

Gosling, J. and Mintzberg, H. (2003). 'The Five Minds of a Manager.' *Harvard Business Review*, November 2003, 54–9.

Handy, C. (1976). *Understanding Organizations*. London: Penguin.

—— (1994). *The Empty Raincoat*. London: Hutchinson.

Makin, P., Cooper, C. L., and Cox, C. (1996). *Organizations and the Psychological Contract*. Leicester: BPS Books.

Mant, A. (1977). *The Rise and Fall of the British Manager*. London: Pan.

Russell, B. (1962). *In Praise of Idleness*. London: Unwin.

Trice, H. M. and Beyer, J. (1991). 'Cultural Leadership in Organizations', *Organizational Science*, 2(2), 149–69.

Part I

Challenges of the Business Environment

1

Four Great Conflicts of the Twenty-First Century

William H. Starbuck

What Happened?

In the final years of the twentieth century, their world looked wonderful to people living in developed nations. Employment levels were high. People seemed to be acquiring amazing wealth and they had great confidence in financial leaders. National and local governments were attacking problems, and with the support of high tax revenues, they were producing good results— lower crime, less poverty, better schools. Charismatic and successful business leaders were all around. Globalization was spreading affluence to the less developed nations, where new businesses were springing up and forming alliances with established businesses in the developed nations.

Or so it seemed.

In the early years of the twenty-first century, the euphoria withered, and the economies of developed nations were struggling. The United States, which had generated 40 per cent of the world's apparent economic growth from 1996 to 2000, went into recession and became a drag on the rest of the world (Roach, 2001). Unemployment levels rose in the US, and many Americans lost a third to a half of the wealth they once imagined they had. In Europe and North America, financial leaders have been unable to halt four years of decline, and Japanese leaders have failed for a decade to correct the faults in their economy. National and local governments are running large deficits and abandoning social programmes that had been producing good results. Economic decline exposed some ugly aspects of business behaviour. Once-admired business leaders turned out to be crooks and liars; once-respected professionals proved to be greedy frauds; governmental bodies have made only weak responses. During 2002, armed conflicts involved more than fifty nations, approximately one-quarter of the nations surveyed (National Defense Council Foundation, 2002).

Furthermore, on 11 September 2001, the developed world received an SOS message from the under-developed world. Desperate men from some very traditional nations attacked symbols of military and economic power in the earth's richest nation, one that violates the standards of many traditional societies. Although the motivations for this attack had been rising gradually for many decades, the wealthy and developed nations had depreciated these developments and had continued to behave as if their current policies were effective. Likewise, the large multinational corporations had paid little attention to these developments and had continued to behave as if their current methods of operation were succeeding. In the immediate aftermath of the attacks, two years after them, it is not at all clear that developed nations or multinational corporations understand why the attacks took place. Certainly, they disagree with each other about why the attacks occurred and how to respond to them. Indeed, business and governmental leaders disagree about whether they should cooperate with each other in making responses.

Thus, a few dramatic events revealed serious problems. But these problems did not arise suddenly and they are not ephemeral. They existed long before they made their presence undeniable, and versions of these problems are certain to manifest themselves repeatedly in the future because they have deep roots in human behaviour.

The prevalence of warfare demonstrates humans' propensity for conflict. One can see wars over control of geography, wars between religions, wars between ethnic groups, wars over economic disagreements, wars about political control, wars about control of resources, wars to defend traditions against change, wars to impose change upon traditional societies, and wars over possession of armaments. Large proportions of citizens back leaders who issue violent threats or order armies to war. Where violence is not overt, one can see conflicts about political philosophy, the roles and status of women, social mores, and friendships and alliances. Older people disapprove of younger ones, believers strive to convert doubters, enthusiasts jeer at sceptics, and students calling themselves 'skinheads' confront ones calling themselves 'hippies'. People are jealous, territorial, aggressive, cliquish, quick to anger, grudge-holding, and capable of disagreeing for a multitude of reasons.

Because conflicts are so prevalent and have so many justifications, it would be foolish to predict that some conflicts are going to be especially visible or important. However, four, mutually interdependent arenas of conflict seem likely to have special relevance for managers of large organizations through coming decades:

the conflict between the affluent and the moderately poor,
the conflict between companies and nations,
the conflict between top managers and other stakeholders, and
the conflict between the short run and the long run.

These conflicts are probably going to continue to plague humanity even if they become less noticeable at times. They are not problems that have identifiable solutions. However, managers will exert strong influence over their prominence and pervasiveness, and in the aggregate, managers' actions will influence how much trouble the conflicts generate.

This chapter seeks to identify issues that managers should consider as they choose actions for themselves and their organizations. The chapter explicitly avoids recommendations about how to resolve issues or how to mitigate conflicts. One reason is that the many readers of this book could generate more ideas and better ideas than those of the author. A second reason is that the conflicts manifest themselves in very diverse ways that probably call for very diverse responses. A third reason is that people are more likely to act if they formulate actions for themselves. Although conflicts create turbulence, they also breed opportunities for significant change, and people may be able to extract benefits from this turbulence. Turbulence can spawn innovations and it can stimulate actions that not only reduce the turbulence but improve the lives of many people. Managers will strongly influence humans' ability to see opportunities in turbulence and to take advantage of them. Not only do there seem to be several opportunities for significant restructuring of organizations, of relations between organizations, and of societies, but also new organizational forms have emerged and more will do so.

The Conflict between the Affluent and the Moderately Poor

Even the oldest written documents report arguments about differences in social status, dissatisfaction by those with fewer resources, and protective measures by those with more resources. These disagreements grow much more violent at some times and in some places, as when citizens overthrew aristocracies in France, Russia, China, and Iran. Although disagreements about unequal social statuses pervade human history (Rindova and Starbuck, 1997), technological and social changes over the last 400 years have both increased the differences between the affluent and the poor and made these differences more visible to the poor, thus intensifying their dissatisfaction. Thus, the twenty-first century promises to involve turmoil fed by extreme differences in wealth.

One very important causal factor is population growth. Demographers estimate that the earth's population grew slowly until roughly 1600, when growth accelerated. By the late 1600s, the population was growing twelve times as rapidly as it had over the preceding 2000 years, and it continued to grow at this higher rate until the twentieth century, when it accelerated again. These accelerations resulted from better diets, better sanitation, better housing, better medical care, and higher standards of living[1]: Human fertility increased, child-bearing extended over much longer periods, infant mortality declined precipitously, and life expectancies doubled. By 1950, the population was growing more than twice as rapidly as during the 1800s and almost four times as rapidly as during the 1700s. As a result, the population expanded 60 per cent from 1750 to 1850, and more than 100 per cent from 1850 to 1950. By 1987, the earth held ten times as many people as it had in 1650 (Reinhard *et al.*, 1968; Wrigley, 1969; Cameron, 1993; United Nations, 1998).

Living standards have also gone up. Indeed, some people benefited from dramatic increases at times. For example, Crafts (1985) estimated that British income per person rose 28 per cent from 1700 to 1800, and another 88 per cent between 1800 and 1860. Hourly earnings of American manufacturing workers quadrupled between 1920 and 1970. However, changes in health, longevity, and living standards have been very uneven, and in 2003, many, many people are facing famine or live in abject poverty. Indeed, many people live no better in 2003 than did their ancestors 2000–4000 years ago. In 2002, the United Nations' Food and Agriculture Organization was estimating that 826 million people were seriously undernourished, 792 million of these in developing nations and 34 million in developed nations (United Nations (2002), see also Doering *et al.*, 2002). These starving people comprise one-seventh of the earth's population, and more people than were living on earth in 1750.

Of course, starving people face immediate challenges to survive so they pose little threat to the affluent. But another three billion people, half of the earth's population, while not starving, live in low-income nations with inadequate nutrition and no access to effective medical care. They decimate forests and agricultural lands and drink lead-laden water. Many of these people resent their disadvantaged circumstances and yearn for higher incomes. Some load too many people on small boats and attempt to cross from Africa to Europe, or from Haiti or Cuba to the United States. In addition, where high percentages of the populace have low incomes, the middle classes feel great sympathy for their less-well-off neighbours. It is middle-class men who have been gathering in mosques to conspire and then to protest by stealing aircraft and crashing them into symbols of affluence and military domination.

According to the World Bank, the numbers of unhappy disadvantaged are going to grow for at least half a century. The Bank classifies nations into four categories: low income, lower-middle income, upper-middle income, and high income. The Bank is forecasting that the low-income nations will expand from 59 per cent of the earth's population to 64 per cent over the next fifty years, while upper-income or upper-middle-income nations will contract from 24 per cent; of the earth's population to 18 per cent;. These changes are likely mainly because the low-income nations have such high birth rates, too high for improving technologies to counteract. As has already been demonstrated in Indonesia, central Africa, and South America, wars break out when more people struggle to share limited resources.

These wealth differences have sociological and ideological components as well as economic ones. At least since the industrial revolution, wealth has been associated with the overturning of social traditions. The developed nations are the ones that have moved most aggressively to exploit new technologies, and the greatest shares of wealth have gone to the individuals who took advantage of new technologies. New technologies have brought not only greater affluence but also non-traditional ways of thinking and behaving. For instance, mechanization of production created industrial jobs for women, which eventually led to women being treated more equally (Starbuck, 2003). The employment of women created a need for child-care that stimulated the creation of public schools, which homogenized cultures and spread literacy.

The under-developed world, hampered by a lack of resources, has generally adopted new technologies slowly and the poorest people are generally those who have adhered to traditional technologies, traditional behaviour patterns, and traditional ways of thinking. Thus, to people in the developed nations, the under-developed world appears unaccountably backward, rigid, and ignorant; and to people in the under-developed world, the developed nations appear inexplicably arrogant, depraved, and disrespectful of tradition.

The affluent are strongly disinclined to accept lower standards of living in order to share their wealth with those less fortunate. They use armies, technology, political influence, and economic and geographic barriers to suppress rebellions and to enforce trade balances that favour themselves, and they have nearly always succeeded in maintaining their favoured situations. Shell International (2002: 36) has pointed out that economic flexibility and better communication generally benefit the affluent:

The logic of global capitalism leads to a relentless pursuit of efficiency, which in turn, leads to a high polarization and volatility because capital and high quality labour move quickly to where the profits are made—the affluent get richer because they're better placed to take advantage of opportunities.

However, there have been occasions when the outrage of dissenters overwhelmed efforts to suppress them.

Although disadvantaged people have been protesting or trying to change their circumstances for tens of thousands of years, the twentieth century expanded awareness that may have redoubled their efforts. Movies, television, and air transportation have made affluence more visible. Affluent people are travelling in much greater numbers and to many more locations. Transoceanic travel has become commonplace. Television and movies have shown affluent people driving luxury cars, living in stately mansions, bathing on the Riviera, eating sumptuous feasts, and generally behaving as if they have neither wants nor cares. That these images sometimes represent unrealistic fantasies or portray abnormal lives is not clear to everyone who sees them, so a significant fraction of the disadvantaged people believe that many others are enjoying incredible wealth.

Thus, the affluent face intimidating challenges. Can affluent people sustain their standards of living only by using military force to suppress the impoverished? Is it even physically possible, without destroying the earth's ecology through global warming and demolished natural resources, to generate enough food and energy to raise the living standards of large fractions of the earth's populace high enough to satisfy most people? One argument holds that birth rates decline as people become more affluent and more educated, so resource problems can become more solvable. Both national and multinational organizations can raise standards of living and offer incentives towards education. Another argument says that improving under-developed economies will depend on the creation of substantial middle classes and that multinational firms are the best means of creating middle classes. Yet another argument asserts that the most developed countries have such low birth rates that their economies will falter unless they import substantial numbers of migrants from under-developed countries. But all these arguments are highly speculative and their validity may never clarify.

The Conflict between Companies and Nations

As early as the 1930s, Berle and Means (1932: 313) surmised, 'The rise of the modern corporation has brought a concentration of economic power which can compete on equal terms with the modern state.' When they said this, Berle and Means were living in a rather insular world. Not many corporations had ventured outside their home nations, and Berle and Means were concerned with the power of large corporations within their home nations. Subsequently, large corporations have indeed demonstrated economic power but the competition between large corporations and governments, if competition is an appropriate word, does not resemble the competition in theoretical economic markets. Obviously, large companies cooperate with national governments as well as compete with them. Executives often move from business to government or from government to business. Large companies participate actively in the political processes both in their home nations and in the nations that host them abroad, and national and local governments actively solicit investment and employment by large companies. The 'competition' that this chapter emphasizes occurs because some activities of large corporations undermine the loyalties that citizens feel toward their nations and their national governments. In particular, companies may offer their employees benefits that bind them to their employers more strongly than to their governments, and companies may undertake activities that undermine nationalistic loyalties of their customers and suppliers. Thus, allegiance to corporations may replace and weaken nationalism.

In the years following the Second World War, many large companies developed personnel policies that bound employees to them. There were implicit understandings that corporations would provide reliable employment as well as benefits such as medical care and insurance, but in exchange, the corporations expected employees to commit themselves to their jobs. Some corporations had explicit policies of moving personnel among locations to strengthen their intrafirm ties and to weaken their ties to communities and states. Thus, corporations were supplanting other social aggregates, including nations, at least for some people. In the latter part of the 1950s, *The Organization Man* and *The Man in the Grey Flannel Suit* made the public aware of organizations' influence on lives outside of jobs (Wilson, 1955; Whyte, 1956), and the social importance of large corporations was widely debated. There was also widespread discussion during the 1950s of the idea that, far from competing, business and government had formed coalitions. 'Engine Charlie' Wilson, a former CEO who became the US Secretary of Defense, set off alarms when he declared 'What is good for the country is good for General Motors, and what's good for General Motors is good for the country.' A few years later, outgoing President Dwight Eisenhower (1961) warned Americans 'In the councils of government, we must guard against the acquisition of unwarranted influence, whether sought or unsought, by the military-industrial complex. The potential for the disastrous rise of misplaced power exists and will persist.'

Although it appeared around 1960 that large corporations might take over many of the functions performed by national, state, and local governments, their integrative human-resource practices ran into financial problems. A symbolically significant turning point occurred when IBM made massive layoffs. IBM had long been renowned for offering job security in exchange for organizational commitment and conformity to organizational norms, and wags had declared that IBM stood for 'I've Been Moved.' The company had been able to maintain this policy partly because it made substantial profits in an industry that grew consistently and partly because its practice of renting equipment tended to stabilize its revenue flows. In theory, IBM's commitment to employees was supposed to translate into happy employees who worked productively and provided good service for customers. However, IBM's immunity to market fluctuations made IBM less sensitive to customers' feelings and market trends. IBM continued to emphasize mainframe computers after a large demand began growing for minicomputers, and IBM's indifference alienated customers. After 1989, IBM's profits turned into losses. To regain profitability, IBM made large budget cuts and personnel layoffs in 1993, thus breaking its implicit contract with employees to provide job security (Mills and Friesen, 1996).

Although IBM's financial problems had idiosyncratic elements, IBM's behaviour towards employees resembled that of many other companies. During the 1950s, the public viewed many corporations as stable, encompassing aggregations that employees could rely on to provide reliable career paths. Corporate management in the 1950s placed some importance on long-term goals and long-term financial planning, and they retained large amounts of cash to absorb short-run fluctuations. Then the 1980s brought a wave of aggressive takeovers. These takeovers frequently used targets' own cash reserves and liquid assets to pay for their acquisition and they often produced layoffs and actions to raise short-run profits. Executives discovered that they needed written employment contracts and that they could lose their jobs if they did not achieve short-run goals. The 1990s also brought management fads—reorganization, re-engineering, and downsizing—that emphasized efficiency and profitability and de-emphasized loyalty to employees, paternalism, and continuity.

Thus, companies retreated from the human-resources practices that made them appear to be trustworthy alternatives to governments, but during this same period, large companies accelerated a long-term global expansion that infringes on national loyalties and the prerogatives of national governments (Vernon, 1977, 1998).

Nearly all of these large companies, although headquartered in developed countries, have sales units, production facilities, and management units all around the world. From 1985 to 2000, companies created about 600 million new jobs worldwide but only 5 per cent of these jobs emerged in Europe, Japan, or North America. This lopsided development has been powered by the low birth rates and high wages in the developed nations as contrasted with the high birth rates and low wages in the less-developed nations. Driven in part by economic globalization, transoceanic travel more than tripled from 1985 to 1998, and transoceanic communications multiplied twenty-eight times from 1986 to 1997. In 2002, the company with the largest revenues in the world was Wal-Mart, which had stores in only ten countries, but many companies operate in scores of nations. For instance, McDonald's has restaurants in 118 nations. Exxon operates refineries in twenty-six nations, retails fuels in 100 nations, and sells lubricants in 200 nations and territories. British Petroleum has facilities in 100 nations. Daimler Chrysler manufactures in thirty-seven nations and has sales organizations in nineteen nations, and its stock trades on nineteen exchanges in seven nations. Mitsui has offices or subsidiaries in eighty-seven nations and its stock trades on eight exchanges in four nations.

Of course, many nations have much less economic power than the large companies they host, and many badly need the jobs and wages that large companies can bring, so the globalizing firms are able to exert strong influence on governmental policies and to dictate terms to local suppliers. The World Bank publishes data about the governments of 116 nations. In 1999, the median budget of these governments was only $5.5 billion (US$)[2] so only fifty-eight nations had annual budgets over $5.5 billion. It is unclear how many companies have budgets larger than \$5.5 billion, but it is many more than 500, for *Fortune Magazine* reported that the 500th largest company had revenues of \$10.1 billion in 2002. On the other hand, the largest company in the world, Wal-Mart, has only 1.4 million employees, which translates to roughly seven million employees, spouses, and children. The World Bank says that eighty-seven countries have populations over seven million.

Even people in large nations sometimes see globalizing firms as invaders who use non-traditional business methods (Hymer, 1960). Wal-Mart has long been a source of controversy within the USA, where it has avoided large cities and focused on smaller communities. A frequent complaint has been that the arrival of Wal-Mart dooms long-standing small-scale retailers because they cannot match Wal-Mart's range of merchandise and low prices. But residents flock to Wal-Mart nonetheless. When large firms enter new markets, they bring in business practices that appear non-traditional in other ways than merchandise quality and pricing. According to the *Wall Street Journal* (2003), 'Wal-Mart's foray into Japan spurs a retail upheaval: As giant confronts barriers, local competitors rush to emulate its methods.' In Paris, there is a privately owned School for Economic Warfare that teaches French-speaking executives how to combat their international competitors (*www.ege.eslsca.fr/*). The School enrols thirty-two students who pay 10,000 euros per year to learn the arts of economic warfare. According to this School's advertising, 'The new economic antagonisms arising from the globalization of markets have generated some novel competitive practices. Offensive strategic manoeuvres have multiplied (rumours, disinformation, destabilization, manipulations, dynamic encirclement of markets) and threaten enterprises that have not prepared for this type of stimulus. From now on, the mastery of information has become a major challenge for organizations.'

Thus, like the conflict between the affluent and the moderately poor, the conflict between companies and nations also arouses resistance against change or innovation in host countries. To many indigenous people, multinational firms introduce non-traditional and unreasonable ways of thinking and behaving, while people within the multinational firms see their own behaviours as forward-looking and modern. In extreme cases, multinational firms see their host nations as outdated and corrupt, while people in these host nations see the multinational firms as greedy and unfair.

One recent change in corporate governance has been increasing separation of corporate control from nationality. With some stocks trading on exchanges in multiple countries and some mutual funds holding shares around the world, the owners of corporate stock may live anywhere. Similarly, companies may borrow money from lenders around the world, and even if these lenders have no formal participation in corporate governance, they are likely to restrict corporations' actions. As companies have expanded globally, more and more senior executives have come from outside the companies' home nations; today, many companies have multinational top-management groups. Some companies have been emphasizing their multinationality as an attraction to potential employees and host nations. Some companies have moved their locations of incorporation to nations that offer them tax advantages or legal ones. Many companies that originated in nations using other languages now state that their official language is English. A few large companies declare that they have no specific national identities.

These changes suggest that the world is witnessing an evolution in which large corporations are challenging the traditional roles of nations. In many instances, multinational firms have brought much more benefit to people in host nations than have their national governments. Some people are defining their identities and loyalties in terms of the firms that employ them as well as their nationalities. Some younger people are defining their identities in terms of the clothing they wear, the foods they eat, and the music they listen to as well as their nationalities. For people who work in globalizing firms or who buy their products or who supply their inputs, elements of organizational culture are overlapping and competing with national cultures. Five months after the USA and UK invaded Iraq, the number-one topic of discussion in Arab nations was not the autonomy of Arabic culture but a television contest in which viewers voted by telephone for the next 'Superstar'. This television contest was a direct imitation of contests that had occurred in the UK and the USA.

A gradual substitution of corporations for national governments seems almost inevitable in the face of free commerce and advanced telecommunications, which give mobility and flexibility to corporations. National governments draw power from geographic location and societal traditions, but these also limit what national governments can do and stabilize their behaviours. Geography imposes resource constraints that create unsolvable problems and dominate social and economic development. The national governments that are trying to reconcile contending political groups probably act more lethargically than do corporations, which not only have clear hierarchical structures but also tie promotions and wages to compliance. Corporations also have the advantage of sheer numbers: There are many millions of corporations and only a few hundred nations. As a result, corporations can undertake many more experiments and when these experiments fail, the impacts are usually much smaller. The advantages of multiplicity increase in turbulent times, when familiar solutions are becoming obsolete and unfamiliar challenges are emerging (Omae, 1999).

To deal effectively with globalization, national governments would have to form worldwide coalitions that have legislative, taxation, and police powers. The European Economic Community approximates such a coalition on a regional scale: However, hobbled by the need to build consensus, the EEC has tended to move more slowly than the corporations it is trying to control, and corporations can sidestep EEC regulations by operating outside of Europe. On a global scale, the United Nations is asking corporations to abide by a Global Compact concerning human rights, the treatment of labour, and protection of the environment, but the United Nations has no ability to compel corporations to conform to this Global Compact and no ability to assess degrees of compliance. Will nations form additional regional coalitions and give them effective regulatory powers? Do nations have the will to regulate corporations on a global scale? Should corporations voluntarily conform to standards such as the Global Compact, both because the standards represent good social policy and because good behaviour helps to guarantee continued freedom? Will large corporations and international governmental bodies such as the United Nations create a world regulatory system that will dominate national governments?

On the other hand, many corporations are large enough to deserve seats at the United Nations, and the comparative advantages of corporations and governments imply that both can benefit from alliances. For example, national governments and international governmental bodies have demonstrated ineffectiveness in raising the economic capabilities of under-developed economies, whereas multinational corporations have actually enriched some under-developed economies. Might cooperative action between governments and corporations yield more significant improvements? Might people come to view some corporations as being equivalent to nations? Might some corporation-government alliances become as influential as NATO or OAS?

The Conflict between Top Managers and other Stakeholders

Whereas conflict between wealthier people and poorer ones has been endemic throughout human history, one version of such conflict is rather new: strife between the very affluent and the middle and working classes is occurring within large companies, where top managers have been enriching themselves at the expense of everyone else who has a stake. Two centuries ago, managers were very few and they received no respect, being seen as low-level instruments of the wealthy (Starbuck, 2003). Before and around the beginning of the twentieth century, law and public opinion viewed businesses as property owned by identifiable individuals, who employed managers to oversee their property. Such managers kept records and relayed instructions, but few of them exercised power on their own. However, such a conceptualization of managers grew less and less tenable throughout the twentieth century. Berle and Means (1932) reported that stock ownership in large US corporations had so dispersed that nearly all stockholders held very small fractions of the stock, with the result that stockholders of about half of the largest corporations could not exert effective control. Thus, in many cases, it was unrealistic to think of managers as agents who represented owners:

On the one hand, the owners of passive property, by surrendering control and responsibility over the active property, have surrendered

the right that the corporation should be operated in their sole interest
... At the same time, the controlling groups [managers], by means of
the extension of corporate powers, have in their own interest broken the
bars of tradition which require that the corporation be operated solely
for the benefit of the owners of passive property.

(1932: 311–12)

The prescience of these observations has grown increasingly
evident over the ensuing seven decades. Large fractions of stockholders cede their voting rights to companies' senior executives,
who therefore control the decisions made at shareholders' meetings, including the 'elections' of directors. Grateful directors
have rubber-stamped executives' decisions and endowed executives with vast wealth. The magazine *Business Week* has reported
escalating differentials between the compensation of chief executives and those of ordinary workers. Whereas the average
chief executive of a large US corporation made forty-two times
the pay of a typical American factory worker in 1980 (Reingold,
1997), this ratio then rose to eighty-five times in 1990, and to 411
times in 2001. Outside the USA, these ratios are lower but
extensive use of perquisites provides executives with income-
equivalents beyond the purview of tax authorities. As well,
outside the USA, more companies are under the control of
small groups or governments.

The spiralling compensation of senior executives has borne
weak relationship to their contributions to corporate performance, and in far too many instances, has involved schemes that
patently diverted corporate wealth to executives personally. In
2002, twenty-three large American companies were under investigation for accounting irregularities: compensation of the CEOs
of these companies averaged $62 million from 1999 to 2001,
compared with an average of $36 million for all CEOs of large
companies (United for a Fair Economy, 2002). Stocks of the

companies under investigation lost 73 per cent of their total value, and these companies laid off 162,000 workers. After business profits declined for two consecutive years, many of the executives who supposedly had their compensation linked to corporate performance had lost very little and some had made large gains. For example, boards of directors had issued additional stock options to offset their senior executives' losses on previously issued options (Lavelle *et al.*, 2002; Craig, 2003). Paywatch, a web site maintained by American labour unions, argued in 2003 that 'The flagging economy and poor corporate performance—including falling stock prices, declining profits and big layoffs—have barely made a dent in executive pay. Median pay actually grew by 7 per cent—meaning half of all executives made more and half made less. This rate is twice the growth of workers' paychecks. Elite corporate chiefs at the top of the CEO pay range took some cuts—lowering average CEO pay by 8 per cent—but the majority of CEOs got raises. In contrast, a typical company's corporate profits declined by 35 per cent in 2001.'

The generous use of stock options has partly undermined Berle and Means' idea that management was gaining autonomy from owners; some senior executives have become major stockholders. Lavelle *et al.*, (2002) remarked, 'Salaries and bonuses are now afterthoughts compared with the potential wealth that options represent.' However, options are not true ownership, and to assure that options become valuable, executives need to increase companies' short-run profits. If these short-run gains come at the expense of long-run profits, only the executives themselves benefit (Kay, 2003). Moreover, executives rarely gain enough stock via options to give them direct control of companies, and other stockholders have been taking action to alter corporate governance (Deutsch, 2003). Stockholders are proposing limitations on executive compensation, changes in accounting practices for executive compensation, and changes in the compositions of boards of directors. However, legislated changes may have negligible effects. A few companies have been cutting back on stock options ... by issuing stock or cash bonuses instead (Lublin, 2003*a*, *b*)! Sonnenfeld, who has studied boards of directors, says, 'The key isn't structural, it's social. I'm always amazed at how common groupthink is in corporate board rooms. Directors are almost without exception intelligent, accomplished and comfortable with power—but if you put them into a group that discourages dissent, they nearly always start to conform' (Hymowitz, 2003: R3).

Executives' financial gains have cost them respectability. Since 1977, The Harris Poll (Taylor, 2001) has surveyed Americans regarding the prestige of seventeen occupations. In 2001, the occupation of 'businessman' was the least prestigious of these occupations. Only 12 per cent of the respondents rated 'businessman' as having 'very great prestige'. A year later, Taylor (2002) reported that 87 per cent of the surveyed Americans believed that top managers receive more pay than they deserve. The same percentage said that they believe top managers have become rich at the expense of ordinary workers. About half of those surveyed described themselves as 'very angry' about executives' compensation.

Governments tend to react to perceived problems. At various times in the past, public outrage over business behaviour has spawned restrictive legislation or reinterpretations of existing legislation. Aggressive behaviour during the late eighteenth century stimulated antitrust legislation and the creation of government agencies to monitor competitive behaviour. Fraudulent behaviour during the 1920s stimulated legislation about accounting practices and financial disclosure. Conspiratorial behaviour has sometimes drawn attention to troublesome practices in specific industries, with one result being that executives have gone to prison. Defective products have led governments to create agencies to monitor product quality and to force product recalls, and environmental pollution has motivated legislation and policing agencies.

One can observe over the last decade rising concern about corporate governance and the control exercised by senior executives. These issues have elicited discussion in the mass media, in the publications of labour unions and business associations, in legislative bodies, and in governmental agencies. Although governmental bodies have taken actions, those actions have aimed at specific behaviours rather than at the basic structure of corporate governance.[3] The US government has been slow to require governance changes that would give stockholders greater power, and sceptics have argued that the actions so far are inadequate to reduce abuses significantly (Morgenson, 2003). Thus, senior executives, stockholders, and governments still face challenging issues concerning the governance of corporations. How much do executives want to regain some of the public respect they have lost? Are they willing to trade wealth for respectability? Can senior executives persuade other stakeholders that they deserve their extremely high compensations?

Many large corporations differ radically from nineteenth-century ideas about businesses run for the benefit of owners (Ackroyd, 2002). In these corporations, small groups of managers control policies and resource allocation and choose their own successors. Insofar as owners have representation, their representation comes through the actions of financial markets rather than through their words or votes. If senior executives continue to dominate corporate governance, as seems likely, will such corporations lose legitimacy and attract closer governmental control? What indeed are the foundations of these companies' legitimacy?

The Conflict between the Short-Run and the Long-Run

Throughout the twentieth century, organizations endlessly shifted their attentions back and forth between short-run targets and long-run goals. Periods of prosperity elicit long-range planning, statements about long-term missions, large-scale construction projects, and personnel policies that confer benefits on employees with longevity. Recessions induce organizations to abandon long-range plans, to attend to immediate problems, to liquidate underutilized facilities, and to lay off personnel. Although economic cycles have important influence, they are not the only factors that shift time horizons. Management fads sometimes have countercyclical effects. Waves of downsizing and re-engineering occurred during the otherwise munificent 1990s. The munificent 1980s and 1990s also brought many aggressive acquisitions that generated actions to quickly boost short-run profits. It became very important to please the stock analysts at brokerage firms. Corporations focused strongly on quarterly results and in some cases, executives lost their jobs because they failed to attain quarterly targets. New financial television channels tried to portray each tiny fluctuation as dramatic news. In some instances the strong emphasis on short-run results became an important stimulus for deceptive accounting (Glassman, 2002; Rockwood, 2002).

Long-run plans and policies are usually advantageous and sometimes essential. For instance, criteria for acceptable investments can keep people from over-investing when good alternatives are sparse and thus can preserve funds for periods when good alternatives abound. The paternalistic human-resource policies of the 1950s and 1960s elicited employees' commitment to their employers quite effectively. Problems that might become unsolvable after they build up for a long time may be solvable with small effort if forecasted and dealt with early: Global warming and over-population may be examples (Natural Resources Defense Council, 2003; World Population Awareness, 2003).

An obvious weakness of long-run plans and policies is the unreliability of long-run forecasts. Almost all long-run forecasts turn out to be very wrong. Forecasting models that have credible face validities make no more accurate forecasts than models that have poor face validities. Simple, crude models tend to forecast more accurately than complex, subtle ones, and the most accurate forecasts are generally no more accurate than naive linear extrapolations that anyone can make (Pant and Starbuck, 1990). But simple, linear extrapolations generally work well only for short intervals; after several periods, trends no longer adhere to linearity. Quite a few studies have found that an average of five or six forecasts was usually more accurate than any of the component forecasts; this led Makridakis and Winkler (1983) to infer 'that there is no such thing as a best model'. After assessing the performance evidence, Armstrong (1985: 91) advised: 'Do not hire the best expert you can—or even close to the best. Hire the cheapest expert.'

So it is also usually advantageous and sometimes essential to deviate from long-run plans and policies. Adhering to a long-run plan will eventually bring ruin, and it may do so abruptly if its premises become invalid suddenly. Miller (1990) has documented many cases in which firms focused so intently on what they perceived as being their strategic strengths that they overlooked important developments; a focus on core competence that makes an organization successful tends to grow narrower over time and to evolve into a liability. The people and organizations that succeed repeatedly come to expect success and they develop great confidence in their current methods of operation (Starbuck and Hedberg, 2001). They create habits and routines to repeat their successes, but these habits and routines turn into breeding grounds for crises that threaten companies' existence.

Perceptions focus on events that have been important in the past, so people and organizations overlook other events that sometimes turn out to be even more important. Within the frames of reference created by experience, habits and routines tend to appear to be working well, but the data about performance are biased. In the face of social and technological change, too strong commitments to current methods of operation gradually render people and organizations incapable of responding to current challenges. Indeed, they may not even understand new challenges when they arise.

Unexpected, fleeting opportunities may be extremely profitable, and to ignore immediate threats can be extremely costly. The ITT Corporation and Tyco International grew large and ostensibly profitable by acquiring undervalued companies, a strategy that can never succeed for more than a few years. Every year brings fads that some vendors exploit to their profit—such as hula hoops, Cabbage Patch dolls, CB radios, re-engineering, quality circles, outsourcing, derivatives, or hedge funds.

Recent years have clearly emphasized short-run performance, and executives who appeared to deliver excellent short-run results profited handsomely as individuals. But it is doubtful that most shareholders, most employees, and most suppliers participated in these benefits, which have often proved non-renewable and unsustainable. In many cases, managers enhanced short-run performances through accounting manipulations that gave immediate credit for hoped-for future achievements. Many large companies, like IBM, abandoned long-run commitments to employees in order to achieve more 'flexible workforces'. Cooper (1999) has argued that in Britain, these changes have lowered job satisfaction and morale and they are challenging notions that work ought to provide workers with more than financial benefits. Hirakubo (1999: 44) suggested that commitments towards long-run employment encourage Japanese companies to do more training, but he also proposed that 'Japanese companies have practised lifetime employment not because it is superior, but because it is convenient.'

Two obvious weaknesses of short-run targets are fickle policies and inadequate provision for long-run needs. Executives who know they will remain in their jobs for only two or three years, whether they succeed or fail, have strong incentives to appear to succeed in the short run whatever the long-run consequences. Warren Buffett, frequently lauded as the most successful investor of all time, has chosen companies for their long-run prospects and has eschewed companies with short-run orientations. Simon (1996) studied 500 very profitable small and medium-sized companies: among their significant characteristics was long-run thinking and avoidance of management fads such as diversification, outsourcing, and strategic alliances. Miller and Le Breton-Miller (2005) argued that some large family controlled companies have been significantly more successful than large publicly owned corporations. According to Miller and Le Breton-Miller, publicly owned corporations too often pursue short-run goals that divert them from more valuable long-run goals, whereas control by a family gives some companies long-run viewpoints that enable them to gradually achieve dominant positions in specialized domains.

However, the long-run success stories highlighted by Simon and by Miller and Le Breton-Miller had to have been rare exceptions. For each company that developed a strategy that proved successful over the long run, many other companies determinedly pursued strategies that they expected to succeed but that failed. Some strategies were never good ideas. Some strategies were good ideas for a time but became bad ideas as technologies evolved and societies changed. Statistics indicate that strategizing has erratic effects and it produces harmful results nearly as often as it produces beneficial results (Starbuck, 1992). Starbuck and Nystrom (1981: xiv) observed:

... the most impressive characteristic of current organizations is how unsuccessful they are. Large organizations do not grow out of small ones: nearly all small organizations disappear within a few years, the great majority of middle-sized organizations are just a few years old, and many large organizations are new organizations. For a small organization to grow into a large organization is very rare, and it is quite unusual for a middle-sized organization to grow large. The very smallest organizations are more prone to disappear ... but so are the largest new organizations ... Three-eighths of all new corporations reach the age of five; 65 per cent of the ten-year-old corporations attain the age of 15; 83 per cent of all 50-year-old corporations survive to the age of 55. Thus, older organizations are more likely to survive. But even very old organizations are far from immortal: approximately one-eighth of all 100-year-old corporations disappear without reaching the age of 105.

Managers will continue to struggle with the dual attractions of short-run and long-run opportunities and the dual challenges of short-run and long-run threats. And managers will continue to confront fashions that encourage them to concentrate on long-run goals and to disregard short-run opportunities, or to seize short-run opportunities at the expense of long-run goals. The struggles will continue because there is no way to resolve the conflicts, and the managerial fashions will continue to appear and fade because everyone dreams of a resolution.

But business firms or markets may be able to create additional ways to moderate the struggles between short-run and long-run goals. Hedging is a financial strategy that allows businesses to avoid losses arising from likely price fluctuations; insurance is a financial strategy that allows individuals and businesses to avoid disastrous losses caused by infrequent misfortunate events; diversification smooths outcomes by distributing investments and commitments among heterogeneous markets. Could managers create similar products or apply similar policies to a wider range of issues—numbers of employees, skills, knowledge, locations?

Conclusion

The twenty-first century promises to be turbulent, and turbulent periods nurture social innovation. One component of social innovation might be changes in legal and popular concepts about corporations. There are many reasons to question the usefulness and validity of current beliefs about what corporations are, what they can do, and what structures they should have. Widespread mythology says corporations are legally equivalent to individuals, they are owned by and run for the benefit of stockholders, and they are subordinate to local and national governments. These myths also assert that managers serve the interests of stockholders, and other stakeholders (employees, customers, suppliers, neighbours) should have no voice in corporate governance. Observation says tens of thousands of corporations are wealthier and more powerful than nearly all individuals, and corporations wield significant political power—

locally, nationally, and around the world. Observation also indicates that insofar as owners have voice in corporations, this voice comes indirectly through financial markets, whereas some other stakeholders have stronger voice in corporate governance; these other stakeholders are mainly large powerful organizations. Mostly, small groups of managers control corporate policies and resource allocations and choose their own successors. Thus, it is time for people to rethink their ideas about large business organizations. Should there be several distinct categories of 'corporation' with different rights and different responsibilities? Where should people draw the boundaries between private rights and public responsibilities? Should some corporations have to consider explicitly the interests of employees, customers, suppliers, and the public at large? Are there governance processes that might allow corporations to hear multiple voices without becoming bogged down in conflict and uncertainty?

There are also powerful social and technological forces pressing organizations to innovate. For example, various forces—telework, diversity, globalization, and technological change—suggest that traditional hierarchies are becoming less useful and interorganizational networks are becoming more useful. This may imply that top managers need to focus their efforts on culture-building and the management of trust, and it may imply that alliances and interorganizational networks will replace many organizations (Baumard and Starbuck, 2001). Several authors have asserted that virtual organizations or imaginary organizations will become socially and economically prominent (Monge and DeSanctis, 1998; Hedberg and Maravelias, 2001; Hedberg et al., 2002).

An even more radically different approach to organization may already have emerged. The Islamic countries have produced an organizational force-field that causes actors to spring into action very nearly at random over a vast geographic area (Bell, 2002). In its initial manifestations, this force-field has been the medium for terrorist activities. But there are other applications, especially in a globalizing world.

This force-field approach treats an organization not as a control structure or a system of rules but as a potential for actions that hover just below the brink of happening. Which people actually act and which actions do occur can appear to be quite random because they are specific instances from very large pools of latent possibilities. The emergent organization may take different specific forms and pursue different missions in different ways at different times, yet one can regard it as a single organization because its varied manifestations express a common integrating motive. This integrating motive facilitates the organization of those people that do act and of those actions they do take. The current Islamic organization draws integration from outrage, but one can imagine an organizational force-field forming because of shared utopian dreams or philosophical tenets. As low-cost and high-speed communications interlace the world, force-fields could well become more and more prevalent.

Notes

I owe thanks to Juan Alcacer, Michel Anteby, Philippe Baumard, Cary Cooper, Mathilde Dufour, Joan Dunbar, John Mezias, John Naman, Narayan Pant, and Malcolm Warner for suggestions and information concerning this chapter.

1. An interesting nuance is that medical care provided to individuals appears to have contributed very little in comparison with more basic factors such as food, clothing, housing, and sanitation. For

example, in 1840, tuberculosis was causing 4000 deaths per million people in England and Wales. This death rate dropped by 90 per cent before a vaccine became available (McKeown, 1979).

2. It is possible to debate at length the appropriate statistics to compare companies with nations or with national governments. Corporate revenues may include rather fictional accounting entries that inflate them. Because the sales of nearly all companies include charges for inputs that are actually the outputs of other companies, De Grauwe and Camerman (2002) argued that the appropriate measure would be value-added. But national GDPs include the values-added by corporations, so to compare corporations with national governments, it might be reasonable to subtract the corporate contributions from GDPs. Corporate revenues may better indicate the visibility of corporate activities, and hence the influence of corporations on social values, than do values-added. The median budget of national governments is only about one-third of their nations' GDPs.

3. Germany requires corporations to have Supervisory Boards (Aufsichtsrats) that incorporate employee representatives as well as stockholder representatives, but no other stakeholders have representation.

References

Ackroyd, S. (2002). *The Organization of Business: Applying Organizational Theory to Contemporary Change.* Oxford: Oxford University Press.

Armstrong, J. S. (1985). *Long-Range Forecasting: From Crystal Ball to Computer.* 2nd edn, New York, Wiley-Interscience.

Baumard, P. and Starbuck, W. H. (2001). 'Where are Organizational Cultures Going?' pp. 521–31 in C. L. Cooper, S. Cartwright, and P. C. Earley (eds.), *The International Handbook of Organizational Culture and Climate.* Chichester: Wiley.

Bell, J. B. (2002). 'The Organization of Islamic Terror: The Global Jihad.' *Journal of Management Inquiry*, 11, 261–6.

Berle, A. A., Jr and Means, Gardiner C. (1932). *The Modern Corporation and Private Property*. New York: Macmillan.

Cameron, R. E. (1993). *Concise Economic History of the World* (2nd edn). New York: Oxford University Press.

Cooper, C. L. (1999). 'The Changing Psychological Contract at Work.' *European Business Journal*, 11, 115–18.

Crafts, N. F. R. (1985). *British Economic Growth during the Industrial Revolution*. Oxford: Clarendon Press.

Craig, S. (2003). 'Wall Street Pains Stops at the Top.' *Wall Street Journal*, 4 March 2003, c1 and c3.

De Grauwe, P. and Camerman, F. (2002). 'How Big are the Big Multinational Companies?' Manuscript, Catholic University of Louvain.

Deutsch, C. H. (2003). 'Revolt of the Shareholders: At Annual Meetings, Anger will Ratchet up a Notch.' *New York Times*, 23 February 2003, section 3, pp. 1 and 12.

Doering, D. S., Cassara, A., Layke, C., Ranganathan, J., Revenga, C., Tunstall, D., and Vanasselt, W. (2002). *Tomorrow's Markets: Global Trends and Their Implications for Business*. Washington, DC: World Resources Institute.

Eisenhower, D. D. (1961). 'Military-industrial Complex Speech: January 17, 1961.' *Public Papers of the Presidents, Dwight D. Eisenhower, 1960*, 1035–40.

Glassman, J. K. (2002). *How to Protect against Another Enron*. Testimony before the House Committee on Financial Services, 13 March 2002. Washington, DC: American Enterprise Institute for Public Policy Research.

Hedberg, B. L. T. and Maravelias, C. (2001). 'Organizational Culture and Imaginary Organizations.' pp. 587–600 in C. L. Cooper, S. Cartwright, and P. C. Earley (eds.), *The International Handbook of Organizational Culture and Climate*. Chichester: Wiley.

——Baumard, P., and Yakhlef, A. (eds.) (2002). *Managing Imaginary Organizations*. New York: Pergamon Press.

Hirakubo, N. (1999). 'The End of Lifetime Employment in Japan.' *Business Horizons*, November–December 1999, 41–6.

Hymer, S. (1960). *The International Operations of National Firms: A Study of Foreign Direct Investment*. Doctoral dissertation, Massachusetts Institute of Technology. Published in 1976 by MIT Press.

Hymowitz, C. (2003). 'How to fix a Broken System: A Rush of New Plans Promise to make Corporate Boards more Accountable. Will they Work?' *Wall Street Journal*, 24 February 2003, R1 and R3.

Kay, I. (2003). *Corporate Governance in Crisis: Executive Pay / Stock Option Overhang 2003*. Watson Wyatt Worldwide (www.watsonwyatt.com/research/)

Lavelle, L., Jespersen, F. F., and Arndt, M. (2002). 'Special Report: Executive Pay.' *Business Week*, 15 April 2002

Lublin, J. S. (2003*a*). 'With Options Tainted, Companies Award Restricted Stock.' *Wall Street Journal*, 3 March 2003, B1 and B3.

——(2003*b*). 'Why the Get-Rich-Quick Days may be over.' *Wall Street Journal*, 14 April 2003, R1 and R3.

Makridakis, S. and Winkler, R. L. (1983). 'Averages of Forecasts: Some Empirical Results.' *Management Science*, 29, 983–96.

McKeown, T. (1979). *The Role of Medicine: Dream, Mirage, or Nemesis?* (2nd edn). Oxford: Blackwell, and Princeton, NJ: Princeton University Press.

Miller, D. (1990). *The Icarus Paradox: How Exceptional Companies Bring About Their Own Downfall*. New York: HarperCollins.

——and Le Breton-Miller, I. (2005). *Managing for the Long Run: Lessons from Remarkable Family Controlled Businesses*. Boston, MA: Harvard Business School Press.

Mills, D. Q. and Friesen, G. B. (1996). *Broken Promises: An Unconventional View of What Went Wrong at IBM*. Boston, MA: Harvard Business School Press.

Monge, P. and DeSanctis, G. (eds.) (1998). Special Issue on Virtual Organizations. *Journal of Computer-Mediated Communication*, 3 (June).

Morgenson, G. (2003). 'Plan Restricting Stock Options Stalls at SEC.' *New York Times*, 13 March 2003, A1 and C5.

National Defense Council Foundation (2002). *World Conflict List 2002.* (www.ndcf.org/)

Natural Resources Defense Council (2003). *Global Warming.* (www.nrdc.org/globalwarming/)

Omae, K. (1999). *The Borderless World: Power and Strategy in the Interlinked Economy,* revised edn. New York: HarperBusiness.

Pant, P. N. and Starbuck, W. H. (1990). 'Innocents in the Forest: Forecasting and Research Methods.' *Journal of Management*, 1990, 16(2), 433–60.

Paywatch. www.aflcio.org/corporateamerica/paywatch/

Reingold, J. (1997). 'CEO Pay—It's Out of Control.' *Business Week*, 21 April 1997.

Reinhard, M. R., Armengaud, A., and Dupaquier, J. (1968). *Histoire Générale de la Population Mondiale.* Paris: Éditions Montchrestien.

Rindova, V. P. and Starbuck, W. H. (1997). 'Distrust in Dependence: The Ancient Challenge of Superior-Subordinate Relations' pp. 313–36 in T. A. R. Clark (ed.), *Advancements in Organization Behaviour: Essays in Honour of Derek Pugh.* Ashgate Publishing.

Roach, S. (2001). 'Global: Debating Globalization'. *Global Economic Forum*, Morgan Stanley, 26 October 2001.

Rockwood, R. M. (2002). *Accounting: Focus on the Red Flags.* FocusInvestor.com (www.focusinvestor.com/AccountingRedFlags. pdf).

Shell International (2002). *People and Connections: Global Scenarios to 2020.* London: Shell International.

Simon, H. (1996). *Hidden Champions: Lessons from 500 of the World's Best Unknown Companies.* Boston, MA: Harvard Business School Press.

Starbuck, W. H. (1992). 'Strategizing in the Real World.' *International Journal of Technology Management, Special Publication on Technological Foundations of Strategic Management*, 8(1/2), 77–85.

——(2003). 'The Origins of Organization Theory' pp. 143–82 in H. Tsoukas and C. Knudsen (eds.), *The Handbook of Organization Theory: Meta-Theoretical Perspectives*. Oxford: Oxford University Press.

——and Hedberg, B. L. T. (2001). 'How Organizations Learn from Success and Failure' pp. 327–50 in M. Dierkes, A. Berthoin Antal, J. Child, and I. Nonaka (eds.), *Handbook of Organizational Learning and Knowledge*. Oxford: Oxford University Press.

——and Nystrom, P. C. (1981). 'Designing and Understanding Organizations' pp. ix–xxii in P. C. Nystrom and W. H. Starbuck (eds.), *Handbook of Organizational Design*, vol. 1. New York: Oxford University Press.

Taylor, H. (2001). *Doctors the Most Prestigious of Seventeen Professions and Occupations, Followed by Teachers (no. 2), Scientists (no. 3), Clergy (no. 4) and Military Officers (no. 5)*. The Harris Poll no. 50, 10 October 2001.

——(2002). *The Enron Effect: The American Public's Hostile Attitudes Toward Top Business Managers*. The Harris Poll no. 55, 18 October 2002.

United for a Fair Economy (2002). *Executive Excess 2002: CEOs Cook the Books, Skewer the Rest of Us*. Boston, MA: United for a Fair Economy, 26 August 2002.

United Nations (1998). *World Population Prospects: The 1998 Revision*. New York: United Nations. (www.popin.org/pop1998/default.htm)

——(2002). *The State of Food Insecurity in the World*. Rome: United Nations' Food and Agriculture Organization.

Vernon, R. (1977). *Storm Over the Multinationals: The Real Issues*. Cambridge, MA: Harvard University Press.

——(1998). *In the Hurricane's Eye: The Troubled Prospects of Multinational Enterprises*. Cambridge, MA: Harvard University Press.

Wall Street Journal (2003). 'Wal-Mart's Foray into Japan Spurs a Retail Upheaval: As Giant Confronts Barriers, Local Competitors Rush to Emulate its Methods.' *Wall Street Journal*, 19, September, 2003, A1 and A6.

Whyte, W. H. (1956). *The Organization Man*. New York: Doubleday.

2

Discretionary Leadership: From Control/ Co-ordination to Value Co-Creation Through Polylogue

Nada Kakabadse
and
Andrew Kakabadse

Considerable easing of the restrictions on world trade and the impact of the information revolution has undermined the importance of national boundaries (Kakabadse and Kakabadse, 2001). Within the international workplace, leaders are increasingly being held accountable, not only by their corporations, but also by the wider community. In effect, contemporary leaders are faced with greater demands from both shareholders and other stakeholders, whereby the requirement for shareholder return is counterbalanced by those who question the benefits of globalization and demand a fairer distribution of wealth, locally and globally.

With such developments, old models of leadership, based on assumptions of control and coordination, are increasingly viewed as falling short of adequately preparing the new generation of leaders. In order to explore fully the models of leadership desired for the future, this chapter examines the changes required in leadership thinking in order to appropriately balance growing shareholder and stakeholder requirements. Examination of contrasting perspectives of leadership as prelude to an in-depth analysis of the challenges that face leaders in today's world, is undertaken. Through such analysis, it is posited that leadership thinking has to encompass the concept of cadre, or shared leadership. Due to the intricacies and complexities of enterprises today, it is proposed that a number of leaders exist in the organization, each of whom utilizes their discretion to make choices that suit each particular person according to their circumstance. Reconciliation of different views and positions as a result of the exercise of discretion is posited as a present-day reality. The challenge for the future will be to harness the ever greater number of contrasting perspectives of different leaders into a more cohesive whole. In order to realize greater cohesion among such actors, who, from their perspective, appropriately adopt different viewpoints, the urgency to conduct multiple conversations simultaneously, is recognized. Thus, the conduct of polylogue, namely, multiple dialogue, is considered a critical capability that future leaders will need to develop.

Models of Leadership

Emerging out of the 'what makes for outstanding leaders' school of thought, which dominated thinking prior to the 1970s, is the distinction drawn between transactional and transformational leadership (Burns, 1978; Bennis, 1989). Transactional leadership, namely, managing, refers to the means to bring about, to accomplish, to have responsibility for, to conduct. In contrast, transformational leadership is more concerned with influence, guiding in a particular direction, to chart a course of action and/or drive opinion (Shelton and Darling, 2001). The difference between the two foci lies between 'activities of communication and co-ordination among people which facilitate effectiveness as a leader, versus activities of controlling resources, and mastering procedures and routines, which facilitate efficiency as a manager' (Darling, 1999: 316). Thus, the argument holds that managers are transactional technologists who maintain the balance of operations and are process- or means-oriented (Burns, 1978). They are 'caretakers of the *status quo*' (Warburton, 1993: 28) who think in terms of explicability, with a focus on control and accountability (Bennis, 1984). Managers relate to other actors in role-terms and favour loyalty, conformity, co-ordination, and team spirit (Bradford and Cohen, 1984; Nibly, 1984; Manz and Sims, 1990; Fairholm, 1991, 1996). They prefer security and are effective in situations where they can direct the desired behaviour, control deviation from set norms, and punish recalcitrance (Zemke, 1987). Managers favour proven technologies and hierarchical structures as they are predictable and are, in themselves, a lever of control (McDermott, 1969: 35). Instinctively, managers avoid complexity and attempt to ensure tangible, detached control to limit the danger and insecurity of uncertainty (McAdam, 1993: 8) and, through efficiency, are in danger of producing mediocrity and suffocating innovation and creativity when major steps forward are required by the organization (Fairholm, 1991).

Thus, from the transactional leadership perspective (Burns, 1978; Bass, 1985a), leadership is modelled on economic transactions and encompasses a number of leadership theories, such as expectancy theory (Vroom, 1964), path-goal theory (House, 1971; House and Mitchell, 1974), exchange/equity theory (Homans, 1958; Homans, 1961; Adams, 1963) and re-inforcement theory (Scott and Podsakoff, 1982; Luthans and Kreitner, 1985). The transactional leader position conceptualizes leaders as inter-organizational power sensitive (French and Raven, 1959), directive (McGregor, 1960), adjusting organizational structures (Fleishman, 1953), task oriented (Katz et al., 1950), disciplinary and punitive (Korukonda and Hunt, 1989; Sims, 1980), veering towards consolidation and output maximization (Quinn et al., 1990).

In contrast, Burns' (1978) 'transformational' leadership is closely related to the charismatic model defined by Weber (1947). Weber's (1947) original sociological concept of leadership charisma emphasized a capability to inspire new forms of organization, the perspective adopted by House (1977) in the formation of his charismatic leadership theory. The concept of transformational leadership grew in popularity and was further developed by others (Bass, 1985b; Quinn et al., 1990; Kakabadse, 1991). Burns (1978), in particular, viewed the leader/ follower relationship as key in determining the impact of charisma in improving the motivation and morale of subordinates. Thus, charisma, a transcendental idea of supernatural, super-human, or, at least, exceptional quality (Weber, 1968), also incorporates ideas of strong emotional bonding between leaders and followers. Burns (1978: 442) argued that 'charismatic leadership is an attribution based on followers' perceptions of their

Tayloristic measurements of 'good' and 'bad' behaviours, is seriously challenged as being inappropriate to effectively interacting in social and organized settings, where contextual dynamics are intense, rapid, chronically 'turbulent' and often critical (Korac-Boisvert and Kouzmin, 1994a, 1994b). A brief overview of the last decades of the past century reveal the impact of Anglo-American corporations in their pursuit of maximizing greater shareholder value with little regard to other stakeholders. Such effect, particularly on operatives, has led to a 600:1 ratio of CEO reward in comparison to that of the average worker (Kochan, 2002). Wall Street analysts and institutional shareholders encouraged corporate leaders towards focusing on the short term in order for corporations to boost earnings and thus enhance the value of stocks (Useem, 1987, 1996; Kochan, 2002). As a result, board remuneration committees and compensation consultants became engaged in better aligning management incentives with investors interests. In turn, this encouraged a search for the CEO who could best manage relations with the financial investment community and equally project an image of confidence (Kochan, 2002), leading to renewed interest in the charismatic top executive and, in many cases, attributing to the person celebrity status. The popular press, autobiographies and management genre of 'I did it my way' (Clegg and Palmer, 1996) for decades, glorified and promoted images that 'corporations are lead by heroes' (Wilson, 1992; Khurana, 2002a, 2002b). The leadership stories of Jack Welch suggest that he single handedly changed GE, while Sir Collin Marshall, ex CEO of British Airways, transformed the culture of British Airways from pleasing the boss to pleasing the customer. Similarly, Gordon Bethune (ex CEO of Continental Airlines, USA) is attributed with turning around the airline from worst to first by using motivational techniques. Similar tales surround William McKnight (ex CEO of 3 M), the person considered to have made 3M the most innovative company in the world, while Lee IaCocca (ex President of Ford and ex Chairman of Chrysler) took risks even when Chrysler was sinking.

However, these stories do not emphasize that most of these leaders joined their respective organization quite some time in the past, possibly as young trainees/first-level officers, and thus were intimately aware of the intricacies of their enterprise. Such insights took years to nurture. Nor do these stories provide information about others who worked with the hero leader and the joint effort necessary to promote the image of success and thus, that of hero. The degree of organizational insight required to lead effectively through change is conveniently omitted.

Through an examination of the literature, what can be concluded is that intimacy with context is downplayed, for charismatic leaders are portrayed as individuals who are dissatisfied with the *status quo*; are restless and energetic; are action oriented and whose discontent pushes them into searching for new opportunities (Kakabadse, 1991). Charismatic leaders are often presented as potent and virile individualists, fighting battles for the good of others and enabling empowerment, (Bass, 1985a, 1990; Avolio and Bass, 1988; Kets de Vries, 1998), images that run counter to being a long-standing organizational employee. Furthermore, charismatic leaders are projected as entrepreneurial, impatient and gifted at articulating a vision by making the big picture seem within the reach of their followers through building alliances and making people feel special (Avolio and Bass, 1988; Bass, 1990; Kets de Vries, 1998). These portrayals are glorified by the press, as with Alfred Sloan (ex CEO of General Motors) talking to 10–12 dealers in a day and thus taking corrective measures, or Bar Nabe's (the CEO of Eni Oil Company, Italy) refusal of a company house and car, thus liberating him to take stern measures. Charismatic leadership is promoted even within the servant-leadership model (Green-leaf, 1998), typified by Herb Kelleher's (CEO of South West Airlines) philosophy of love and kindness, in that, even when he dismissed an employee, the said employee named his newly born child 'Kelleher'. In effect, the concept of the charismatic hero has created an unprecedented demand for men and women of unassailable virtues, unstained by scandals of financial con-flicts of interest or that of an un-virtuous personal life (Marcus, 1961; Blau, 1963; Dow, 1969; Wilson, 1992).

In parallel to the charismatic leader perspective, models of the ideal institution have emerged, legitimated by occidental man-agement practice and exemplified by management consultants, business school activities through MBA and other programmes, the quasi-professional management bodies, the management gurus, and the popular management texts (De Bettingies, 2000; Ball and Carter, 2002). It has become commonplace for profes-sional managers to draw upon these sources for guidance through recipe-like 'best' practice without encouraging consider-ation of alternatives (Mingers, 2000; Ball and Carter, 2002). Business schools that, for example, teach liberal-economics 'do great damage by teaching three million students a year that to be selfish is to be efficient' (Etzioni, quoted in Kozlowski and Doherty, 1989: 16) and thus perpetuate current social disson-ance. Many socially conscious managers may have been sur-prised and disappointed to realize that their MBA is linked to the rise of the new right and the privatization wave of the mid 1980s (Ball and Carter, 2002: 554). Moreover, business school discip-lines have been 'cut off' from humanistic thinking and, as such, promote solutions of universalistic applications based on ab-stracted general theory that is divorced from the nature of differ-ent contexts (Kakabadse, 2001; Zald, 2002). For example, a survey by Wood et al. (2002), of the curricula of some 102

US-based business schools (including *Business Week's* Top 50 Business Schools) found that corporate citizenship—corporate involvement in the community—has not been considered as a stand-alone course at any of the surveyed schools. Moreover, they found that because the business schools' curriculum was heavily oriented towards personal and organizational self-interested goals, the challenging issues of social justice, of social responsibility and citizenship, were not clearly articulated. Thus business schools and other professional bodies are viewed by many as the first that need to change in their education and development of current and future leaders (De Bettingies, 2000; Kakabadse, 2001; Adler, 2002; Wood *et al.*, 2002 Zald, 2002;).

Due to scandals, corruption, lack of preparedness, poor or inappropriate training and development to confront personal, and institutional ethical challenges, the confidence in the viability of the transformational charismatic hero model of leadership has been severely undermined. The search for alternative models of leadership which not only encompass force and drive, but equally collegiality, sensitivity and sharing, has had to take into account powerful demographic forces that are altering our economic, political, and social landscape. In fact, three critical forces are identified; the impact of globalization, the effect of information technology on the structuring and functioning of organizations and society, and the evolving and maturing needs of ever greater educated followers.

Globalization

As the degree to which national economies becomes ever more integrated increases due to government policy, supported by ever evolving, innovative information, and communication

technology (ICT), action taken at a distance (non-local caus-
ation) is transforming life within localities. In effect, strategic
decisions taken in one part of the world have far-reaching consequences in other parts. The forces of globality have positioned
two systems, multinationals and the nation state 'each legitimated by popular consent, each potentially useful to the other, yet
each containing features antagonistic to the other' (Vernon,
1991: 191). Thus, individuals and communities are being challenged to come to terms with the changes that globalization
brings to one's working life (Eden and Lenway, 2001). The
need to adjust to increased pressures for job mobility allows
people greater opportunity to enjoy diversity and provides for
greater returns from acquiring new skills. The reduced barriers
to trade and investment accentuates the 'asymmetry between
groups that can cross international borders and those that
cannot' (Rodrik, 1997: 4). Therefore, those holding a local
focus will feel the effects of globalization as multinationals
span national borders, promoting common controls, common
goals, and common ownership of geographically spread resources, thus challenging the very concept of the nation state
(Vernon, 1991).

Although many criticisms of the global economy and global
institutions are well founded, it is hard to conceive of a future in
which international trade and global institutions play no part
(Kakabadse and Kakabadse, 2001). We cannot turn the clock
back. In developed and developing societies, both public and
private organizations are currently forming partnerships with
enterprises in recipient economies, on transactional joint ventures requiring dependency on each other, collaboration and
even compromise of domestic technological skills and capabilities. Contemporary executives operate within a global socio-

economic-political network where the internal organizational context (internal cultural values and work standards) are only one part of the diversified global context.

Undoubtedly, emerging technology will promote greater visibility. The Earth Simulator software/hardware, for example, currently runs at more than 35 trillion calculations per second, allowing researchers to 'plug in' real-life climate data from satellites and ocean buoys to generate an electronic virtual model of the entire plant (Grossman, 2002). Such a platform allows for forward projections in order to ascertain what will happen to our environment (Grossman, 2002). Soon policy makers will be able to plug their parameters in the virtual Earth model and then evaluate the effect of their policies (Grossman, 2002), or what Shoemaker (1997: 46) calls a 'scenario planning disciplined method for imagining possible futures'.

In effect, the globalization of work environments adds to the cultural diversity of constituencies and stakeholders and provides for additional complexity to the management of those interactions and intimate relationships between transnational organizations and their domicile societies. Actors in leadership roles need to address the requirements of critical groups who have a stake in the success of the organization. Dealing effectively with contradictions, ambiguities, different values and measurement standards, and conflicting goals requires a plurality of methods. Leaders will need to synthesize and reduce ethnocentrism and arbitrarily manipulate cultural relativism, because in their extreme forms, both sources of diversity pose equal dangers to transnational communication and understanding. Unfortunately, the former becomes insensitive to cross-cultural differences while the latter becomes blind to cross-cultural similarities.

ICT Development and Proliferation

The information revolution of the 1990s was epic in scale and significance and even daunting in its consequences (Korac-Boisvert and Kouzmin, 1994a). ICT, as a process, induces greater complexity in the organizational landscape. The ICT employed deeply influences the patterns of independencies within the organization and hence the power relations between different actors and groups (Morgan, 1986; Arhne, 1990). Emerging ICT allows for multiple points of access to common knowledge databases and to the joint possibility of greater local independence and yet further centralized control (for example, centralizing on-going surveillance over performance). Actors are provided with more comprehensive, immediate, and relevant data relating to their tasks (Korac-Boisvert and Kouzmin, 1994b). However, irrespective of increased centralization or greater de-centralization, but depending on the intent of the organization's management (Huber, 1990), ICT has a powerful impact on key leadership roles through emergent virtuality. In particular, the internet (e.g. e-mail, bulletin board, Web) facilitates communication between non-linearly-connected actors and increases the level of coupling between previously uncoupled entities in a 'network structure' (Boettinger, 1989; Korac-Boisvert and Kouzmin, 1994b).

The combined effects of IT-mediated communication (increased flows of information), electronic brokerage (electronic market, e-business) and ICT integration (tighter coupling between inter-organizational processes—electronic hierarchies) have resulted in emergent value-adding partnerships (Malone *et al.*, 1987) generating new patterns of interaction. These new patterns are as much 'processes' as they are emerging structures being continually shaped and re-shaped by the actions of actors who, in turn, are constrained by the structural position in which they find themselves (Korac-Boisvert and Kouzmin, 1994a). Sometimes, these developments are clearly demonstrated by organizational re-structuring. At other times, change occurs slowly, more in terms of image than in form. It should be noted that ICT-based developments do not inherently imply organizational democratization. The impact of ICT applications may promote pseudo-devolved structures, where strategic control is centralized while operational decision making is being de-centralized, thus replacing the top-down power relationship with a centre-periphery one, which is less easily discernable (Korac-Boisvert and Kouzmin, 1994b). Thus, ICT adoption 're-defines the work content, changes managerial styles and culture, re-shuffles power hierarchies and spawns a series of both man designed and spontaneous adaptions' (Zelany, 1982: 58; Nohria and Eccles, 1992). In this sense, the challenges of ICT proliferation can appear as ideological conflict concerning particular roles, such as, the removal of a considerable number of operational roles thus inducing large-scale redundancies and hence creating policy challenges.

The proliferation of new ICT, which both facilitates and challenges cross-functional and intra-functional integration (Boettinger, 1989), or 'networks' (Powell, 1990), forces changes of mindset concerning leadership roles and hierarchies. Leaders are faced with making the difficult call between what is local and valuable to their function and what is global to the business. Equally, they are required to differentiate between decisions that are more operational and task focused against those that are strategic and have greater policy relevance. Greater inter-dependencies create the need for more sharing of tasks, information and decision-making accountability (Boettinger, 1989; Fairholm, 1991; Korac-Boisvert and Kouzmin, 1994a). Adaptation in planning and operational parameters is required, thus promoting a need for greater interaction with a wider range of stakeholders. In effect, ICT development and distributed decision-making accountability induces a mutation of traditional managerial prerogatives.

The ICT potential to transform hierarchical organizations is enormous, generating 'information-based organizations' (Drucker, 1988, 1990) or 'network organizations' (Powell, 1990). Such transformation can be realized in four ways. First, information technology (IT) makes possible the reduction of management levels by providing a dramatically enhanced potential for control (Beniger, 1986). Second, network structures facilitate fluid, flexible, and dense patterns of inter-connections that cut across various intra- and inter-organizational boundaries (Drucker, 1988, 1990). Third, ICT provides real-time communication across social time and space (Sproull and Kiesler, 1991). ICT also improves communication between systems, thus blurring the boundaries of organizations beyond market or hierarchical exchange (Malone and Rockhardt, 1991).

Fourth, ICT contributes to flexibility through electronic storage, data manipulation (Walton, 1989) and simulation that facilitates 'networked organizations' (Powell, 1990), characterized by relations that are based on neither authority nor market transactions but on the network structure of ties (relationships) among actors in a social-context (Powell, 1990). Such configurations are radically different from the Weberian model of bureaucracy (Baker, 1992; Nohria and Eccles, 1992), but are fundamental to the concept of social capital (Lin, 2001).

Organizational and social networks, facilitated by ICT, are now more distributed and are gaining acceptance as a more effective organizational form for the achievement of objectives through social information processing. ICT has made networks a critical mode of organizational communication by enabling relational proximity (Rogers and Kincaid, 1981) and accessibility throughout the organization and across geographical boundaries (Forester, 1987; Mathews, 1989). The organization's actors are better connected with one another as well as with customers, vendors, and strategic partners (Malone and Rockhardt, 1991). The reality of 'networked', 'global', and 'virtual' organizations becomes synonymous with 'electronic networks' where remote, asynchronous and, often dysfunctional, communication may replace face-to-face communication further re-defining and distorting relationships, actions, and formal roles. For example, the Society for Worldwide International Funds Transfer (SWIFT), shared by a growing international consortium of banks and other financial institutions, changes many of the basic dynamics of its members' core business, re-designing the meaning of organization within a context of tightly coupled and shared electronic operations worldwide. SWIFT necessitates competitors, on the one hand, to cooperate by establishing close, structure-independent, linkages between banks, while on the other hand, induces greater competition by enhancing the range of services provided.

Greater global communication mobility transforms predominantly ethnocentric organizations into multicultural ones. ICT increasingly invalidates traditional management assumptions, such as strategy and structure are closely correlated (Mathews, 1989). The emergence of the 'meta-business' or the networked-organizations, a quasi-firm created through ICT linkages and dependencies between organizations, leads to a situation where actors are tightly coupled, making it difficult to define where the boundary of one organization ends and the boundary of another begins. Examples can be found in supply chains, where competition between firms is replaced by competition between supply chains, and where suppliers cooperate with customers in order to contribute to the overall competitiveness of the chain (i.e. supply system) in which both operate. For example, in the air-transport industry, the One-World Alliance (BA, AA, Aer Lingus, etc.) competes with Star Alliance (UA, Lufthansa, etc.). If the dynamic partnered arrangements in the chain work efficiently in market terms, individual and mutual prosperity for its members emerges (Lammin, 2001).

Rhetorical management actions (giving orders, setting procedures, supervision) are extrinsic and cannot solely be assumed to be effective in such networked structural futures. Actors in the leadership roles will have to accommodate less arbitrary, more culturally ambiguous, globally transacted, collegial, decisions arrived through protracted negotiation, formal discussion, compromise and high levels of residual and personal uncertainty. The fundamental changes in agency relationships are accompanied by an ever greater emphasis on added value and insightful understanding of consumers. The move is from learning organizations to learning chains with ICT providing the essential lubricant.

Awareness of Followers

The commonplace conceptualization of leadership, embedded in the dualistic nature of leader-follower with one holding power over the other is traditionally underpinned by the Judeo-Christian struggle between good and evil. Cain's problem with Abel involved inequality of power and influence, while Moses parried with the Pharaoh to let his people go and later represented the epitome of leadership and organizational power as he sat in judgement over the people of Israel during their forty-year pilgrimage (Korac-Boisvert and Kouzmin, 1994a). As highlighted, many leadership and management models are underpinned by this dualistic differentiation, leader-follower, leader-manager and transactional-transformational leader, each implicitly portraying a struggle of power, whereby traditionally, the word 'leader' has conjured up visions of an individual who has the authority to command others (the followers) and displays heroic capabilities such as courage and intellectual, physical and/or spiritual boldness. Further, the 'age of value' (*circa* 1980–1990) and the emerging 'age of ideology' (*circa* 1990–2000) added weight to the viability of the notion of shareholder value emphasizing the charismatic leader as critical to the survival of this philosophy.

Yet, with the new century, serious questions are being asked of the 'shareholder value' ideology as a discipline for running large public companies, and thus, in turn, the appropriate models of leadership that will be required. Shareholder value, being increasingly viewed as rooted in greed through worshipping stock price and considerably enhancing the wealth of corporate leaders, while most others are worse off, has led to deep reconsiderations concerning the philosophies of leadership to be adopted (Favaro, 2002).

Simultaneously, with the demise of the industrial/manufacturing era and the rise of the information era, the nature of the work, and the profile of the workforce has changed. The rise of knowledge workers has been accompanied by a decline in the importance of physical capital in determining competitive advantage. The realization of competitive advantage has migrated from a reliance on modes of production to intellectual capital and information, and is currently moving to knowledge and social capital, thus challenging the leader–follower relationship concept (Kakabadse and Kakabadse, 2001). Information 'as a commodity that can be bought and sold has become insufficient to define competitive advantage' (Bassi, 1997). Social capital is increasingly being recognized as the means for achieving competitive advantage. Social capital is viewed as an attribute of individuals in social contexts (Bourdieu, 1986), defined as 'resources embedded in a social structure that are accessed and/or mobilised in purposive actions' (Lin, 2001: 29). These, in turn, nurture the emergence of networks that are built around and further propagate common social attributes embedded within 'formative contexts' such as institutional arrangements, cultural values, ethnic tastes, training, background, and cognitive frames that shape the daily routines of actors, their ideology, and desired objectives (Unger, 1987; Korac-Boisvert and Kouzmin, 1994*b*).

Considering that the concept of social capital is a resource that is derived from the relationship between individuals, organizations, communities and/or societies, it does not easily lend itself to notions of heroic leadership (McDermott, 1987). The underlying philosophy, however, is that of emergent strong interpersonal relationships within organizations and communities (Nahapiet and Ghoshal, 1998). Although one can acquire social capital through purposeful action and can transform social capital into conventional economic gains, the ability to do so depends on the nature of social obligation, strength of connections, and network amiability (Table 2.1). At the heart of social capital theory is the notion that internal and external social linkages between organizational actors, usually translated into social networks, are resources with a positive organizational value (Bolino *et al.*, 2002). The growing consensus is that social linkages or relationships *can* secure benefits for those people involved (Portes, 1998) and ultimately the organization gains from these benefits. These linkages embrace both intra- (Tsai and Ghoshal, 1998) and inter-firm linkages (Newell and Swann,

Table 2.1 Models of Capital

	Physical Capital	Human Capital	Social Capital
Reflected by:	Tools Machines	Education Training Experience Tacit knowledge/know-how	Existence of close interpersonal relationships among individuals
Characteristics:	Deliberate sacrifice for future benefits Alienability Rate of return can be measured by summing up past investment net of depreciation	Deliberate sacrifice for future benefits Can be measured (productivity measure) Appreciates with use	Acquired with(out) calculations or/and sacrifice for future benefits Difficult to measure Appreciates with use

Source: Bourdie (1986); Arrow (1999); Ostrom (1999); Solow (1999); Lin (2001).

2000), as organizations increasingly require access to resources which they do not have within their boundaries.

Discretionary Leadership

With the shift from physical capital to the 'softer' models of capital spawning the emergence of network-based organizations, the emphasis has changed from one person clearly highlighting the pathways forward, to a group-based view of leadership, whereby, understanding and being responsive to multiple stakeholders in their context, is the prime concern. However, being adaptive to multiple contexts introduces greater complexity to leadership application, for greater acknowledgement has to be given to the needs and demands of contrasting stakeholders (Kakabadse, 2000). Effectively addressing multiple stakeholders, means recognizing and responding to multiple agendas. Transversing pathways through a multiplicity of issues and circumstances, would be near to impossible for any one individual to effectively confront. Thus, network-based organizations, by their very configuration and purpose, require more actors to adopt the leadership mantle, allowing the organization to be responsive to a greater volume and variety of organizational and environmental demands (Fondas and Stewart, 1990; Kakabadse, 2001). The neat coupling of more issues to address and a greater number of actors to address them invites the application of choice from those occupying leader roles. Thus, the new generation of leaders are required to exercise discretion extensively in order effectively to address the issues facing them.

Thus, the roles of leadership are ones that require its incumbents to exercise broad discretionary judgement (Jaques, 1992). In effect, the individual shapes the role and determines its more intricate nature (Kakabadse and Kakabadse, 1999). Discretionary roles vary according to the degrees of freedom they offer their incumbents (Fig. 2.1). Certain roles will only allow for changes to the configuration of particular jobs, whereas ultimate discretion encourages for making a profound impact on the strategic future of the enterprise (Kakabadse, 1991; Kakabadse and Kakabadse, 1999, 2000*a*).

A role with clearly assigned parameters is one where the incumbent is assigned resources and given the specific brief to pursue particular courses of action (prescribed). The limited freedom of the role holder requires the person to leverage existing resources, irrespective of whether those resources are considered adequate to do the job. The role holder may even be directed to act in a manner considered suitable to achieve the

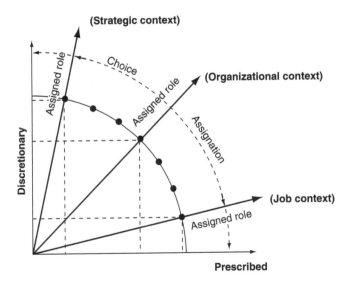

Figure 2.1 *Role Discretion.*
Source: Kakabadse and Kakabadse (2000b).

goals of the task, team, department, or organization (Kakabadse, 1991). Roles with broader discretion require the role
holder to establish the parameters of the role, the direction
they are to pursue and to be responsive to the circumstances
they face. Accordingly, the discretionary element inherent in
roles encompasses 'the choices that the role incumbent needs
to make in order to provide shape and identity to his/her role
and, by implication, to that part of the organisation for which
he/she is accountable' (Kakabadse and Kakabadse, 2000*b*).
Ultimately, discretionary roles are considered as those positions
for which organizationally beneficial behaviours and gestures
can neither be enforced on the basis of formal role obligation nor
elicited by contractual guarantee or recompense (Organ, 1990:
46; Barksdale and Werner, 2001). The degree of discretion may
be planned for in the role but is, 'principally driven by the
incumbent's capability to influence and determine the boundaries, responsibilities and accountabilities of that position' (Kakabadse, 2001: 553). In response to the pace and pressure of
organizational change, the nature of role discretionary boundaries is increasingly determined by personal views, concerning the
challenges leaders face and the nature of those with whom they
interact (Kakabadse, 1991; Kakabadse and Kakabadse, 1999,
2000*b*). Thus, the idiosyncratic nature of the organization, the
peculiarities of each leader role and characteristics of the individual occupying such a role, are critical considerations in determining role boundaries and parameters (Kakabadse and
Kakabadse, 1999).

Indeed, making such a distinction illustrates that those with a
broader role remit are in a position to influence substantially
their situation (Kakabadse, 1991; Bowman and Kakabadse,
1997; Tompson and Werner, 1997; Kakabadse and Kakabadse,
1999, 2000*b*). Further, the number of discretionary roles

that exist in an organization determine the number of visions and ways of operating that can shape, positively or negatively, the future of the enterprise (Fig. 2.2; Kakabadse and Kakabadse, 1999). The greater the number of discretionary roles, the greater the number of visions that can be pursued and thus, the greater the leadership challenge in attaining cohesion and a sharing of philosophy among the leadership cadre of the organization.

Accordingly, leaders exercising their discretion are required perpetually, deliberately, and reflexively to consider the nature of the linkages that connect their every action. Leadership is not just concerned with the exercise of control and co-ordination in the pursuit of a particular direction, but also with a sensitive understanding of the context in which actions are exercised and the appropriate mobilization of others, in essence, the

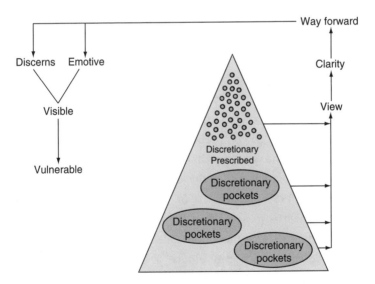

Figure 2.2 *Discretionary Role Analysis.*
Source: **Kakabadse and Kakabadse, 1999.**

generation of social capital. Through so doing, the shape of organizations, supported by technological systems are increasingly designed around intellectual flows rather than configurations of command, where performance measures and incentive systems reward individuals for the creation of value. For the flatter, more network-based organization, which, by nature, house a greater number of discretionary roles, the need to promote positive interdependency, is paramount. Responding to multiple stakeholders' requirements obviates identifying the 'one best way to manage' (Quinn *et al.*, 2001). Only through nurturing a shared value system are the tensions inherent in the network-based enterprise minimized and that energy focused towards achieving positive ends.

However, where discretionary role analysis highlights variation of experience, capability, values, personality, behaviours, and the exercise of choice among the leaders of the organization, tension and conflict become endemic with potentially disastrous consequences for individuals and the organization (Kakabadse, 1991; Finkelstein and Hambrick, 1996). Where continuous tension and an evolving but negatively inclined organizational landscape become the norm, leaders, particularly within network-based organizations, require an overarching analytical perspective that can comprehend the totality of the state of the organization and yet, simultaneously, understand the nature of each interaction within the enterprise (Whittington, 1988; Boettinger, 1989; Powell 1990). A first step towards such enlightenment is to appreciate the level of migration from the control/transactional model of leadership to that of discretionary leadership which can induce a transformational impact (Table 2.2).

As the effectiveness of organizational performance considerably rests on the quality of interactions, communication, and co-

Table 2.2 Migration of Leadership Models

Characteristics	Control/Transactional	Transformational	Discretionary
Projected image	'Strong Man' Rational Man Omnipresent	Hero Superman (Ubermensch) 'Maverick' Merlin Athlete Omnipotent	Professional executive Co-creator Distributed
Metaphor	Manager (individual)	Leader (individual)	Leadership cadre
Conceptualizedas	Leader/followers relationship (e.g. 'instrumental relationship')	Leader/followers relationship (e.g. followers' identification with the leader)	Role discretion contextually defined (e.g. shared power)
Emphasis on	Power and control	Extraordinariness of a leader	Development of others/ organization
Attributes	Powerful Autocratic	Charismatic Restless/dissatisfied with the *status quo*	Emotionally mature Reflexive decision maker

(*Continues*)

Table 2.2 Continued

Characteristics	Control/Transactional	Transformational	Discretionary
	Directive (e.g. path-goal setter)	Energetic/virile	Mindful of self, others and society
	Initiator of structure	Risk taker	Responsible
	Disciplinarian	Fighter	Accountable
	Punitive	Action oriented/potent	Networked
	Task oriented	Visionary	Communicative (engaged in polylogue)
	Consolidator	Determined	Influencer
		Communicator	Negotiator of paradoxes
		'Rational' (logical, practical)	Inquiring learner
		Good listener	Coach/developer of intellectual and social capital
		Passionate	Co-create differentiation
		Alliance builder	Change mindset
Key tasks	Planning (charting)	Provide vision/focus	Co-create beliefs
	Organizing (structuring)	Challenge *status quo*/impetus for change	
	Controlling	Stimulate and inspire	
	Reviewing	Empower others	

Key needs	Skills	Competence	Capability
Impact	Transactional	Transformational	Contextual (transactionally and transformationally appropriate)
Resources mobilization	Physical capital (reflected by tools, machines)	Physical capital (reflected by portfolio investment)	Social capital (reflected by existence of close interpersonal relationships among individuals)
	Human capital (reflected in number of employees)	Human capital (reflected by education training, experience)	
Role theory explains	Role expectancy	Role modelling	Role discretion
	Role clarity	Role/frame alignment	Role accountability/responsibility
		Role assignment/followers perceptions	Role representation
		Role clarity/ambiguity	

(Continues)

Table 2.2 *Continued*

Characteristics	*Control/Transactional*	*Transformational*	*Discretionary*
Communicative strategies to	Give direction	Influence followers to 'buy into'	Shift mindset
Focus on	Output maximization	Results/outcomes—shareholder value	Intrinsic values/sustainability
Influential theories	Two-factor theory of leadership (McGregor, 1960)	Sociology of charisma (Weber, 1947)	Role discretion (Jaques, 1951)
	Equity theory (Adams, 1963)	Social cognitive theory (Bandura, 1986)	Corporate social responsibility (Davis, 1973)
	Expectancy theory (Vroom, 1964)	Charismatic leadership theory (House, 1977)	Self-management theory (Thorenson and Mahoney, 1974)
	Path-goal theory (House, 1971)	Transformational leadership (Burns, 1978)	Leadership capability (Kakabadse, 1991)
	Contingency theory (Tannenbaum and Schmidt, 1958)	Empowering leadership theories—Super leadership (Manz and Sims, 1991) and Servant leadership (Greenleaf, 1998)	Stewardship model of leadership (Block, 1996)

Situational theory (House and Dessler, 1974)	Visionary leadership (Tichy and Devanna, 1986)	Ecological theory of inter-dependence (Gilpin, 1995)
Exchange theory (Homans, 1961)	Value-based leadership (Covey, 1989)	Discretionary leadership (Kakabadse and Kakabadse, 1999)
Leadership behaviour theories—Reinforcement theory (Thorndike, 1911); directive/structuring (Fleishman, 1953); autocratic and punitive (Halpin and Winer, 1957); task orientation (Katz et al., 1950); Punitive (Arvey and Ivancevitch, 1980)	Leadership competence (Bennis, 1993)	Leadership cadre (Kakabadse, 2001)
Transactional leadership (Burns, 1978)	Spiritual leadership (Fairholm, 1996)	Social capital theory (Lin, 2001)

Source: Compiled by the authors.

ordination between stakeholders, leaders will be challenged to
share their leadership and, as a result, will need to enhance their
maturity in order to share authority and responsibility effectively
across the leadership cadre (Korac-Boisvert and Kouzmin,
1994*b*). Ever greater innovation in ICT and the growing globalization of trade will further induce the proliferation of networked organizations of alliances, emphasizing joint ventures
based on collaboration and dependent on situational authority.
The 'new-age-capabilities' of pursuing multiple dialogues
simultaneously, namely, polylogues and co-creating value, are
posited as becoming fundamental elements of organizational
functioning.

Value Co-Creation

In the quest for differentiation, scholars and practitioners alike
have, for several decades, sought, through vivid and rich debate,
how to secure competitive advantage as well as understand its
sources. The emerging debate in economics posited that superior
and sustainable performance could not be attributed to industry-
wide structural determinants, since within each industry, there
existed high and low achievers. Thus, attention focused on
individual firm performance, with the aim of enquiring about
the heterogeneity of firms. The resource-based view (RBV)
emerged as the new paradigm judged to be best suited to understanding differences in enterprise performance (Penrose, 1959;
Mahoney and Pandian, 1992; Peteraf, 1993; Spanos and
Lioukas, 2001). From the RBV perspective, the firm is seen as
a bundle of tangible and intangible resources (i.e. tacit know-
how) that could be identified, selected, developed, and deployed
to attain superior advantages (Cool *et al.*, 2002). The basic

argument of RBV is that Ricardian rents come from resource heterogeneity between firms, which can be sustained if certain conditions are met, namely, market imperfections and resource immobility. The crux of the argument states that when firms have VRIN attributes (valuable, rare, inimitable, and non-substitutable) they can achieve sustainable competitive advantage by implementing value-creating strategies that cannot be easily duplicated by competing firms.

Based on RBV thinking, value creation and value drivers differ among organizations. Many firms have pursued a production and service orientation, based on the belief that production/service efficiencies, cost minimization and mass distribution can be used effectively to deliver quality goods and services to the consumer at attractive prices, while others concentrate on R&D and others on merger and acquisition. However, despite a growing trend for copyright and patent registration, those strategies for differentiation provide only short-term advantage, due to their 'mimicability' by competitors.

In contrast to the notion of tangible based capital, Nahapiet and Ghoshal (1998) posit that the development of social capital within an organization is likely to be a source of competitive advantage. That is, networks or a community approach to nurturing strong inter-personal relationships within an organization, ultimately facilitates a level of differentiation that is difficult to replicate (Coleman, 1984). The uniqueness of the organization is attained through pursuing a particular cognitive phenotype (shared language, shared narrative, communicative ability), through adopting particular structural arrangements (network ties, network configuration, network appropriability) and aspiring towards desired relational dimensions (high level of trust, shared norms, perceived obligations, sense of mutual identification) (Nahapiet and Goshal, 1998).

A subsequent challenge is to attract, continuously develop and retain talent which in addition to acquiring generalist and specialist skills and competencies, needs to harbour a willingness to subordinate individual interests for the good of the collective. Maintaining such a value base does require each actor to be accessible to project a willingness to trust others.

However, as already highlighted, interacting within a network as much engenders a complexity of tensions as promoting a humanistic concept of development. Demands are made on the whole person rather than on some range of skills or functions (Lonergan, 1992: 239). Community decisions can violate the rights of individuals as every choice involves limited knowledge and limited understanding of the issues at stake and the consequent implications of one's actions. History shows that every community is shaped as much by failed choices as by the realization of good ones (Lonergan, 1992: 254–7). Communitariansim can exhibit tendencies towards inflexibility and suppression of initiatives through censure and force. In resisting such negativities, building a 'natural', social, and cultural critique as a dynamic of community is critical to the continued progress of the community and to realizing the quest for differentiation and advantage.

Polylogue: Continuous Shifting of Mindsets

The current dominant market paradigm of neo-liberalism treats values such as, trust, friendship, and loyalty, in an instrumental manner (De Bettingies, 2000: 177), which in turn, has provoked a reaction that values 'cannot be legitimately subsumed by value performance maximisation' (Shaw, 1998: 294). Thus, the switch from the charismatic leader model of communication concerned with 'the manufacture and maintenance of meaning' (Hopfl, 1992: 29) in order to sell the leader's vision and get 'buy-in' from followers, to that of discretionary leadership which aims to influence the mindset of others in the network and through such shift work towards a shared philosophy, requires movement from singularly created meanings to co-created meanings (Table 2.3).

In so doing, the leader needs to be an active listener in order to gain the necessary understanding of follower needs and use that insight to shape his/her vision in a fashion that appeals to the followers, thus engendering inspired followers.

Such bonding and bridging of social capital in order to promote a shared philosophy, not only depends on the leaders' cognitive phenol type but also on the 'social time' devoted to addressing the formal and tacit relational dimensions within the organization (Coleman, 1984; Bourdie 1986; Putman, 2000). Open information organizations are characterized by lateral and horizontal patterns of exchange, interdependent flows of resources and reciprocal lines of communications (Fig. 2.3). The diverse interests and priorities of varying stakeholders

Table 2.3 Communication Models of Leadership

Communication	Transactional	Transformational	Discretionary
Purpose	Give direction to subordinates	Influence followers to 'buy into leader's vision'	Co-create meanings with others
Strategy	Planning	Manufacture and maintain meanings	Mind-shift
Outcome	Clarity of goals	Inspired followers	Shared philosophy

Source: Complied by the authors.

Figure 2.3 *Open Information Interactions.*

requires the discretionary leader to navigate through a multiplicity of interests, identifying shared commonalities and ensuring that benefit is derived from participation. Dialogue, a form of communication between two actors, is insufficient when sense making conversations are simultaneously required across multiple actors. Thus, dialogue is substituted by polylogue (Greek—root poly, suggesting numerous) (Gergen, 2000: xxiii) or multilogue (Duke, 1974).

Within polylogue communication, conversations abound, at times being experienced as productive and other times, being viewed as repetitive and fruitless. Emotionally and contextually driven conversations require re-inforcement, often involving repetition of the same conversation, as much to help individuals face their challenges as to provide them with insights to better enable them to move forward (Cooper, 2002). Providing support, displaying empathy to others, making allowance for people to express their frustrations and going over the same issues so that each individual can gain a greater understanding of the issues facing them, can be perceived as pointless repetition. Reinforcing messages can also, unfortunately, lead to unproductive repetition. However, through greater intimacy of appreciation of each stakeholder and by judging the degree to which a new convergence of opinion emerges, a breakthrough in terms of mindset shift can be achieved (Fig. 2.4).

As polylogue requires ceaseless conversations, negotiations, compromise, mutual exploration, and inquiry, where the range of participants encompassed not only covers the trusted, but also 'strange and alien voices' (Gergen, 2000: xxxiii), it is critical also to achieve closure on discussions through establishing a new

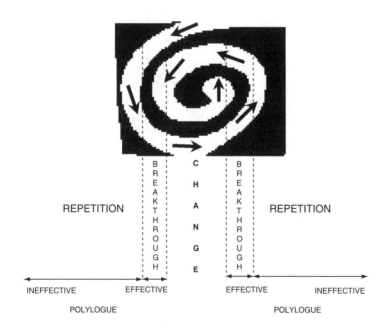

Figure 2.4 *Polylogue Pathway: Shifting Mindsets.*
Source: Compiled by the authors.

platform of awareness reinforcing the changed mindset
(Fig. 2.5). The challenge of achieving closure is clearly identified
by Cooper (2002: 86) who remarks, '. . . inclusive doesn't mean
being touchy feely' and continues that shared and inclusive
leadership equally has little to do with popularity.

Once established, the philosophical platform enables integration of contrasting perspectives, such as, concern for others

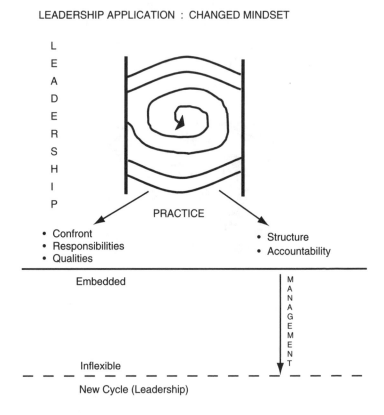

Figure 2.5 *Discretionary Leadership Communication for*
Platform Building.
Source: **Compiled by the authors.**

(people), economic efficiency (profit), environmental care (planet), and establishing an environment conducive for future generations (posterity) (Kakabadse, 2003). The discretionary leader's challenge is to promote a polylogue environment by providing intellectual as well as process contributions. Teams become as much units of action as learning groups, whereby reflection on experience and learning, combined with action, are accepted as an everyday norm. Adopting a polylogue mindset better enables the community to address and discuss the 'undiscussable' issues that require open examination. Thus, the discretionary leader promotes a value trajectory, in which participatory methods used for debate and procedures and tools for guiding debate, form as much the leadership kitbag of skills as do fiduciary and accountability mechanisms, a point supported by research examining policy application effectiveness in government which concludes that leadership has to be considered as a pluralist activity and not an individual cluster of qualities and requirements (Giacchino, 2003).

Conclusion

In this chapter, it is contended that individuals who find themselves in a leadership position bear the responsibility for the moral state of their constituency. Such responsibility however, does not require establishing only the leader's values. Moral effectiveness requires balancing and, if possible, integrating the constituent members' desires and perspectives, and emerging with a collective sense of moral integrity and responsibility. Such considerations are particularly critical in today's complex organizations where leadership is 'shared'. Certain individuals promote leadership from the centre, others hold leadership responsibility on a country or regional basis, still others on a

functional/professional basis and yet others have a 'line of business' or product or service responsibility. Simply because leadership responsibilities and accountabilities are shared that does not
mean a sharing of philosophy, objectives, attitudes, or even mission and vision for the organization. On the basis that the greater
the number of leaders potentially the greater dissonance, the
requirement for polylogue-based communication is heightened,
for otherwise the erosion and tearing of the social and economic
fabric of organizations will become an everyday experience
(Greenleaf, 1998). Thus, the balance lies between desire and a
personal sense of responsibility; between the demands of economies of scale and the social needs of the community (Fig. 2.6).

Responding to the economic realities confronting leaders (the
right hand, masculine arm, Fig. 2.6), balanced against providing a
sense of care for the community (the left hand, feminine arm,
Fig. 2.6), are paradoxes that any one individual would be unduly
challenged to reconcile. Thus, the need for the discretionary leader
to co-create futures with others, through involvement and continuous examination of ways forward, balancing short-term, operational demands captured in the accountabilities that confront
each leader against attending to the sustainable development of
the enterprise. Thus, the philosophy of shareholder wealth is
impregnated by the philosophy of stakeholder development. Polylogue, the desired philosophy of communication underpinning
discretionary leadership, requires the suspension of judgement
until the other's point of view has been examined, and reflection
over one's own practice has been undertaken. Discretionary leadership adopts the Socrates perspective of the examined life—'an
unexamined life is not worth having' (Aristotle, 1911)—and only
through such enrichment, can all jointly progress beyond leader/
follower and shareholder wealth, to shared responsibility and
enterprise and community sustainability.

Figure 2.6 *The Polylogue Scales.*
Source: Compiled by the authors.

References

Adams, J. S. (1963). 'Wage Inequities, Productivity and Work Quality.' *Industrial Relations*, 3, 916.

Adler, P. (2002). 'Critical in the name of whom and what?' *Organisation*, 9(3), 387–96.

Ahrne, G. (1990). *Agency and Organization: Towards an Organizational Theory of Society*. London: Sage.

Aristotle (1911). *The Nicomachean Ethics* (translated by Chase, edited by Dutton). London: Oxford University Press.

Arrow, K. J. (1999). 'Observations on social capital.' In *Social Capital: A Multifaceted Perspective*, (eds.) P. Dasgupta and I. Seregeldin. Washington: World Bank, pp. 3–5.

Arvey, R. D. and Ivancevitch, J. M. (1980). 'Punishment in Organizations: A Review, Propositions, and Research Suggestions.' *Academy of Management Review*, 5, 123–32.

Avolio, B. J., Waldman, D. A., and Yammarino, F. J. (1991). 'Leading in the 1990s: The Four I's of Transformational Leadership.' *Journal of European Industrial Training*, 15(4), 9–16.

—— and Bass, B. M. (1988). Transformation Leadership, Charisma, and Beyond. In *Emerging Leadership Vistas*, (eds.) J. G. Hunt, B. R. Baliga, H. P. Dachler, and C. A. Schreisheim, pp. 29–50. Lexington, MA: Lexington.

Baker, W. (1992). 'The Network Organization in Theory and Practice.' In *Networks and Organizations: Structure, Form and Action*, (eds.) N. Nohria and R. G. Eccles, pp. 397–429. Boston, MA: Harvard Business School Press.

Ball, K. and Carter, C. (2002). 'The Charismatic Gaze: Everyday Leadership Practices of the "New" Manager.' *Management Decision*, 40(6), 552–65.

Bandura, A. (1986). *Social Foundations of Thought and Action: A Social Cognitive Theory*. Englewood Cliffs, NJ: Prentice Hall.

Banner, D. K. and Blasingame, J. W. (1988a). *Toward a Developmental Paradigm of Leadership*. School of Business and Public Administration, University of the Pacific, Stockton.

—— (1988b). 'Towards a Developmental Paradigm of Leadership.' *Leadership and Organisation Development Journal*, 9(4), 7–16.

Barksdale, K. and Werner, J. M. (2001). 'Managerial Ratings on In-Role Behaviors, Organisational Citizenship Behaviors, and Overall Performance: Testing Different Models of their Relationship.' *Journal of Business Research*, 51, 145–55.

Bass, B. M. (1985a). *Leadership and Performance Beyond Expectations*. New York: Free Press.

—— (1985b). 'Leadership: Good, Better, Best.' *Organizational Dynamics*, 13(4), Winter, 26–40.

—— (1990). Bass *and Stogdill's Handbook of Leadership: Theory, Research and Managerial Applications*, 3rd edn. New York: Free Press.

Bassi, L. (1997). 'Harnessing the Power of Intellectual Capital.' *Training and Development*, 51(12), 25–30.

Beniger, J. (1986). *The Control Revolution*, Cambridge: Harvard University Press.

Bennis, W. (1984). 'Where Have All the Leaders Gone?' In *Contemporary Issues in Leadership*, (eds.) W. E. Rosenbasck and R. L. Taylor, pp. 42–60. Boulder, CO: Westview Press.

—— (1989). *Why Leaders Can't Lead*. San Francisco, CA Jossey-Bass.

—— (1993). *An Invented Life: Reflections on Leadership and Change*. Reading, MA: Addison-Wesley.

Blau, P. (1963). 'Critical remarks on Weber's theory of Authority.' *American Political Science Review*, 7(2), 87–94.

Block, P. (1996). *Stewardship*, San Francisco, CA: Berrett-Koehler Publishers.

Boettinger, H. M. (1989). 'And That Was the Future Telecommunications: From Future-Determined to Future-Determining.' *Futures*, 21(3), June, 277–93.

Bolino, M., Turnley, W., and Bloodgood, J. (2002). 'Citizenship Behavior and the Creation of Social Capital in Organizations.' *Academy of Management Review*, 27(4), 505–22.

Bourdieu, P. (1986). 'Forms of Capital'. In *Handbook of Theory and Reach for the Sociology of Education*, (ed.) J. G. Richardson, pp. 241–60. Westport, CT: Greenwood Press.

Bowman, C. and Kakabadse, A. (1997). 'Top Management Ownership of the Strategy Problem'. *Long Range Planning*, 30(2), 197–208.

Bradford, D. L. and Cohen, A. R. (1984). *Managing for Excellence*. New York: Wiley.

Burns, J. M. (1978). *Leadership*, New York: Harper and Row.

Clegg, S. and Palmer, G. (1996). Producing Management Knowledge. In S. Clegg and G. Palmer, *The Politics of Management Knowledge*. London: Sage.

Coleman, J. S. (1984). 'Social Capital in the Creation of Human Capital'. *American Journal of Sociology*, 94 (supplement), S95–S120.

Cool, K., Almeida Costa, L., and Dierickx, I. (2002). 'Constructing Competitive Advantage.' In *Handbook of Strategy and Management*, 1st edn, (ed.) A. Pettigrew, H. Thomas, and R. Whittington, pp. 55–71, London: Sage.

Cooper, C. (2002). Quoted in the Director Magazine, special section on 'Leadership, The Ego has Landed'. *Director*, November, 82–6.

Covey, S. R. (1989). *The Seven Habits of Highly Effective Leaders: Restoring the Character Ethic*. New York: Simon and Schuster.

Darling, J. R. (1999). 'Organizational Excellence and Leadership Strategies: Principles Followed by Top Multinational Executives.' *Leadership and Organisation Development Journal*, 20(6), 309–21.

Davis, K. (1973). 'The Case For and Against Business Assumptions of Social Responsibilities.' *Academy of Management Journal*, 16, 312–22.

De Bettingies, H-C. (2000). 'The Corporation as a Community: An Oxymoron? Can Business Schools Re-Invent Themselves?' The Inaugural Dean G. Berry Memorial Lecture, *Concepts and Transformation*, 5(2), 165–211.

Dow, T. E. Jr (1969). The Theory of Charisma. In J. A. Conger and R. N. Kanungo, *Charismatic Leadership: The Elusive Factor in Organisational Effectiveness*. San Francisco, CA: Jossey Bass.

Drucker, P. (1988). 'The Coming of the New Organizations'. *Harvard Business Review*, 66, January–February, 35–53.

——(1990). *The New Realities*. New York: Harper and Row.

Duke, R. D. (1974). *Gaming, The Future's Language*. Beverly Hills, CA: Sage.

Eden, L. and Lenway, L. (2001). 'The Janus Face of Globalization', *Journal of International Business Studies*, Fall, 32(3), 383–9.

Fairholm, G. W. (1991). *Values Leadership: Towards a New Philosophy of Leadership*. London: Praeger.

——(1996). 'Spiritual Leadership: Fulfilling Whole-Self Needs At Work'. *Leadership and Organisational Development*, 17(5), 11–17.

Favaro, K. (2002). 'How Shareholders Value Let Shareholder Down'. *Opinion*, Marakon Associates, 1–3.

Finkelstein, S. and Hambrick, D. C. (1996). *Strategic Leadership: Top Executives and Their Effects on Organisations*. New York: West Publishing Company.

Fleishman, E. A. (1953). 'The Description of Supervisory Behavior'. *Personnel Psychology*, 37, 1–6.

Fondas, N. and Stewart, R. (1990). 'Developing Role Theory for Research on Managerial Jobs and Behaviour'. *Templeton College Management Research Papers*, MRP 90(1), 1–40.

Forester, T. (1987). *High-Tech Society*. Oxford: Basil Blackwell.

French, J. R. P. and Raven, B. (1959). 'The Basis of Social Power'. In *Studies in Social Power*, (ed.) D. Cartwright, pp. 150–65. Ann Arbor Institute for Social Research, University of Michigan, MI:

Freud, S. (1922). *Group Psychology and the Analysis of the Ego*. London: International Psychological Press.

—— (1953). *The Complete Psychological Works of Sigmund Freud*. London: Hogarth Press.

Gergen, K. J. (2000). *The Saturated Self: Dilemmas of Identity in Contemporary Life*. New York: Basic Books.

Giacchino, S. (2003). 'Bridging the Politico-Administrative Divide', Unpublished Doctoral Thesis, Cranfield School of Management.

Gilpin, A. (1995). *Environmental Impact Assessment (EIA): Cutting Edge for the 21st Century*. Cambridge: Cambridge University Press.

Greenleaf, R. K. (1998). *The Power of Servant-Leadership*. (ed.) L. C. Spears, San Francisco, CA: Berrett-Koehler Press.

Grossman, L. (2002). 'Earth Simulator', *The Times*, 160(22), SR. 4.

Halpin, A. W. and Winer, B. J. (1957). A Factorial Study of the Leader Behavior Descriptions. In *Leader Behavior: Its Description and Measureinent*, ed. R. M. Stogdill and E. A. Coons. Columbus, OH: Ohio State University, Bureau of Business Research.

Homans, G. C. (1958). 'Social Behaviour as Exchange'. *American Journal of Sociology*, 63, 597–606.

—— (1961). *Social Behaviour: Its Elementary Forms*. New York: Harcourt Brace.

Hopfl, H. (1992). 'The Making of the Corporate Acolyte: Some Thoughts on Charismatic Leadership and the Reality of Commitment'. *Journal of Management Studies*, 29(1), 23–31.

House, R. J. (1971). 'A path goal theory of leader effectiveness'. *Administrative Science Quarterly*, 16, pp. 321–38.

—— (1977). 'A 1976 Theory of Charismatic Leadership.' In *Leadership: The Cutting Edge*, (eds.) J. G. Hunt and L. L. Larson, pp. 76–94. Carbondale, IL: Southern Illinois University Press.

House, R. J. and Dessler, G. (1974). The Path Goal Theory of Leadership: Some Post Hoc and a priori Tests. In *Contingency approaches to leadership*, (eds.) J. G. Hunt and L. L. Larson. Carbondale, IL: Southern Illinois University Press.

House, R. J. and Mitchell, T. R. (1974). 'Path-Goal Theory of Leadership'. *Journal of Contemporary Business*, 3, 81–97.

Huber, G. P. (1990). 'A Theory of the Effects of Advanced Information Technologies on Organizational Design, Intelligence and Decision Making'. *Academy of Management Review*, 15(1), January, 47–71.

Jaques, E. (1951), *The Changing Culture of the Factory*. London: Tavistock.

—— (1992). *Requisite Organization The CEO's Guide to Creative Structure and Leadership*, US edn. Cason Hall & Co.

Kakabadse, A. (1991). *The Wealth Creators: Top People, Top Teams and Executive Best Practice*. London: Kogan Page.

—— (2000). 'From Individual to Team to Cadre: Tracking Leadership for the Third Millennium.' *Strategic Change*, 9(1), 5–18.

—— (2001). 'Leadership for the Third Millennium'. In *Handbook of Management*, (eds.) S. Crainer and D. Dearlove, pp. 551–5. Financial Times and Prentice Hall.

Kakabadse, A. and Kakabadse, N. (1999). *Essence of Leadership*. London: International Thomson.

—— (2000b). 'Future Role of IS/IT Professionals.' *Journal of Management Development*, 19(2), 97–154.

—— (2001). *The Geopolitics of Governance*. New York: Palgrave.

Kakabadse, N. (2003). 'Polylogue as a Platform for Governance: Integrating People, Planet, Profit and Posterity.' *Corporate Governance: International Journal of Business in Society*, 3(1) (forthcoming).

Kakabadse, N. and Kakabadse, A. P. (2000*a*). *Creating Futures: Leading Change Through Information Systems*. England: Ashgate.

—— (2002). 'Making Modernising Government Initiative Work—A Culture Change through Collaborative Inquiry.' *Public Administration and Development*, 22(3), 337–62.

Katz, D., Maccoby, N., and Morse, N. (1950). *Productivity, Supervision, and Morale in an Office Situation*. Ann Arbor, MI: Institute for Social Research.

Kets de Vries, M. F. R. (1998). 'Charisma in Action: The Transformational Abilities of Virgin's Richard Branson and ABB's Percy Branevik.' *Organizational Dynamics*, 26(3), 6–21.

Khurana, R. (2002*a*). 'The Course of the Superstar.' *Harvard Business Review*, September, 60–6.

—— (2002*b*). *Searching for Corporate Saviour: The Irrational Quest for Charismatic CEOs*. Princeton, NJ: Princeton University Press.

Kochan, T. A. (2002). 'Addressing the Crisis in Confidence in Corporations: Root Causes, Victims. And Strategies for Reform.' *Academy of Management Executive*, 16(3), 139–41.

Korac-Boisvert, N. and Kouzmin, A. (1994*a*). 'The Dark Side of Info-Age Social Networks in Public Organizations and Creeping Crisis.' *Administrative Theory and Praxis*, 16(1), April, 57–82.

—— (1994*b*). 'Soft-Core, Disasters: A Multiple Realities Crisis Perspective on IT Development Failures.' In *Trends in Public Sector Renewal*, (eds.) H. Klages and H. Hill, pp. 71–114. Berlin: Peter Lang Publishing House.

Korukonda, A. R. and Hunt, J. G. (1989). 'Pat on the Back vs. Kick in the Pants: An Application of Cognitive Inference to the Study of Leader Reward and Punishment Behaviors.' *Group & Organization Studies*, 14(3), September, 299–324.

Kozlowski, S. W. and Doherty, M. L. (1989). 'Integration of Climate and Leadership: Examination of a Neglected Issue.' *Journal of Applied Psychology*, 74(4), August, 546–53.

Kozmetsky, G. (1985). *Transformational Management*. Cambridge: Harper and Row.

Lammin, R. (2001). Supply Chain Management. In *Handbook of Management*, (eds.) S. Crainer and D. Dearlove, pp. 395–404. Financial Times and Prentice Hall.

Lin, N. (2001). *Social Capital: A Theory of Social Structure and Action*. New York: Cambridge University Press.

Lonergan, B. (1992). *Insight: A Study of Human Understanding*. Toronto: University of Toronto Press.

Luthans, F. and Kreitner, R. (1985). *Organizational Behavior Modification and Beyond*. Glenview, IL: Scott-Foresman.

Mahoney, J. T. and Pandian, J. R. (1992). 'The Resource-Based View Within the Conversation of Strategic Management.' *Strategic Management Journal*, 13, 363–80.

Malone, T. W. and Rockhardt, J. F. (1991). 'Computers, Network and the Corporation.' *Scientific American*, 265(3), 128–37.

——Yates, J., and Benjamin, R. I. (1987). 'Electronic Markets and Electronic Hierachies.' *Communication of the ACM*, 30, 484–97.

Manz, C. C. and Sims, H. P. Jr (1990). *SuperLeadership*. New York: Berkeley Books.

——(1991). 'SuperLeadership: Beyond the Myth of Heroic Leadership.' *Organizational Dynamics*, 18–35.

Marcus, J. T. (1961). 'Transcendence and Charisma.' *The Western Political Quarterly*, 14, 236–41.

Mathews, J. (1989). *The Tools of Change: New Technology and the Democratisation of Work*. Sydney: Pluto Press.

McAdam, N. (1993). 'In Search of the "Sensitive New Age" Leader: Brain Dominance and Leadership Style.' *Management*, November, 5–8.

McDermott, L. C. (1969). 'Technology: the Opiate for the Intellectuals.' *New York Review of Books*, 31 July, 25–31.

—— (1987). 'Keeping the Winning Edge: Strategies for Being a Business Partner.' *Training and Development Journal*, 41(7), 16–19.

McGregor, D. (1960). *The Human Side of Enterprise*. New York: McGraw Hill.

Mingers, J. (2000). 'What is it to be Critical? Teaching a Critical Approach to Management Undergraduates.' *Management Learning*, 31(2), 219–37.

Morgan, G. (1986). *Images of Organization*. Beverly Hills, CA: Sage.

Nahapiet, J. and Ghoshal, S. (1998). 'Social Capital, Intellectual Capital and the Organisational Advantage.' *Academy of Management Review*, 23(2), 242–66.

Newell, S. and Swann, J. (2000). 'Trust and Inter-Organizational Networking.' *Human Relations*, 53(10), 17–23.

Nibly, H. (1984). 'Leadership versus Management.' *BYU Today*, February, 16–47.

Nietzsche, F. (1976). *The Will to Power*. New York: Vintage.

Nohria, N. and Eccles, R. G. (1992). 'Face-to-Face: Making Network Organizations Work.' In *Networks and Organizations: Structure, Form and Action*, (eds.) N. Nohria and R. G. Eccles, pp. 288–308. Boston, MA: Harvard Business School Press.

Organ, D. W. (1990). 'The motivational basis of organisational citizenship behavior.' *Research in Organisational Behavior*, 12, 43–72.

Ostrom, E. (1999). 'Social capital: A fad or a fundamental concept.' In *Social Capital: A Multifaceted Perspective*, (eds.) P. Dasgupta and I. Seregeldin, pp. 172–214. Washington: World Bank.

Penrose, E. T. (1959). *The Theory of the Growth of the Firm*. New York: Wiley.

Peteraf, M. A. (1993). 'The Cornerstones of Competitive Advantage: A Resource-Based View.' *Strategic Management Journal*, 14, 179–91.

Peters, T. and Austin, N. (1985). *A Passion for Excellence: The Leadership Difference*, New York: Random House.

Portes, A. (1998). 'Social Capital: Its Origins and Applications in Modern Sociology.' *Annual Review of Psychology*, 24(1), 1–24.

Powell, W. W. (1990). 'Neither Market Nor Hierarchy: Network Forms of Organization.' In *Research in Organizational Behaviour: Volume 12*, (eds.) B. Staw and L. L. Cummings, pp. 295–336. Greenwich, CN: JAI Press.

Putman, R. (2000). *Bowling Alone: The Collapse and Revival of American Community*, New York: Simon and Schuster.

Quinn, J. B., Anderson, P., and Finklestein, S. (2001). 'Leveraging Intellect.' In *Handbook of Management*, (eds.) S. Crainer and D. Dearlove, pp. 587–594, Financial Times and Prentice Hall.

Quinn, R. E., Faerman, S. R., Thompson, M. P., and McGrath, M. R. (1990). *Becoming a Master Manager*. New York: Wiley.

Rodrik, D. (1997). *Has Globalization Gone Too Far?* Washington: Institute for International Economics.

Rogers, E. M. and Kincaid, D. L. (1981). *Communication Networks: Towards a New Paradigm for Research*, New York: Free Press.

Scott, W. E. and Podsakoff, P. M. (1982). 'Leadership, Supervision and Behavioral Control: Perspectives from an Experimental Analysis.' In *Handbook of Organizational Behavior Management*, ed. L. Frederickson. New York: Wiley.

Senge, P. (1992). *The Fifth Discipline: The Art and Practice of the Learning Organization*. Sydney: Random House.

Shaw, B. (1998). 'Community: A Work in Progress.' *Business Ethics Quarterly*, 8(4), 669–81.

Shelton, C. K. and Darling, J. R. (2001). 'The Quantum Skills Model in Management: A New Paradigm to Enhance Effective Leadership', *Leadership and Organization Development Journal*, 22(6), 264–73.

Shoemaker, P. J. H. (1997). 'Disciplined Imagination: From Scenarios to Strategic Options.' *International Studies of Management and Organisation*, 27(2), 43–70.

Sims, H. P. Jr (1980). 'Further Thoughts on Punishment in Organizations.' *Academy of Management Review*, 5, 133–8.

Solow, R. M. (1999). 'Notes on Social Capital and Economic Performance.' In *Social Capital: A Multifaceted Perspective*, ed. P. Dasgupta and I. Seregeldin, pp. 6–10. Washington: World Bank.

Spanos, Y. E. and Lioukas, S. (2001). 'An Examination into the Causal Logic of Rent Generation: Contrasting Porter's Competitive Strategy Framework and the Resource-Based Perspective.' *Strategic Management Journal*, 22(10), 907–34.

Sproull, L. and Kiesler, S. (1991). 'Computers, Networks, and Work.' *Scientific American*, 265(3), 1492–512.

Tannenbaum, A. and Schmidt, W. H. (1958). 'How to Choose a Leadership Pattern.' *Harvard Business Review*, March–April, 36, 95–101.

Thorenson, E. E. and Mahoney, M. J. (1974). *Behavioral Self-Control*. Holt, Rinehart and Winston.

Thorndike, E. L. (1911). *Animal Intelligence: Experimental Studies*. New York: Macmillan.

Tichy, N. M. and Devanna, M. A. (1986). 'The Transformational Leader.' *Sloan Management Review*, July, 27–32.

Tompson, H. B. and Werner, J. M. (1997). 'The Impact of Role Conflict? Facilitation on Core and Discretionary Behaviors: Testing a Mediated Model.' *Journal of Management*, 23, 583–601.

Tsai, W. and Ghoshal, S. (1998). 'Social Capital and Value Creation: The Role of Intrafirm Networks.' *Academy of Management Journal*, 41(4), 312–24.

Unger, R. M. (1987). *False Necessity*. Cambridge: Cambridge University Press.

Useem, P. (1987). *The Inner Circle*. Cambridge: Harvard University Press.

Vernon, Raymond V. (1991). 'Sovereignty at Bay: Twenty Years After. Millennium.' *Journal of International Studies*, 20(2), 191–6.

Vroom, V. H. (1964). *Work and Motivation*. New York: John Wiley.

Walton, R. E. (1989). *Up and Running: Integrating Information Technology and the Organization*. Boston, MA: Harvard Business School Press.

Warburton, F. E. (1993). 'Enhancing Competitiveness Through Leadership in Management.' *Business Council Bulletin*, October, 28–30.

Weber, M. (1947). *The Theory of Social and Economic Organization*. Henderson, A. M. and Parsons, T., Parsons, T., New York, NY: Free Press.

Weber, M. (1968). *On Charisma and Institution Building*. Chicago, IL: University of Chicago Press.

Whittington, R. (1988). 'Environmental Structure and the Theories of Strategic Choice.' *Journal of Management Studies*, 25, 521–36.

Wilson, I. (1992). 'Realizing the Power of Strategic Vision.' *Long Range Planning*, 25(5), 18–28.

Wood, J. D., Davenport. K. S., Blackson, L. C., and Van Burn III, H. J. (2002). 'Corporate Involvement in Community Economic Development: The Role of US Business Education.' *Business and Society*, 41(2), 208–41.

Zald, M. N. (2002). 'Spinning Disciplines: Critical Management Studies in the Context of the Transformation of Management Education.' *Organisation*, 9(3), 365–85.

Zelany, M. (1982). 'High Technology Management.' *Human System Management*, June, 57–9.

Zemke, R. (1987). 'The Gulf of Mutual Incomprehension.' *Training*, August, 8.

3

Managers' Lives, Work, and Careers in the Twenty-First Century

Prabhu Guptara

Let me begin by reporting a snippet from a meeting with one of the most experienced, respected, and intelligent senior executives whom I know. I had gone to take up an invitation to dinner and, as he came out of his office and shook my hand, I saw that he was looking crestfallen, so I asked if he had had a long day. He shook his head and said 'No, Prabhu, it's rather that I don't understand the world any more.'

Was this mere world-weariness or was it unusual sensitivity to what is going on in the world? I reflected on that statement and that conundrum, and have come to the conclusion that he is not the only senior executive who does not understand the world any more, and that no economist or politician understands our world either. That is at least partly because few people attempt to think systematically and thoroughly about the world any more.

So let us attempt to think systematically about some of the radical changes the world is going through.

First the impact of technology. We know that this has grown quickly over the last 200 years, and with increasing speed over the last few years. Though its impact may have slowed since the bursting of the bubble in Spring 2000, the fundamental research, and the development of new applications and products which will continue to drive that impact with yet more speed in the days ahead, has not stopped, and has profound implications for our immediate future. We all must not merely become IT literate, but also at least begin to understand how IT is changing society, government, politics, economics, corporations, industries, and indeed the boundaries between industries.

In 1996, I published research into the Global 100 companies[1]—the largest companies in the world. We explored the degree of IT-competence of the top teams in these companies (i.e. the five to ten most senior people in a company, including the MD and the Chairman). The results were not surprising, yet shocking: hardly anyone understood how IT is reshaping business; worse, few seemed to be doing anything about ameliorating their incompetence.

Today, only seven years later, I would guess that most senior executives are in fact IT literate, though I doubt if there is any greater understanding of the impact of technology in terms of how it is changing our world, and why.

Let me offer a simple 5-Way Model which helps explain the five different ways in which technology makes an impact, using descriptors that are arranged alphabetically to make the model easily memorizable:

A Technology *Automates* existing processes

This is simple to see and understand yet the impact even of this simple way in which technology impacts our world is every bit as profound as the subsequent ones, and neither businesses nor society have yet come to terms with it, for even simple automation increasingly abolishes whole classes of occupation. Take the example of an executive dictating a letter to a secretary: it was usual for the dictation to be taken down in short-hand, typed and presented to the executive for proof-reading and amendment; a back and forth process of several iterations. One little machine, a word-processor, considerably cut down the entire process and made life efficient for everyone. But the process of automation did not end there. Today there are cheap machines that recognize the voice and turn speech into digital form automatically. So we don't need typists, filing clerks, and the rest any more. Anyone who types at less than forty words a minute is actually costing a company money. Voice-recognition software will revolutionize the appeal and reach of technology manyfold as children and old people, the disabled and everyone who hates machines, in other words all who are outside the IT world at present, will find it easy to enter it: the consequent increase in user-friendliness, will also therefore result in much greater and indeed manifold job-reduction as vastly greater categories of repetitive jobs are eliminated, including some fairly sophisticated ones.

Perhaps you don't think of a doctor's job as repetitive or an equity trader's job as repetitive, since the average equity trader in good times can earn $6 million (1996). But do we need equity trading to be done by human beings any more, when we are developing software systems that can emulate what they do? These can capture that elusive and very personal 'know-how' gathered over years of experience. And, so far as doctors are concerned, not merely the efficient working out of prescriptions but even surgery need no longer be done by human beings: the Lausanne University School of Medicine has invented a robot that can carry out brain operations.

In ten years, will there be any job not deeply changed by the impact of automation alone? Is there any job which has not been already profoundly reshaped by the impact of automation over the last ten years?

The key point is that, not only in manufacturing, but also in the service industries, we will continue to need to employ fewer and fewer people to produce vastly greater output much more economically. And the individuals we do need to employ will continue to be only those who are faster, more creative, and skilled at a greater number of activities than any single robot or other machines at that point in time—or those who can use the potential of these machines more creatively than is allowed autonomously by the level of automation at that stage in the development of technology. Naturally, as automation continues its onward march, this puts a premium on what is called 'life-long learning'—the downside is that not everyone has the ability, the inclination, the means or the leisure to pursue this desirable goal in the particular areas which will provide what I call 'employability-advantage'—that is, competitive advantage in the employment stakes.

B Technology *Builds Bridges* between parts of a corporation that had little to do with each other

For example, marketing and R&D did not have much contact with each other twenty years ago. But now, information can be moved easily from one domain to another, closer to where it is really needed without intervening 'silos' of command and control. Result? Actually, the entire value chain has changed from (functional) silos to horizontal processes, which is at least partly what led to the revolution called Business Process Re-engineering. It is true that many BPR efforts failed to deliver all that they promised in terms of bottom-line benefit. However, that was for the same human reasons due to which we find it difficult to eliminate the repetitive jobs which are in principle eliminable by automation: you still find secretaries in most organizations and you still find vertical processes in many organizations. That does not mean that secretaries are necessary or that vertical processes are necessary. It simply means that most organizations have so far failed to leverage the benefits of these two initial stages in the impact of IT. But we must be aware that it is only those organizations which succeed in utilizing each of the radically different and themselves rapidly progressing ways in which technology impacts our world, that will have any chance of succeeding in the intense battle for survival of our times.

The outsourcing of certain parts of the value chain is another result of this move of the value chain from vertical to horizontal. Look at the call centres set up to handle customer requests on behalf of a wide range of companies who would otherwise have to carry a substantially greater cost. At present, these employ tens of thousands of people and there is no doubt that businesses that specialize in these sorts of outsourced functions will grow both in number and in size in the near future, but their long-term future is at best uncertain: what outsourcing means in terms of management is that managers are having to learn by trial-and-error the vicissitudes of managing service-level contracts and remote workforces. In time, it will become evident that such services can be better provided to customers and better controlled in terms of cost and availability if they are brought back into the centre—not least because maturing markets worldwide will mean a more frenetic search for new sources of profitability, and it is easiest to extend one's efforts to the nearby parts of the value-chain rather than to unrelated businesses.

Outsourcing (and its converse, insourcing, if you already have an operation large and sophisticated enough) is only one impact of business process re-engineering. Lean production is another, reducing the cycle time from concept to product-launch, resulting in an enormous increase in the speed with which new products can be launched. This is excellent for customers (even though they may not always want all the new products that are launched!) but, from the producers' point of view, this means of course a shorter and shorter shelf-life for all products, and a shorter and shorter time in which to recoup investments in research, design, manufacture, distribution, sales, marketing, and infrastructure—making all enterprise inherently more uncertain than it was earlier, and increasing risks in all sophisticated manufacturing activity.[2]

C Technology *Cancels* traditional divisions and *Creates* entirely new ways of organizing companies

Until five years ago most financial services companies were organized along national lines; now they are organized in global sub-businesses because IT has made it possible, and indeed necessary, for businesses to be organized in that way. This now applies also to most other sorts of business, except extraction and construction, which are probably the only businesses that, because of their very nature, will continue to be organized by nation (or, in the case of large nations, by region or even locality). In the future, however, as a result of the continuing impact of technology as well as the globalization of businesses, even such industries will increasingly be organized globally: witness the increasing globalization of the real estate industry (see the summary of the Wolfsberg Think Tank on this subject on 7 February 2002, *www.wolfsberg.com*).

As companies have reorganized along lines that cross international borders, they have had to form transnational teams for each business line. The result is that earlier problems in communication and synergy between people from different countries have been ameliorated, and problems in communication and synergy between global business lines have increased.

D Technology increasingly *Destroys* the walls between an organization's internal divisions (this has not yet had a great impact, but it will happen)

For example, in boom times, we in the financial services industry need lots of equities traders, but, in times of recession, we need more bonds traders instead. Why do we go into the market looking for such people when there are shortages … and sack them at times when nobody wants them … paying them high salaries when they are wanted, and having to bear high redundancy costs when they are not wanted? Such inefficiency will become completely untenable.

But if you speak to the people who run these businesses they will tell you: 'Prabhu, these are very special people … you can't teach a Bonds Trader to be an Equities Trader … these are entirely different animals.' This is sheer mythology, and expensive mythology at that. In future, we will look for people who have the capacity to do both jobs. Very few such people, do you say? Well, as I hope I have demonstrated by discussing the impact of automation and bridge-building alone, we will in fact need to employ very few people and the people we will need, in all industries, will need to be multiskilled at a far higher level than we have dreamed of yet. All of our systems for recruitment, training, and retention will have to change to take account of the rather fewer but rather different kinds of people who are all that will be 'needed' by companies. This raises the question of what society is going to do with all the rest of the people[3] who are not only unemployed but unemployable—a question that I will attempt to tackle after I have discussed the fifth and most stunning way in which technology is impacting and will impact business.

E Technology *Eliminates* the boundaries between industries

The 'financial services industry' was traditionally confined to banks, financial brokers, and so on. Today, this industry is being attacked by companies from every conceivable sector. Manufacturing companies like GE, retail chains like Marks and Spencer, oil companies such as Shell, airlines such as BA, voluntary organizations such as the Automobile Association in the UK, computer companies such as Microsoft (and Quicken), Internet companies such as Yahoo, new internet-based companies such as E*Trade and Schwab, information providers such as Reuters—everyone is in financial services. I foresee games companies such as Nintendo, news providers such as Pearson, TV companies such as CNN, and even Hollywood filmmakers entering financial services as further developments in IT make further integration possible. At present, the 'merging' is one-way. That is, companies formerly involved only in retailing, manufacturing, information services, leisure, or transport are entering the financial services field. Naturally, this cannot remain a one-way affair. Financial services companies, notwithstanding Deutsche Bank's abandonment of its cross-sectoral portfolio, will enter other industries—if for no other reason than through mergers and acquisitions. In any case, the result will be that the category called the 'financial services industry' will not exist in the very near future, as this industry integrates with the information industry, the entertainment industry, the retail industry, the manufacturing industry, and so on.

Of course that means that these other industrial categories will also be fundamentally reshaped, because some companies which are at present 'only' in financial services will expand their areas of operation into manufacturing and/or retail and/or extraction and/or travel/entertainment and/or computing/internet, and so on. On the other hand, some companies currently in financial services as a whole, will have to limit their areas of operation and specialize much more, becoming niche companies as a result. Clearly, the world market will be split much more than it is between niche players and entirely new entities which I call 'megacorporations', spanning all, or at least very many, of the existing industrial divisions.

How will these megacorporations be different from old-fashioned conglomerates? Conglomerates hold an unrelated portfolio of business for the purpose of balancing potential income over differing business cycles in different industrial sectors, and the reason they generally failed (though let us not forget that there are some outstanding successes such as GE in the USA and Virgin in the UK) was that understanding and experience of one industry does not necessarily enable you to manage another industry;

moreover, having a conglomerate was fine when the various industries in your portfolio were performing as you expected, but the structure of world industry has changed since 1989 and we have seen supposedly counter-cyclical industries converge, so that they have turned sour at very similar times. Since the business cycles have changed and the world has become increasingly chaotic, it is not possible to identify counter-cyclical businesses with confidence any more. In any case, the essential difference between the old-style conglomerates and the new megacorporations is that the latter will leverage the emerging changes in the relationship between customers and producers on the one hand, and between producers and supplier, producers and marketers, and producers and financiers or investors, across industries.

Megacorporations will need to employ very few people and will entirely reconstruct the value chain—again across industries—by providing customers with a confidential, convenient, quick, cheap way of getting an extremely wide range of products and services (or indeed ALL products and services) with the assistance of worldwide electronic networks stretching from production to delivery. We can see this already beginning to happen with companies such as Amazon and e-bay: the first warehouses products, the second does not, since it simply acts as a marketing arm. I think neither model will obtain, but rather a megacorporation model, in which the company handles not only the marketing, warehousing, and delivery, but also the manufacture of all its products and services. That Amazon and e-bay have been able to do reasonably well, even in the current world of text-based electronics, should persuade us that the tendency to move in the direction of supplying all possible goods and services will be multiplied, as video-based electronic nets come into being and are complemented by networks which are designed to carry Virtual Reality as well.

There is much talk of core competences at present. But a 'core competence' by itself means nothing. For example, if I am the world's expert in the structure of the Mongolian language, that by itself may not enable me to make a living. The question is always, *what* core competences will *which* market pay *how much* for? So let us think in a clearer way about the core competences which will be required by the best-paying markets in the future. If the megacorporations about which I have theorized do in fact come into being, as I think they will, then it is fairly evident that the core competences of that world will be three principal ones: marketing-related, logistics-related, and innovation-related. Anyone who can help in the brand wars which are ahead will be worth a lot. So will anyone who can help re-engineer the logistics-chain. And finally, innovation will be much in demand, whether it is a rich elite who come to dominate the world, or a just world for everyone.

In this new world, the new core competences are not going to be along the old lines of industry. The core competences of the future are going to focus on only three areas:

- excellence in marketing (or, rather, excellence in recruiting and retaining a loyal base of customers);
- excellence in organizing and operating an 'intelligent'/robot-ized value chain; and,
- excellence in innovation (new products, services, ways of marketing and ways of organizing logistics, perhaps through technological creativity and innovation).

These could form the basis of the 'industrial divisions' of the immediate future, though it is likely that even more genuinely massive mega-corporations will already emerge first, which will integrate such 'industry divisions'.

So what are the key competences that will enable *companies* to survive and flourish? Let us think of that question along the following lines. At present, we are going through another phase in the world economy in which the slogan of the day is 'return to roots' or 'back to the core'. Executives do not seem to understand that while we built up our present level of success on the basis of our original core business, returning to that core in the current situation does not guarantee survival. One cannot 'return to innocence'. An angel with a flaming sword guards the way back to Eden! Radically new strategies are needed for our times. The key competence for the future is the willingness and ability to recreate one's company in radical fashion: much bigger or much smaller.

The question is going to be: who are the people who will either shrink their companies down to niches in order to enable them to continue being profitable, or who will integrate existing corporate giants or, alternatively, build from scratch the chain across industries which can supply a range of cross-sectoral products and services to the customer? Some people do not and will not believe that this is possible. They will, of course, never attempt to build such megacorporations. But some people do believe this is possible. Clearly, the people who will attempt to build these megacorporations will come from the ranks of such 'believers'. Many such people may fail in their attempts to build these megacorporations. It could be argued that AOLTimeWarner and Vivendi Universal were attempts to create the first such megacorporations and that these attempts have failed. But the point to remember is that just because those executives failed, or some others fail in their attempts, does not mean that every one of those who try to create a megacorporation will fail. Many people die in their attempts to scale mountains, but that does not prevent others from trying and, when the first hardy soul succeeds in climbing a particular mountain, he or she makes history—and not only reshapes our horizons regarding what is possible but also changes our perception of reality.

In any case, you don't need many megacorporations to succeed. In fact, not many can succeed. There is room for somewhere between, say, twelve and twenty-five megacorporations, depending on antitrust activity on the part of governments. Without that activity, there is room for perhaps five megacorporations in the world. The point to keep in mind is that today's industrial, technological, and economic logic is undoubtedly in favour of the creation of megacorporations, and that the limits to the creation of such megacorporations lie not in the worlds of industry, business, management, technology, finance, and economics, but in the worlds of society and politics.[4] However, megacorporations are in the future, even if the not-very-distant future. Let us look in a little greater detail at *the impact of technology on our world at present.*

As a Result of the Technology Revolution, the World is Flying Blind

(1) Never before have we been confronted with such over-capacity and over-supply in every single industry across the entire globe (for example, over-capacity in steel has been forcing down prices by more than two per cent annually for the past twenty-five years (*The McKinsey Quarterly*, June 2002) till President Bush's recent intervention to shore up falling prices by political fiat. There is almost infinite over-capacity in telecoms. In the auto sector, the over-capacity is 33 per cent, not including the new factories that are coming on stream in India, China, Brazil, *et al.* The single most important assumption upon which economic theory is based is

scarcity of resources, not super-abundance. So all economic theory is in principle obsolete and we need to revisit the fundamentals of economics. This is one reason why economists are having such trouble understanding today's world and why economic forecasters are so consistently getting things wrong.

(2) Yet, in this world of over-supply and over-capacity, 3,500 children will die today . . . because there is not enough food and not enough water for them. Forty thousand adults died yesterday for the same reason. Eight hundred million went to bed last night without enough food, shelter, or clothing. Roughly one person out of every four in the world lives in absolute poverty with an income of less than a dollar a day, 'and poverty is growing . . . over a hundred countries are worse off today than fifteen years ago'[5] as the United Nations Development Report reminded us even at the height of the recently ended boom. Today, after the bust of Spring 2000 has not only lasted much longer than most people anticipated but has also caused much more paper value to be lost, the global situation regarding poverty is much worse.

What was merely a tragedy yesterday is both a tragedy and an obscenity today because none of this needs to happen; we can provide for the poorest in the world with no perceptible difference to the quality or standard of life in the developed world. In fact, it is estimated that the additional cost of achieving and maintaining universal access to basic education for all, basic health care for all, reproductive health care for all women, adequate food for all, and clean water and safe sewers for all is roughly $40 billion a year—or less than four per cent of the combined wealth of the 225 richest people in the world! This raises questions about the kind of world we are living in. It forces us to revisit the assumptions behind the services we all provide in terms of not just *what* we do, but also *why* we do them.

In any case, we can forget trickle-down theory—it doesn't work in reality; or, at best, it works only in a limited sense in particular areas and in particular circumstances.

Though there is over-supply, there are entire nations that are poorer than they have ever been, and the split between rich and poor has widened both within countries and across countries. The challenges within countries are often to do with a kleptocracy or robber-class ruling the country (consider Sudan and North Korea, where the rulers have prevented aid from reaching their people).

(3) Theoretically, in capitalism, there should be no booms or busts, because the free market should take care of individual distortions in the marketplace. Until the fall of the Berlin Wall, we all worked within very strong national boundaries and that was held up as one reason for 'market distortions'. Today, we have a global market, with far fewer national distortions, much greater capacity and speed of communications, and much less distortion and information opacity, yet the reality is that there is more boom and more bust than ever before. The result of a global marketplace has been, in some respects, *unprecedented* boom and bust. Clearly, something is wrong with, or at least lacking in, our theories.

(4) The result of this globalized economy is that it makes the developed world vulnerable to parts of the world that we do not know or even care very much about. Who cared about the Baht? Or had heard of the Baht? Foreign Direct Investment into China by starry-eyed Western capitalism created a flood of cheap exports from China which was the fundamental, though not the immediate cause of the devaluation of the Thai Baht … which created a knock-on effect in SE Asia and thence to all emerging markets in 1997–8 … Russia went into a tail-spin … which unleashed a global credit crunch and market jitters to this day. Let me emphasize this point: where did the problem start?

Not with econo-political incompetence in Thailand (which was almost usual), but with a rush of capital into China! This is a strange world we have never been in before.

(5) The result is that we need to be prepared for a whole range of scenarios—something which we have never had to do earlier. Companies and individuals need to prepare for *all eventualities*.

As an example close to home, let's look at the present uncertainty regarding the half-century-long project to create a more and more united Europe. If one selects for attention only the economic dimension, the intention of the euro was (and is) European competitiveness, through elimination of the inefficiencies caused by the need to stabilize exchange rates across Europe, through greater economies as a result of increases in the scale and scope of production, through easier trading across what till recently were borders within Europe, and through the creation of European multinationals that can compete with American and Japanese multinationals.

Has the European project worked? Undoubtedly, in certain areas, such as its original goal of keeping peace within what has from time to time been defined as Europe. Is the effort going to continue to be effective, and be effective overall in creating a European social, political, and economic entity (whether thoroughly federal or increasingly unitary)? There are in fact, so far as I can see, five different scenarios which might result, even from the viewpoint of business.

Scenario 1: Rapid corporate consolidation, and therefore immense socio-political problems

If there is rapid corporate consolidation, this should be excellent for European customers, in terms of prices. It should also be excellent for company executives and shareholders in terms of European competitiveness against players from other parts of the world. Just think: ABN-Amro which controls about half of the Dutch market has only two per cent of Europe's market in financial services; and Deutsche Bank has only five per cent even of the German market! The down side is that corporate consolidation will lead to a huge loss of jobs, at least in the short term. At the time of writing, something like twenty million are unemployed in Europe. How many more jobs will be lost? We don't know. What will be the impact on the bottom line of each country's social and economic balance sheet? We don't know. Will the Stability and Growth Pact hold? We don't know. But let us imagine, for miraculous reasons, that a different result obtains.

Scenario 2: Rapid corporate consolidation and *socio-political success*

If this happened, the euro would quickly supplant the dollar as the world reserve currency. The impact? A tidal shift in geo-economics. Currently 70 per cent of world trade is denominated in the dollar, even though the US has 24 per cent; of world GDP, and the euro-zone (as distinct from Euroland) has 29 per cent;. Remember too that the long-term fundamentals of the dollar are weak: it is still overvalued, there is an unprecedented current account deficit, a growth slowdown, and US household savings are at a historic low. For these reasons, my view is that it is not so much a case of IF the euro takes over from the dollar, but a case of WHEN. And if there is rapid corporate consolidation in Europe combined with socio-political success, there is no doubt in my mind at all that there would be an enormous geopolitical shift to the euro very quickly. However, a third scenario is possible too.

Scenario 3: Economic and socio-political failure

Let us face the fact: never have so many people been subjected to so astonishing an economic experiment (economic integration without political integration). The creation of the euro without the creation of a European political entity is a triumph of a particular political ideology which elevates market forces above politics. What if the experiment fails? Will the patient and till-now prosperous German tax-payer, who has borne the bulk of the cost of integration for half a century, revolt? Will there be other, at present unforeseeable reasons causing the collapse of this unprecedented experiment? In any case, if such a collapse happens, it is fairly clear that Europe will descend into a new dark ages and that will not be fun and games for the rest of the world. So let us turn to a more pleasant scenario.

Scenario 4: Little *economic consolidation but socio-political* stability

Within Europe, it is still possible that little economic consolidation may take place. Why? Because the credit crunch bites and there are not enough resources available; and because people may simply not have the stomach for it. Survival alone is tough enough, and the extra risks from mergers and acquisitions may not be offset by any real advantages for many players. In such a scenario, there would be few benefits to customers, executives, companies, or shareholders but, on the other hand, there would be little increase in political and social instability or upheaval. This leads to what I hope is the most likely possibility.

Scenario 5: Slow *consolidation—with political stability*

The difference between this scenario and the previous ones is simply that of the time-frame: in all the previous scenarios I am looking at developments over five years. In this scenario, I am assuming the fourth scenario, but suggesting that corporate consolidation takes place slowly after that, somewhere between five and twenty-five years, so that we have the time to work through the socio-political issues wisely, for example the issue of the lack of synchronization of political and economic systems in the euro zone.

This is definitely the best scenario overall, and certainly at the level of the middle-sized companies which are the heart and stomach and muscles of Europe (whatever may happen to the few giants we have). I happen to believe that this scenario is what is most likely to happen. It may be that I hope for this scenario simply because I am an optimist! But the point is this: If you are the top team of any company anywhere in the world you have to prepare equally hard for five different worldwide scenarios—simply as the result of this single factor, the introduction of the Euro—and there are numerous other such factors, in the light of each of which you have to prepare for fundamentally different scenarios—and that is something you have never had to do before.

Let me recapitulate up to this point my argument about our being in a world in which we are 'flying blind'. We live today in:

- a world of over-production and over-capacity in every industry (alongside unprecedented starvation and deprivation across the globe), calling all economic theory as well as our current socio-political arrangements fundamentally into question.

- A world of 'booms and busts', which should not in theory be happening in worldwide free markets.
- A world of global interdependence (meaning that relatively small adjustments in one corner of the world can lead to major and emotionally driven over-adjustments in other parts).
- A world where captains of industry need to prepare equally hard for many fundamentally different eventualities.

I come now to the final point which I think is necessary to understand the world in which we are 'flying blind'. The global market by its very structure biases things towards the creation of megacorporations on the one hand, and on the other hand towards an enormous number of niche players, represented by entrepreneurs who are able to move fast and exploit windows of opportunity, either before the big corporations step in, or in relation to which big corporations are blind or uninterested for some reason.[6] That bias towards the mega- and the niche means the stripping out of the middle-sized companies (through merger and acquisition), and the stripping out of the middle classes, as the professions decline in number and each of that number declines in its individual extent.

Let us look first at the stripping out of middle-sized companies and establish that this is in fact happening, and let us look at my sector alone for the moment—but the facts are similar in almost every industry:

- The number of US banks shrank from 14,210 in 1986 to 9,530 in 1996 (a decline of around one-third in ten years!) and to around 6,000 in 2002.

- In 1980, the biggest twenty-five US banks generated one-third of the industry's net income; today they generate well over a half.
- In 1990 the top twenty-five US mortgage originators did 26 per cent of the business, in 1997 they did 45 per cent, today they do something like 70 per cent.
- In 1987, the top ten US credit card companies held 45 per cent of all outstandings, in 1997 they held 57 per cent, today they hold over 80 per cent.
- By 1996, the top ten mutual funds companies controlled 47 per cent of all assets.
- The top fifteen home- and auto-insurers write over two-thirds of all policies.
- In California, Florida- and North Carolina (where the 'big bang' happened long ago), the top three banks control more than 60 per cent of all deposits.

If we agree that the stripping out of middle-sized companies is happening, then it is worth asking why it is happening.

As financial products are commoditized, only the biggest players will be able to support the colossal advertising and promotion efforts—anywhere from $100 million–300 million a year in the USA alone—necessary to build and support a truly national brand. Global branding of course requires somewhere between three and four times that budget. So too with technology. The top ten banks today lavish more than $1 billion on technology every year.

These factors apply in every industry, but an additional factor in other industries is the cost of R&D—for example, it costs many millions, even billions, to discover a new drug, invent a new plane or a new telecom switching system. Further, in the manufacturing industries, the cost of compliance has increased steeply and will increase even more steeply. Finally, the cost of even a day's delay in launching a product now cuts into profits so steeply, that the entire process from conception to delivery of finished and approved products needs to be made as efficient as possible, which means huge continuing investments in every area of a company: in pharmaceuticals, one day's delay in launching a product can mean a million dollars lost in profitability. No wonder middle-sized companies are being squeezed out of the world economy, no matter how good their financing, management, technology, products, and services.

We now come to the most worrying fact: *If the middle-sized company is being stripped out, so is the middle-class individual and the middle-class family.* In the USA and Europe, we see not only blue-collar jobs disappear, but also white-collar workers being stripped out in what is becoming a world of short-term employment, just-in-time production requirement, and substitution of skilled and unskilled work by software. Not surprisingly, real wages have fallen for 80 per cent of Americans for the last twenty years. Sixty per cent of all US jobs created since 1979 pay less than $7,000 a year (Fian Fact Sheet, *Welfare by Corporations is Corporate Welfare*; if you want to check other facts of this nature, please visit *www.foodfirst.org*).

These are revolutionary times. Without a middle class:

how do you hold a society together?
how do you run an economy?
how do you contain the social tensions between the 'haves' and the 'have nots'?
how do you nurture or even preserve democracy?[7]

The middle class is of course a purely post-feudal invention. In England, King Henry VII created the first 'middle' class, due to his need for tax collectors. This was, however, a rather thin middle class, and it was not till Victorian times that a proper middle class emerged, due to the social engineering of right-wing governments which recognized that they needed a middle class to hold society together. Why is a two-tier society so volatile? Because dissatisfied or enlightened lower-class leadership can cause revolutionary upheavals . . . But, despite an illusion created by the media that the middle class is being preserved or is even increasing in size, reversion to a have vs. have-not society is in fact taking place worldwide. Fortunately, there are at least a few people who care enough to think systematically about how to create a world that is safe and just and peaceful for us all.[8]

Let us take the next set of questions: how many people do we *need* to employ in an IT driven world? What sort of people do we need to employ in the not very distant future—say ten years? And what do we do with all the rest of the people in the world? If we take that ten year time-scale, many of the organizations that exist today will cease to exist. This is a hard thing to say and a harder thing to accept. But it is possible that between twelve and twenty-five megacorporations will come to dominate the world—unless you and I and everyone else decides to do something about it politically. Some of what can be done has been thought through, and some is being thought through, though of course there is a lot more which needs to be developed. So if you are an activist-type, there is plenty you can do to get some of the thinking implemented, and if you are a thinker-type, there is still enough scope for you to help pioneer some of the things which need to be developed.

In the meantime, I come back to the question of what sort of people companies will need to employ. The principle that exists even today, though we may not think of it in this way, is that we employ only such people as can offer a price/performance ratio superior to that offered by computers and robots at their current stage of development. In a world where Deep Blue has already beaten the Chess Master, it should be clear that computers can (or will soon be able to) do most single tasks better than human beings. The vast majority of lawyers, doctors, stock and bonds traders, for example, are already (in principle) redundant—even though it will take several years for this to work its way into reality. The kinds of people we will continue to employ will be those who are innovative and creative, and those able to work across a range of disciplines—because it seems extremely unlikely that we will ever be able to produce machines that are creative, innovative, or able to work across disciplines. Matters calling for judgement and service are unlikely to be looked after adequately by robots.

Scared? Don't Be!

These are times of fundamental change for everyone. But these are also times of glorious opportunity for the clear-eyed and daring. What do I mean by clear-eyed? Those who don't duck the new realities but look at them squarely in the eye. (Most of us are running around unable to look at the new realities because we are so completely taken up with busyness and activity!) What do I mean by daring?: Those who face up to the worst that could happen and then decide to create the best that there could be.[9] This is the first time in history that we can really design organizations which will be fit for the future. If we wish to do so, we will need to re-examine:

what we want to achieve (purpose)
how we set about trying to achieve it (methods)
why it is worth achieving (values, ethics, and spirituality).

Unless we look at ourselves very radically as individuals, as families or as corporations, it will be difficult to survive the whirlwinds that are ahead.

At the same time, it will be a wonderful world for quick-eyed and quick-footed entrepreneurs able to see and to move into niches which are either not spotted or not worthwhile for the megacorporations. We need to be clear-eyed. Moving from our current core competences as companies (and, if necessary, as individuals) requires daring. These are terrible times. They are also wonderful times. They are times of which we can make what we will. These are times of opportunity. The question is: will we use the opportunity? And will we use it only to cater to our own greed? Or will we use it also to make the world a place that is at least minimally human?

Finally, how *will* life, work, careers, and companies be different for twenty-first-century managers as compared to those in the last century? As I have tried to explain, that is really up to us, for the first time in history. However, if an insufficient number of people get involved in thinking and action to implement wise political choices, as far as I can see, subject to environmental constraints and assuming that the small number of rich people continue to have a weak social or other kind of conscience, life will be unimaginably wonderful for the fewer and fewer number of people who will be richer and richer.[10]

Here are some other final if somewhat scattered thoughts on the subject:

(1) Though there seems to be a systematic drive on at present to misrepresent facts so as to avoid believing this, the environmental consequences of our current economic–technological way of organizing things will be disastrous, and all the major religious scriptures of the world predict that this is what will

happen, though the point of view of the Bible seems to be that Armageddon is avoidable.[11]

(2) Partly because most people instinctively sense this fact, substantial energy is directed towards improved corporate governance as well as towards greater responsibility for the environment and for society. However, most of the measures which have been proposed are merely cosmetic and do not address the root issues, which are structural. For example, we need to re-think company law and the purpose of companies, and push for the creation of Publicly Approved Companies.[12]

(3) Since most work will be done by machines, employment as we have known it for the last two hundred years will more or less cease to exist. If you want to generate an income, you will need to be imaginative, entrepreneurial, and energetic, spotting opportunities to make money and jumping to take advantage of them before some other person or organization does so. Careers will be non-existent, except in the sense that the imaginative, entrepreneurial, and energetic will career from one risky money-making opportunity to another as the fancy takes them. The result will be that the sort of plague of mental illness which at present afflicts the United States will spread to all parts of the world. Even those people who have more-or-less guaranteed incomes from a large portfolio of diversified investments will feel the increasing pressure of anxiety as many investments disappear because of the increasing number of bankruptcies, while the few investments that continue to yield fruit will do so spectacularly, and portfolios will constantly need to be rebalanced, when the meaning of the world 're-balance' will not at all be clear. Only those who are perennially optimistic, because of their genes or upbringing or active relationship with God, will be able to withstand the pressures on life.

(4) There will be an increase in SMEs, portfolio careers, people working remotely (across and within countries), and a range of organizational structures marked on the one hand by much greater horizontal and vertical integration in mega-corporations, to much more contractual relationships across and within loosely federated companies.

(5) Many white-collar workers who were laid off in heavy manufacturing industries in the past were frequently re-employed when times got better. Will this happen again? Or will this happen only for those who invest in continuing relationships in spite of the bitterness they feel about the way in which they have been treated?[13]

Mrs Thatcher once famously said that there is no such thing as society. There may even be a question about what exactly is a company. However, without organizational structures which provide training, development, and careers, only the fleetest of foot and quickest of mind will flourish. The rest will find it difficult even to survive. 'Only the fittest should survive', say Darwinists, 'let the rest go to the wall'. However, not all of us are Darwinists. Questions such as 'What is society? How to build it sustainably? What are companies? How can they be enabled to contribute to society as well as to individuals? How can individuals and families flourish in the modern world?' remain questions worth pursuing for non-Darwinists. Even Darwinists might want to reflect, however, on whether it is worth living in the kind of world that is being created by current trends in technology, finance, economics, politics, and society. For all of us—for our life, work, and careers—the implications of such reflection are profound.

Notes

I am grateful to Jonathan Winter and other colleagues in the Career Innovation Group (and to those from the member companies) for their ideas and suggestions in response to some of the material in this chapter, which was originally presented at a CiGroup conference in 1998, and published by CiGroup as an internal discussion paper in 1999. All flaws in thinking and articulation are of course not to be attributed to the CiGroup or to the member companies, but to myself. Moreover, I should make it clear that I write in a personal capacity, and not as a representative of any of the universities, business schools, organizations, or companies with which I am connected. This is specifically because I want to practise the art of the caricaturist in order to capture some of the essential features of our times in the short ambit of one chapter. Naturally, I do not expect that readers will agree with everything in this chapter, but I trust my remarks will have some stimulative power and will lead to wider discussion about key questions and dangers that confront the world economy and society and indeed the world—though I don't wish to sound apocalyptic, since many of the prophets were killed, and are still treated in our supposedly tolerant age with disbelief and indifference, rather than with any eagerness to learn.

1. Published by ADVANCE: Management Training Ltd (UK) and the Wolfsberg Executive Development Centre (a Member of the UBS Group), Switzerland, 1998.
2. 'Eighty to eighty-five per cent of all new food products launched in the UK are *not* on supermarket shelves one year later', reported Dr Tim Ambler in his paper 'Innovation Metrics', London Business School Working Paper 98/904, Centre for Marketing, London Business School, 1998.
3. This puts me in mind of the statement made in one of the gospels by Jesus that towards the time of the end of the world (in his view) people would bless barren women—an inversion of the usual situation historically when people blessed fertile women and thought that barren women were accursed.

4. See my review-article on Paul S. Mills and John R. Presley's *Islamic Finance: Theory and Practice* (Macmillan Press, 1999) in *The ACE Journal* 27 (2000), 32–43); also my review article on Susan L. Buckley's 'Teachings on Usury in Judaism, Christianity and Islam' (*Faith in Business Quarterly*, Spring 2002, 25–9).

5. The finding was originally stated in the 1997 UNDP Human Development Report. The finding was repeated and re-emphasized in the 1999 Report as well as in the Human Poverty Report 2000. The latest figures on growing poverty in the world, as well as in particular areas of the world, can nowadays be rapidly accessed by a Google search for 'poverty is growing'.

6. *The New Pioneers* by Thomas Petzinger, Jr (Simon & Schuster, 1999) is a good example of the tendency to think that 'innovative firms in small and medium-sized businesses are creating an opportunity-rich economy', when the fact is that it is not SMEs that are doing so at all. SMEs are simply benefiting from the present phase in the world economy (a fundamental restructuring), in which it is possible for SMEs to flourish. This market environment will come to an end when the megacorporations whose creation I predict come into existence. When these megacorporatons first come into existence, there will be a phase in which several will mushroom. This will result in a battle among these megacorporations in which some will be driven into extinction, and some will emerge winners. These winning megacorporations will then need to snap up smaller and smaller companies in order to maintain innovation, growth in sales, and growth in their share value as well as in their market capitalization. We must also remember that SMEs almost always last only for somewhere between one and three physical generations from the founder, for reasons that are too well documented to bear repetition here.

7. For a related discussion, see my paper: 'An Indian Perspective on Democracy' (presented at the Professorenforum, Frankfurt, Germany, 13 April 2002; copies available on request).

8. See, for example, Michel Albert, *Capitalism against Capitalism*, Whurr Publishers, 1992; Jonathan Boswell and James Peters,

Capitalism in Contention: Business Leaders and Political Economy in Modern Britain, Cambridge University Press, 1997; Hernando De Soto, *The Mystery of Capital: Why Capitalism Triumphs in the West and Fails Everywhere Else*, Perseus Books, 2000; Peter Drucker, *Post-Capitalist Society* (1994); Colin Kirkpatrick and Norma Lee (eds.), *Sustainable Development in a Developing World: Integrating Socio-Economic Appraisal and Environmental Assessment*, Edward Elgar, 1997; David C. Korten, *The Post-Corporate World: Life After Capitalism*, Kumarian Press, 1999; Edward O'Boyle (ed.), *Teaching the Social Economics Way of Thinking*, Mellen Press, 1999; Mancur Olson, *Power and Prosperity: Outgrowing Communist and Capitalist Dictatorships*, Basic Books, 2000; Heinrich Pesch, *Liberalism, Socialism and Christian Order* (4 vols.), Mellen Press, 2000, 2000, 2001, and 2002; Tom Sine, *Wild Hope*, Monarch, 1992; Tom Sine, *Mustard Seed vs. McWorld*, Monarch, 1999; Russell Sparkes, *The Ethical Investor*, HarperCollins, 1995; Alister McGrath, *The Re-enchantment of Nature—Science, Religion and the Human Sense of Wonder*, Hodder & Stoughton, 2003.

9. This involves understanding two things. First, the reasons why the world is in the current mess; and, second, what can be done about it. I explored some of the reasons for both matters in the lecture entitled 'Ethics Across Cultures' that I was invited to deliver at the Royal Society for the Encouragement of the Arts Manufactures and Commerce, London, England (a summarized version of the lecture was published under the same title in the *Journal* of the Society, in issue 2, 1998, 30–2). The reasons were explored a little more fully in the lecture on the topic 'Making the World Better: Why it Does Not Happen and What To Do About It' that I was asked to give at the Dozentenforum, University of Zurich; the audio-recording of that lecture is available from *rbadertscher@coba.ch*. The reader might also want to consult The Other Economic Summit (TOES) and *Sojourners* magazine (USA) for sometimes parallel, sometimes converging, and sometimes diverging, explorations of the reasons.

10. Forty per cent of the gains from the rise in the stock market over the decade (from 1988 to 1998) of the last boom went to one per cent of the US population, according to the US Secretary of Labor—reported in *Financial Times*, 7 April 1999.

11. The Jewish scriptures are ambiguous on this point, and some Jewish folk believe this; others believe the opposite. By contrast, the Koran is quite clear that this is what will happen, and good Muslims have no option but to accept this teaching. Hindus are ambivalent regarding the end of the world, with some believing that the world regularly ends every so many aeons before it is reborn; in any case, the present age (*Kaliyuga*) is supposed to end with the coming of Kalki riding a horse—remarkably similar to the New Testament's view of the end of this world. Some biblical commentators, as in the rage for the *Taken Away* film series, seem to understand the books of Daniel and Revelation as referring to an inevitable timetable. They seem to ignore the book of Jonah, in which the prophet was sent with a very specific warning of destruction (within forty days) to the important city of Nineveh, but when the people changed their way of life, the verdict of destruction was lifted—much to Jonah's chagrin but resulting in a revelation of God's love as the basis both of judgement and of forgiveness.

12. Bob Goudzwaard argues, in *Globalization and the Kingdom of God* (Baker Books, 2001), that private limited companies need to be replaced with 'Publicly Authorized Companies' which take seriously the environment, labour, consumers, and civil society. He also argues for establishing suitable international treaties, for example, regarding international finance, technology, and the environment. Other individuals thinking in similar ways include David Korten, who recommends a rigorous audit, which he calls a Market Efficiency Audit. This audit would measure the external impact of a company, both good and bad, and he compares these external impacts with the profits the company generates. Simon Zadek of the New Economics Foundation in Britain has worked with Richard Evans of Traidcraft to develop a social audit system

based on the ideas of George Goyder. Whole organizations, such as the Council for Economic Priorities (CEP), are not merely beginning to think in this way, but CEP has also developed a system for grading the social responsibility of corporations in seven categories (and published its findings in the book, *Shopping for a Better World*, by Marlin *et al.*, 1992). Goyder's son, Mark Goyder, founded the Centre for Tomorrow's Company (CTC) in London, UK. The findings of CTC's first Enquiry demonstrated that taking all stakeholders seriously is not just idealism but also makes economic sense in terms of sustainable shareholder value and market capitalization. CTC's second Enquiry, currently in progress, is looking wider: at the whole chain of investment from the individual saver to the companies in which the saver's money gets invested. The findings of this Enquiry are expected to be thought-provoking.

13. My friend Joe was dismissed from his job recently in spite of earning consistently as a salesman for his company for thirty-six years, and in spite of the fact that he had only four years to go before his retirement! From a financial point of view, he does not 'need' to earn again, so why should he invest in relationships with people who were his subordinates, and indeed how can he be expected to invest in relationships with new employees he has never met earlier, especially if there are no structures to enable him to do so? In turn, why should the new people respond to any overtures from him when they have their own deadlines and bottom lines to cope with, as well as their own friends and ac-quaintances who may also be out of work and whom they would employ first if there were any opportunity to do so, assuming that they had more or less equal qualifications?

4

Late Twentieth-Century Management, the Business School, and Social Capital

Ken Starkey
and
Sue Tempest

This chapter explores the dubious legacy that late twentieth-century management (LTCM) has bequeathed to the twenty-first-century manager. It argues that some of the guiding principles of LTCM have outlived their usefulness and that we face an urgent need to rethink management. It suggests the concept of social capital as a key focus for the twenty-first-century manager. It also addresses the role of the business school in educating managers, arguing that, just as we need to rethink management, we also need to think critically about the mindset and the values that the business school, particularly through the MBA degree, offers managers.

Late twentieth-century management (LTCM)

It is difficult to imagine management in its current form surviving until the end of the twenty-first century. Grounded in thinking and practices that became the orthodoxy in the late twentieth century, our current way of managing seems to have reached or to be approaching its limits.

Why do we say this? For three main reasons.

(1) The legitimacy of management is under fire as never before. Society is asking questions of management that do not have easy answers. The business crises of the early twenty-first century raise fundamental questions about LTCM and why managers act and feel empowered to act in the ways they do.

(2) Nature cannot support it. While not wanting to revisit limits of growth arguments or to engage with the excesses of green critique of current business practices, there is accumulating evidence that the kind of world we live in will be transformed for the worse (probably irreversibly) unless we rethink the way we manage.

(3) Just as citizens are asking searching questions about the negative aspects of big business, employees are too. Those who have lost jobs in recent rounds of corporate restructuring are, understandably, disaffected. Those who are fortunate enough to have survived the various rounds

of corporate restructuring are disaffected in different ways. Ironically, they lack the time to consume, they suffer the stresses and long hours of operating in the slimmed-down workplace, the negative effects of this on their personal lives, the guilt that comes with having survived less fortunate colleagues and the anxiety, as they grow older, that they will be next to go.

Why are we where we are? The fall of the Berlin Wall in 1989 seemed to mark the end of history in the sense portrayed in Francis Fukuyama's (1992) best-selling book of the same name. Economic, social, and political history, Fukyama argued, had come to an end because there was no convincing alternative to liberal democracy and capitalism with minimal regulation. The late twentieth century saw the triumph of one variant of management—the American Business Model, consisting of the unrestrained pursuit of self-interest, market fundamentalism, minimal state, low taxation (Kay, 2003). The free market economics espoused by Milton Friedman and others were given free rein, driven by the rhetoric of market liberalization and globalization.

The triumphalism expressed by Friedman [and championed in Reagonomics in the US and Thatcherism in the UK] developed into hubris and finally into collective madness . . . The greatest admiration for the American business model was to be found in the American business community. Arbitrariness and disparities in the distribution of income are justified—even morally justified—simply because they are market outcomes.

(Kay, 2003: 6–7)

Arbitrariness itself is finessed out of the picture in a perversely secularized variant of the Puritan ethic. The rich deserve to be rich, the poor deserve to be poor. Greed, to return to a key phrase of the 1980s, was good. Why did managers come to think like this? Part of the issue here is management education. The phrase 'Greed is good' was notorious corporate raider and insider dealer Ivan Boesky's valedictory comment to a group of Stanford MBAs. Presumably he thought it was appropriate to the culture of business and education into which these graduates had been initiated.

The Business School

The business school has been one of the major success stories of higher education in the last hundred years. It has outgrown most other parts of the university and is now a central feature of the higher education map. In the MBA degree it has created perhaps the world's first global degree. Originating in the USA the MBA has grown pervasively and now turns up in all corners of the world, and with a relatively common curriculum policed by influential accrediting bodies.

Yet the MBA is increasingly criticized for an antiquated approach to management, essentially unchanged since the 1950s, focused upon business functions and on analysis and techniques (Mintzberg and Gosling, 2001: 64). The MBA is also criticized for not delivering, possibly because of its outmoded pedagogical assumptions, either for the individuals who pursue the qualification or for the companies that employ them after graduation. 'Although business schools and business education have been commercial successes, there are substantial questions about the relevance of their education product and doubts about their effects on both the careers of their graduates and on management practice' (Pfeffer and Fong, 2001: 78).

Looked at from the perspective of the present, rather than the 1950s when the curriculum started to congeal, the MBA is accused of having a 'weird almost unimaginable design' and for graduating 'critters with lopsided brains, icy hearts and shrunken souls' (Leavitt, 1989: 39). Top MBAs are equipped to perform sophisticated financial analyses of companies to determine which are ripe for takeover (leveraged or otherwise) or restructuring. The analytic brain is greatly developed but there are parts that the MBA does not touch and which it might actually atrophy.

The MBA and the business school were in the firing line of criticisms of the hype and failings of the new economy of the 1990s. Enron, for the latter half of the 1990s the world's most admired company (!), was praised for its innovative recruitment practices focused upon recruiting the best MBA graduates. The accusation is that the business schools helped promote, through their rhetoric and educational offerings, a fixation with unsustainable growth and questionable management practices that attempted to hide the performance void that lay behind the rhetoric. Of course, the business schools were not the only culprits. The dot-coms (soon to be renamed *dot-cons*—Cassidy, 2002) and management consulting firms were also complicit in shaping the *zeitgeist*. But, of course, before the advent of the new economy the career of the choice for the MBA was management consulting, only to be replaced, during the heady days when the new economy was in full flight, by a career in the start-up.com!

In the harsh light of the collapse of the dot-coms and of corporate scandals such as Enron, the business school was charged with having played a significant role in creating the business climate that made these possible.

So many people—most notably investors and employees, but also society at large—have been badly hurt by the Enron debacle. How could it happen? Business schools must accept some of the responsibility. Recent survey data suggest that MBA students graduate with less concern about social and ethical issues than when they entered business school ... Like it or not, business school faculty—myself included—must accept some responsibility for the managers we train. Too often we turn out ambitious, intelligent, driven, skilled over-achievers with one under-developed aptitude. Too many of the business leaders we graduate are hitting the ground running, but we have forgotten to help them to build their moral muscles.

(Salbu, 2002: xiv)

Ironically, business school league tables, which play a key role in the market for management education, measure the added-value of the MBA in terms of differences in graduate salary pre- and post-MBA. What goes missing in the process is the concern with training business leaders to be 'true professionals with true character' (Salbu, 2002: xiv).

Another way of framing the criticism of business school education and of LTCM is in terms of character development. This is the line explored by Richard Sennett (1998) in his coruscating critique of contemporary management and its culture and practices based upon ideas and ideals of permanent restructuring, downsizing, and flexible working. Sennett examines the ways in which the 'new' capitalism corrodes the bases for trust, loyalty, and mutuality in work.

How can long-term purposes be pursued in a short-term society? How can durable social relations be sustained? How can a human being develop a narrative of identity and life history in a society composed of episodes and fragments? The conditions of the new economy feed instead on experience which drifts in time, from place to place, from job to job ... short-term capitalism threatens to corrode ... those qualities of character which bind human beings to one another and furnishes each with a sense of sustainable self.

(Sennett, 1998: 26–7).

Sennett is prone to exaggeration. Not all work is subject to the same extent to the excesses of new capitalism thinking. Yet! But he is right in arguing that this thinking is becoming more pervasive in its impact upon management philosophy. Sennett's rhetoric appeals also, very successfully, to our fears (Chris Argyris, personal communication). But this fear itself speaks to understandable concerns, about identity, for example, which is shaped to a large degree by our work. When we meet someone for the first time we are commonly concerned to situate and to identify ourselves through our work location and allegiance. The question 'What do you do?' usually elicits a response about our occupation. It also speaks to a deep-rooted need for sustainability and for at least a degree of predictability in an uncertain world. Again, work can, for the more fortunate, provide an anchor in shifting times. We know from research into unemployment how destructive the absence of work can be to the sense of self.

Sennett's work gives rise to a crucial question for business school faculty: How can we educate managers to recognize their impact, currently negative, on the construction of the 'sense of sustainable self'? How can management help construct organizations in which this sense of self is sustained and sustainable? One way of framing this is in terms of social capital.

The Task of the Twenty-First-Century Manager—Building Social Capital

We cannot guess what the organisations of 2008 will look like. We do know, though, that trust, community, connection, conversation and loyalty will make them work and will make work meaningful for their members. The value of the social capital elements they embody will be redisovered again and again because they lie at the heart of our humanness and our human ability—and need—to do things together.

(Cohen and Prusak, 2001: 186)

The social capital argument is that successful long-term organizations and institutions are rooted in relationships based upon trust, loyalty, connectivity, and communication. Social relations, if they are to be effective and long-run, depend upon cooperation more than competition. Social capital is 'made up of social obligations *("connections")... convertible, in certain circumstances, into economic capital*' (Bourdieu, 1985: 243).

Features of social organization such as networks, norms, and social trust, the embodiments of norms of reciprocity, facilitate co-ordination, and cooperation for mutual benefit (Putnam, 1995: 67; Woolcock, 1998: 153). In the business context, the management task in building social capital is to develop those aspects of organization that facilitate co-ordinated action to achieve desired goals. In the words of the former chief executive of the Zurich Financial Services, these include 'social norms and values, shared context (strategic agenda, vocabulary, mission, vision) and networks. This includes social capital embedded among the employees of a firm as well as in the networks of relationships the firm has with its customers, suppliers and other constituents that impact on the modern organisation' (Hüppi and Seemann, 2001: 3).

Rooted in sociology and social policy, the concept of social capital was developed to explain how communities work to the mutual benefit of their members through sustaining positive connections among people. Organizational social capital is a resource reflecting the character of social relations within the firm. It is realized through members' collective goal orientation and trust and . . . 'is a major source of relational wealth for a firm' (Van Buren III and Leana, 2000: 233). The strongest contemporary argument for the importance of social capital was elaborated by Robert Putnam in his now classic study, *Bowling Alone.*

For a variety of reasons, life is easier in a community blessed with a substantial stock of social capital. In the first place, networks of civic engagement foster sturdy norms of generalized reciprocity and encourage the emergence of social trust. Such networks facilitate coordination and communication, amplify reputations, and thus allow dilemmas of collective action to be resolved. When economic and political negotiation is embedded in dense networks of social interaction, incentives for opportunism are reduced. At the same time, networks of civic engagement embody past success at collaboration, which can serve as a cultural template for future collaboration. Finally, dense networks of interaction probably broaden the participants' sense of self, developing the 'I' and the 'we', or (in the language of rational-choice theorists) enhancing the participants' 'taste' for collective benefits.

(Putnam, 1995: 67)

At the societal level the emphasis upon social capital goes hand in hand with the emphasis upon investment in human capital (Giddens, 1998: 99–101). This has obvious implications for business schools where some faculty have long championed the cultivation of human potential as their major task.

The debate about social capital is a new theme in management research literature. It can be understood, at least in part, as a reaction against the excesses of LTCM. One strand of management literature integrates seamlessly with the understanding of organizations from a social capital perspective. This is the view in organizational learning that 'a firm be understood as a social community specializing in speed and efficiency in the creation of knowledge' (Kogut and Zander, 1996). Social capital is a crucial resource for creating and sharing knowledge, a process that is facilitated by the mutual influence, trust and empathy associated with its presence. A key factor here is 'associability', 'the willingness and ability of individuals to define collective goals that are then enacted collectively' (Leana and Van Buren, 1999: 542).

This emphasis upon mutuality is at odds with much of the rhetoric of LTCM and its emphasis upon individualism. Greed is good implies the selfish pursuit of self-interest, at the expense of others if necessary. Ghoshal (2003) criticizes the education offered by business schools and particularly the economics taught in MBA courses for the value system it embodies. For example, agency theory, arising out of the work of Michael Jensen, is grounded in a view of human nature that does not accept that managers can be trusted to deliver on what is seen as the key purpose of the corporation—shareholder value. Stock options are justified as a means of aligning managerial concupiscence with this purpose. Transaction cost economics, another staple of the MBA, justifies the existence of companies in terms of tight managerial controls and performance incentives. The touchstone of most MBA strategy courses is the work of Michael Porter, itself grounded in a view of the business environment red in the tooth and claw of competition.

The social capital approach is based on different assumptions about human nature and the nature of organization. It requires that we think of how well-managed organizations can develop high levels of social capital through structural, relational, and cognitive means (Nahapiet and Ghoshal, 1998). *Structural* thinking means we have to consider how the overall pattern of connections between actors can best be managed for mutual gain. Here one can 'measure' the density of connections, structural hierarchy, and connectivity. *Relational* thinking means we have to be sensitive to the quality of personal relationships that exist between individuals and groups in an organization and across its boundaries, for example, with suppliers and customers. From a social capital perspective these relations should be managed to optimize the creation of trust and trustworthiness, obligations, and expectations and a sense of shared identity and identification with organizational goals that subsume or transcend the goals of individuals. Social capital is a relational good. It is 'owned' collectively because it is only activated through and in relational activity.

The *cognitive* task for management is to develop a language and forms of communication that promote genuinely shared cognitive representations and systems of meaning among actors and groups in the organization. These three dimensions are crucial to facilitating collective action that transcends that promoted by tight control or an emphasis upon competition at the expense of everything else. Their implementation requires of managers high levels of *cognitive* and *emotional competence*.

Cognitive competence grows with social capital. In particular, the strong ties that characterize organizations strong in social capital facilitate the transfer of complex information and tacit knowledge (Hansen, 1998). Another way of framing this is to say that social capital supports the generation of intellectual capital. 'Intellectual capital [refers] to the knowledge and knowing capability of a social collectivity . . . Intellectual capital thus represents a valuable resource and a capability for action based in knowledge and knowing' (Nahapiet and Ghoshal, 1998: 245). The greater social capital, the more knowledge managers will be able to assimilate from an informationally enriched social network (Cohen and Levinthal, 1990).

Richard Goleman (1999: 11), the pioneer of emotional intelligence, argues that *emotional competence* is a pre-requisite for coping with the 'war zone' that is contemporary business:

'People are beginning to realize that success takes more than intellectual excellence or technical prowess, and that we need another sort of skill just to survive—and certainly to thrive—in the increasingly turbulent job market of the future. Internal qualities such as resilience, initiative, optimism, and adaptability are taking on a new valuation.' The premise is that our prospects for the future, individually and collectively, depend upon our ability to manage ourselves and to sustain relationships more than ever before. Emotional competence, according to this perspective, is a combination of personal competence (self-awareness, self-regulation, and motivation) and social competence (empathy, awareness of others' feelings, needs and concerns, social skills, adeptness in relating to others).

The Challenge for Business Schools and Managers

The exuberance that characterized the 1990s now looks, in the famous words of Alan Greenspan, Chairman of the Federal Reserve Board, deeply irrational. The NASDAQ index of technology stocks, a key indicator of this irrationality, reached its peak in early 2000. Within two years it had lost 75 per cent of its value. The demise of the new economy, its hubris, reflected the unsustainability of LTCM. It was the result of a way of business having been hijacked by the values of a financial community that is preoccupied with trading and deal-making to the exclusion of a broader sense of purpose. Couched in a simplistic argument about the economic efficiency of capital markets, what goes missing is a sense of the dysfunctional consequences of a narrowly defined bottom line for the general good, for the kind of society we inhabit, for the lives we lead and for those we aspire to lead. Some even go as far as seeing in this period a growing crisis of legitimacy in modern capitalism (Plender, 2003).

A prime characteristic of the 'new' capitalism was the fetishism of the individual and the 'outlawing' of personal dependence on others (Sennett, 1998). Bell argues that: 'Capitalism was not just a system for the production of commodities, or a set of occupations, or a new principle of calculation (though it was all of these), but a justification of the primacy of the individual' (Bell, 1973: 481). But the emphasis upon individualism ignores the hidden dynamics that shape collective behaviour. Kay (2003: 318–19) reminds us that markets only function effectively if they are embedded in social institutions which are themselves grounded in trust and community: 'Corporate cultures, ethical values and the blending of working and social lives are all necessary for effective cooperation.' It is only in this context, grounded in social capital, that we can effectively deal with the demands, the anxieties, challenges, and risks we face, individually and collectively.

It is our contention that management research needs urgently to address the complex relations governing the interactions of social, political, and economic institutions. The economic turmoil of the opening years of the twenty-first century reminds us that the focus on economic capital as the be-all and end-all of management is short-sighted, limited, and ultimately destructive. We need to think again about how effective societies and markets work. The business school has a crucial role to play here in making this a central part of its agenda, though this will involve a degree of self-questioning of its purpose. We have suggested that one possible, though certainly not the only, way of doing this is to apply the lens of social capital to research and management education so that it becomes a core concept for the twenty-first-century manager.

The social capital argument is that good companies thrive on good company (Cohen and Prusak, 2001). Employees are more likely to devote their energy, talent, and loyalty to an organization and to share the fruits of their experience if they feel that such behaviour is likely to be reciprocated and that they are being managed in a fair and equitable manner. In such an organization managers can expect:

- Lower transaction costs (to use the economic rhetoric referred to above), due to a high level of trust and cooperative spirit (both within the organization and between the organization and its customers/partners).
- Lower turnover rates, reducing severance costs and hiring and training expenses, avoiding discontinuities associated with frequent personnel changes, and maintaining valuable organizational knowledge.
- Greater coherence of action due to organizational stability, shared understanding, and shared vocabulary.
- Better knowledge sharing, due to established trust relationships, common frames of reference, and shared goals.

This is not to suggest that social capital is a panacea nor that it does not have potential downsides. The ties that bind can also blind members of a group and leave them self-centred and isolated. Internal networks need to be complemented by external if organizations are to function effectively in staying adapted to their environment. Access to networks—and their information and knowledge—is an extremely valuable social asset. It is, for example, a crucial selling point for top MBA programmes. The negative side of social capital is that, while facilitating cooperative behaviour within groups that it binds together, it can close the minds of members of these groups to outside influence.

In-bred groups can indulge themselves in conspiracies against the public as exchange is enhanced among members but at the expense of others (Portes and Landolt, 1996). Too closely knit social, political, and economic organizations are prone to 'cartelization' and to what economists term 'rent seeking' and ordinary men and women call corruption (Putnam, 1995). Social capital can lead to organizational dysfunction to the extent that it restricts the requisite degree of individual freedom and initiative and strong norms breed conformity or marginalize dissidents so that group-think develops.

We live in a time of flux. Old hierarchies are rightly being dismantled. The context of contemporary work is many-faceted. Some still work in large, complex organizations, though they are smaller than as in their bloated heyday. Others are in smaller organizations, virtual organizations, network organizations, organizations that aspire to last, or organizations that come together for the life of a project and then disband (Starkey, Barnatt and Tempest, 1998). This is the price of a dynamic economy and we are not challenging it. We are, though, asking that we reflect upon why such an economy exists and what is its purpose? What do we risk losing and for what gain, if we cling to LTCM principles?

Careers too are changing. Individuals have become more interested in self-employment and independent consulting, in part as a means of becoming less dependent on large corporations that they now trust less to provide security. For some, careers are synonymous with flexibility. Stability is no longer the most salient component of the employment relationship. However, we do not yet know the price these changes will demand in terms of social capital which is dependent upon developing trust among employees and employers. The signs, though, are not auspicious. Garsten (1999), in a study of temporary workers in

the USA and Sweden, found an emphasis on individuals developing personal skill sets and mindsets and the sense that this
might be to the good of the firm, but not necessarily. The danger
is that we are moving into an era where too much of our thinking
is transactional rather than relational.

How should one manage a career in an environment in which the
establishment of relational wealth has been largely supplanted by the
pursuit of shareholder wealth? . . . The questions facing organizations in
this new employment model is how to balance the objective need for
short-term results with longer-term needs for employee commitment
and involvement. Can organizations devise methods to develop individual human capital and organizational relational capital at the same
time? Can young employees develop the type of human capital and
personal reputation they need in an environment that features little
long-term trust between labor and management? Integrating individual
needs and organizational demands in some new configuration will be
the major career-development challenge facing both young professionals and their employers in the years ahead.

(Feldman, 2000: 171, 180)

The lens of social capital enables us to understand how we
depend upon gradually developed ties of trust and understanding that comes from interaction with known colleagues over
time. But the rhetoric of LTCM is that the most efficient organization is one that consists of 'free agents' who meet briefly to
carry out a particular project and then move on to some other
temporary configuration. This view blinds us to the felt quality
of work, its experiential dimension, its role in creating a sustainable sense of self:

we experience work as a human, social activity that engages the same
social needs and responses as the other parts of our lives: the need for
connection and cooperation, support and trust, a sense of belonging,

fairness and recognition. But analysts still often see organizations as machines (for producing goods, services, or knowledge) or as an assemblage of self-focused individuals—free agents or 'companies of one'—who somehow manage to co-ordinate their individual aims long enough to accomplish a task.

(Cohen and Prusak, 2001: ix–x)

However, the building of such trust relationships is ever more difficult. Indeed, we have seen a general decline in levels of trust in society generally over recent years. Putnam (1995) notes that Americans are increasingly less trusting. The proportion of Americans saying that most people can be trusted fell by more than a third between 1960 and 1993, from 58 per cent to 37 per cent. This is a trend that unites and is shared by all socio-economic groups. Indeed, the overall decrease in social trust is even more apparent if we control for education because social trust is correlated with education and educational levels have risen sharply in this time period.

Historically, part of the 'business' of education has been to promote citizenship and trust—in self, in others, and in the progress that is made possible by the accumulation of human and cultural capital. The business school has played an increasingly central role here but, in its contribution to LTCM, has tended to over-emphasize a limited set of values, narrowly economic and of a particular kind, and a one-dimensional view of character. It has tended to over-emphasize intellectual or rational intelligence (measured as our IQ) at the expense of other features of character. A social capital perspective suggests that intellect needs to be supplemented with emotion, IQ with EQ (emotional intelligence), the latter a mix of personal competence in managing ourselves and social competence in managing our relationships with others.

Management, like education, has been a key force in the march of progress. Yet the idea of progress now comes charged with ambiguity. While welcoming the gifts of an affluent society we are increasingly aware that they are ambiguous gifts and that progress comes at a price. The concept of the 'risk society' captures our growing sense of anxiety. The sense of growing risks with uncertain outcomes—for example, in the degradation of the environment that comes with its exploitation—undermines our sense of security in the world and the optimism of even the most emotionally intelligent. In the process, knowledge, expertise, and authority are increasingly and rightly questioned and more openly disputed.

Science and its application in business to create new technologies that open the way to new products and services, and drive costs from business, is seen both as a blessing and, in its unintended consequences, as a potential threat. LTCM promised much, far more than it delivered or can deliver. It too is now revealed as a sort of Pandora's box. A risk society is a 'self-critical society' in which we see a 'self-opening of the monopoly on truth' (Beck, 1994: 25). It is our contention in this chapter that late twentieth-century management does not hold a monopoly on truth. LTCM is characterized by the limits of its vision and the narrowness of its assumptions.

One of the most pressing tasks for the twenty-first-century manager and for the business school is to evaluate critically the current bases of our management thinking. Our purpose in this chapter has been to challenge this narrowness of LTCM and to challenge managers to question and, where appropriate, to transcend its limits and the limitations. We have suggested areas in which this challenge might be focused. We leave the reader with a question to focus this self-opening to management's limitations. How can social capital and financial capital co-exist for the long-term good of individuals, organizations, and society?

References

Beck, U. (1992). *The Risk Society*. London: Sage.

Bourdieu, P. (1985). 'The forms of capital.' In J. G. Richardson (ed.), *Handbook of Theory and Research for the Sociology of Education*, pp. 241–58. New York: Greenwood.

Cassidy, J. (2002). *dot.con. The Greatest Story Ever Told*. London: Penguin Press.

Cohen, W. M. and Levinthal, D. (1990). 'Absorptive Capacity: A New Perspective on Learning and Innovation.' *Administrative Science Quarterly*, 35, 128–52.

Cohen, D. and Prusak, L. (2001). *In Good Company. How Social Capital Makes Organizations Work*. Boston, MA: Harvard Business School Press.

Feldman, D. C. (2000). 'From the Me Decade to the Flee Decade', In C. R. Leana and D. M. Rousseau, *Relational Wealth*, Oxford: Oxford University Press.

Fukuyama, F. (1992). *The End of History and the Last Man*. London: Hamish Hamilton.

Garsten, C. (1999). 'Betwixt and Between: Temporary Employees as Liminal Subjects in Flexible Organizations.' *Organization Studies*, 20(4), 601–17.

Gerlach, M. L. (1992). *Alliance Capitalism: The Social Organization of Japanese Business*. Berkeley, CA: University of California Press.

Ghoshal, S. (2003). 'Business Schools Share the Blame for Enron.' *Financial Times*, 18 July 2003.

Giddens, A. (1998). *The Third Way*. Cambridge: Polity Press.

Goleman, D. (1999). *Working with Emotional Intelligence*. London: Bloomsbury.

Hüppi, R. and Seemann, P. (2001). *Social Capital. Securing Competitive Advantage in the New Economy*. London: Financial Times/Prentice Hall Executive Briefings.

Kay, J. (2003). *The Truth about Markets*. London: Allen Lane.

Kogut, B. and Zander, U. (1992). 'Knowledge of the Firm, Combinative Capabilities and the Replication of Technology.' *Organization Science*, 3, 383–97.

Leana, C. R. and Rousseau, D. M. (2000). 'Building and Sustaining Relational Wealth.' In C. R. Leana and D. M. Rousseau (eds.), *Relational Wealth. The Advantages of Stability in a Changing Economy*, pp. 277–94. Oxford: Oxford University Press.

Leavitt, H. (1989). 'Educating our MBAs: On Teaching what we haven't Taught.' *California Management Review*, 31(3), 38–50.

Mintzberg, H. and Gosling, J. (2001). 'Educating Managers beyond Borders.' *Academy of Management Learning and Education*, 1, 64–76.

Nahapiet, J. and Ghoshal, S. (1998). 'Social Capital, Intellectual Capital, and the Organizational Advantage.' *Academy of Management Review*, 23, 242–66.

Pfeffer, J. and Fong, C. T. (2001). 'The end of Business Schools? Less Success than Meets the Eye.' *Academy of Management Learning and Education*, 1, 78–95.

Plender, J. (2003). *Going off the Rails. Global Capital and the Crisis of Legitimacy*. Chichester: Wiley.

Portes, A. and Landolt, P. (1996). 'Unsolved Mysteries: The Tocqueville Files II.' *The American Prospect*, 7.

Putnam, R. D. (1995). 'Bowling Alone: America's Declining Social Capital.' *Journal of Democracy*, 6, 65–78.

——(2000). *Bowling Alone: The Collapse and Revival of American Community*. New York: Simon & Schuster.

Salbu, S. (2002). Foreword to *Anatomy of Greed. The Unshredded Truth from an Enron Insider*. London: Hutchinson.

Sennett, R. (1998). *The Corrosion of Character. The Personal Consequences of Work in the New Capitalism*. New York: W.W. Norton & Company.

Starkey, K., Barnatt, C., & Tempest, S. (1998). 'Beyond Networks and Hierarchies: Latent Organizations in the UK Television Industry.' *Organization Science*, 11, 299–305.

Van Buren III, H. J. and Leana, C. R. (2000). 'Building Relational Wealth through Employment Practices: The Role of Organizational Social Capital.' In C. R. Leana and D. M. Rousseau (eds.), *Relational Wealth. The Advantages of Stability in a Changing Economy*, pp. 233–46. Oxford: Oxford University Press.

Woolcock, M. (1998). 'Social Capital and Economic Development: Toward a Theoretical Synthesis and Policy Framework.' *Theory and Society*, 27, 151–208.

Part II

The Academics' View

5

A Next Challenge in Organizational Leadership

Chris Argyris, 2004

There are two mindsets that appear to dominate the world of action. The first is productive reasoning. The second is defensive reasoning (Argyris, 2003 in preparation).

Productive Reasoning is used in the service of producing valid or validatable knowledge, creating informed choices, and emphasizing personal responsibility for the effectiveness of actions. The core of productive reasoning is testing the claims that human beings make to ensure that they are not invalid and the parties involved are not unknowingly kidding themselves.

The design and management of most organizations is based on productive reasoning. The managerial disciplines aim to specify with increasing clarity (a) the concepts and actions that are necessary for each discipline to be effective, (b) the causal connections between the ideas and the actions, and (c) the effective monitoring of their implementation.

The effective implementation of productive reasoning requires that human beings be skilled at this type of reasoning so that they can use it in an on-line real-time manner, whether engaging in face-to-face relationships or developing plans for policies and practices (e.g. strategy, finance, marketing, and information technology).

As each managerial discipline matures in its use of productive reasoning, there is an increasing insistence that the testing of their ideas and implementation be as transparent as possible, and that the logic used to test the claims be as independent as possible from the logic used to create the claims. Without transparency and independence, there is the danger that the tests, using self-referential logic, will produce results that are self-fulfilling and self-sealing. Productive reasoning is the hallmark of effective action and personal responsibility.

Defensive Reasoning is used to avoid most of the features of productive reasoning. It is used to avoid transparency, valid testing of ideas, and personal responsibility for one's actions. The consequences of defensive reasoning include escalating misunderstanding, and self-fulfilling and self-sealing processes. These in turn produce feelings of helplessness and a victim mentality. Moreover, trends develop towards self-protection being more important than genuine learning, especially when the issues are about challenging the status quo in policies and practices.

Because defensive reasoning and actions violate the espoused principles of effective management of organizations, such reasoning and actions are cover-up. In order for cover-ups to work, they too must be covered up. A key strategy to activate this is to make both the cover up and its cover-up undiscussable. This strategy requires further cover-up.

Soon organizations develop an underground culture of managing. Everyone knows its rules. Everyone knows that one of its rules is to deny when they are being used. The creators and users of the underground world maintain that they do so in order to protect the organizations from their own foolishness. Organizational defences are necessary to protect organizations from their own defensiveness.

Organizational Inner Contradictions. The co-existence of productive and defensive reasoning produces inner contradictions. For example, the successful implementation of productive reasoning necessarily strengthens defensive reasoning. Also as the transparent above ground organizational world is strengthened, the underground world will also be strengthened. One important consequence of not dealing effectively with the inner contradictions is that the underground world will be strengthened, as will be the denial of its existence. However if the underground bubble is pierced by a crisis that makes the underground world transparent, the users will deny their personal causal responsibility and place the responsibility on factors other than themselves.

For example, there is the Enron/Arthur Andersen fiasco, the lack of cooperation between the FBI and the CIA, the tragedy of the Challenger flight (Rogers *et al.*, 1986). There is also the cover-up of questionable and, at times, illegal actions by Catholic priests. Finally, there are several cases recently reported in the newspapers where teachers have given pupils the correct answers to test questions so that the schools can get higher evaluations. In all these cases, the participants blame others or the system. They were the victims. They were helpless and they had to cover up. Whistle-blowers are required to surface these features. But, in doing so, whistle-blowers violate the protective games of the underground system. They are often characterized as immature trouble-makers.

A Puzzle. The analysis above contains an important puzzle. Productive reasoning is the basis for the theories that are used to design and implement the managerial disciplines such as accounting, finance, IT, and strategy. The knowledge and skills of the management disciplines are taught in all types of educational programmes as normative theories for effective managing and leading. Not surprisingly, these ideas play a prominent role in the policies of organizations.

What is surprising is that defensive reasoning which is as powerful is not taught as a recommended normative theory for effective action and organizational survival. I do not know of classes at universities or organizations that are dedicated to help individuals and organizations become skilled at defensive reasoning and that recommend and teach the skills required to produce organizational anti-learning consequences such as skilled incompetence, skilled unawareness, and organizational defensive routines. Where and how are the ideas and the skills taught? How come they are maintained even though they inhibit the implementation of productive reasoning and its positive consequences for organizations?

This question has concerned myself and my colleagues for several decades (Argyris, 1982, 1990, 1993, 2000, 2003/in preparation; Argyris *et al.*, 1985; Argyris and Schön, 1996). I will outline, very briefly, some of our attempts to begin to answer the question.

(1) Human beings produce action through the use of their mind/brain. In order for the mind/brain to produce actions effectively, it must have stored designs that specify the actions and their correct sequences in order to achieve whatever consequences they intend.

(2) Human beings hold two kinds of designs. There are the designs that specify their beliefs, values, and attitudes about effective dealing with human beings and effective organizations. These are espoused theories of action.

(3) The designs that human beings actually use to produce action are their theories-in-use. Although human actions vary, the theory-in-use does not, even across cultures, genders, races, and the type, size, and age of organization, wealth, and economic status. This means, for example, whatever variances is observed it is consistent with the theory-in-use that has been labelled as Model I. The core competence of Model I is defensive reasoning.

(4) Model I theory-in-use is produced by individuals but it is *caused* by a massive acculturation process that is worldwide. The acculturation to Model I and defensive reasoning begins early in life, long before human beings enter organizations. They do not need workshops in defensive reasoning because they are already skilled in this human competence and they create organizational defensive routines to protect their defensive reasoning and to deny that such practices exist.

Thus, human beings are skilled at productive and defensive reasoning. They are able to use both. If this perspective is correct, then it is their Model I theory-in-use that is the primary cause of organizational defensive phenomena such as organizational defensive routines. Once in place, the organizational defensive routines feed back to reinforce Model I. Hence we have the generic counterproductive underground processes described above.

The Primary And Secondary Causes Of The Defensive Reasoning Mindset

How is this challenge to be met? In order to answer this question, we begin by making explicit a claim that is at the heart of our analysis. Although the theories-in-use and the organizational defensive routines co-exist, and mutually reinforce each other through circular feedback processes, the Model I theories-in-use are the primary causes and the organizational defensive routines are the secondary causes. If you want to reduce the counterproductive consequences of Model I theories-in-use and organizational defensive routines in such a way that the changes persevere, it is necessary to *begin* by changing the dominance of Model I theory-in-use.

Beginning by focusing first on organizational changes will result in changes that are limited at best. Two examples come to mind. The underlying strategy for creating alternative schools was based on changing the system. Alternative schools have failed because the theory-in-use of the teachers and students was never changed (Argyris, 1974). This is consistent with what Wrong (1961) defined as the over-socialized view of human beings: change the system or context correctly, and the rest will follow.

A more massive example is the experiment of the former Soviet Union. The employees were given power through ownership. Yet, underground defensive routines blossomed and did so by the initiative of the workers. This is one reason why in many Soviet factories political observers were often present during meetings intended to make crucial managerial decisions. Their task was to force the workers to be more proactive and take more initiative in controlling their world (Argyris, 2004 in preparation).

There is a way to field test the claim of primary and secondary causes. *If* we place individuals in settings that are: (a) non-hierarchical or pyramidal, (b) absent of everyday pressures related to achieving organizational objectives, (c) absent of rewarding or punishing people for learning, (d) absent of harming their reputation or their organization, (e) free to leave the setting, and, (f) if these human beings choose to attend these settings because they wish to learn how to strengthen their effectiveness in managing themselves and others as well as designing and implementing effective organizations, *then* these individuals will create actions that are consistent with Model I and 'classroom' defences that are consistent with organizational defensive routines, even though such actions are seen by them, and the faculty, as counterproductive.

I present two illustrations. The first is the Andy Case that, to date, has been used in ten different settings, each ranging from twelve to 120 participants in Europe and in the United States. The second example comes from tape recordings from hundreds of seminars, each ranging from ten to 140 participants. Most of the participants came from different organizations. However, at least twelve seminars were conducted with the participants being from the same 'organic' group. Gender, race, education, position in the hierarchy, type of organization varied widely in eight of the Andy Case seminars and in the seminars used in the second example as well.

The Andy Case. The first example is the Andy Case. The participants in this seminar were thirty-four CEOs. The results are similar on nine different workshops with participants ranging from thirty-four to 120.

The CEOs read the Andy Case ahead of time. It tells the story of how Andy failed to become a CEO in a company that hired him to be the COO, fully expecting that he would become the

CEO. The case describes the authors' (Ciampa and Watkins, 1999) diagnosis of the errors Andy made that led to his demise. They include:

(1) Andy did not learn enough about the politics and the culture of the company.
(2) Andy overemphasized action at the expense of truly understanding what it would take to make changes.
(3) Andy failed to motivate others, especially senior managers in manufacturing and engineering, to abandon their comfortable work patterns.
(4) Andy became isolated. Andy never built coalitions to support his efforts to transform the organization.
(5) Andy did not manage himself well. He was overconfident in himself as a leader and in his plan. (Ciampa and Watkins, 1999: 9)

I acted as the faculty member (FM). I told the CEOs that the purpose of this exercise was to help them to become more aware of their effectiveness in helping others, in this case Andy, to become a more effective leader.

The two sessions (each lasting about two hours) were tape-recorded.

ANDY [As acted by the Faculty Member, FM.] You know folks, I believe the company sucked me in during the courting period. I also believe that I made errors and worse, yet, I was blind while making them. I want your help to overcome my blindness, and correct my errors. I do not want to repeat this failure again.

The advice from the CEOs came fast and can be organized as follows:

(1) Advice that was not actionable. For example, 'you should have met more with your direct reports to win them over'. Andy's response to this was, 'I know that it is important to meet with my direct reports in order to win them over. What I don't know is what I should have said. What kind of talk produces winning them over? My fear is that I would craft my conversation in ways that are counter-productive and I would be unaware of this fact.' No response was given to his request.

(2) Advice that contained inconsistent actions. For example, 'show that you have thought it through, that you have a vision. That you are committed. In other words, show a simple force of strength.'

(3) Advice that was about his past errors without including advice as to how to correct the errors. For example, 'Andy, you should have gotten support from the CEO and the Board before you took action.' Andy agreed that this was an error. He thought he had their support when they had told him to breathe new life into the company. When he asked how he could accomplish this, the response was that he should have gotten the support in writing.

(4) Advice that Andy acted in ways that harmed the organization. Andy responded that he honestly believed that he was doing the right things. One CEO then said, 'Well [if you believe that], I don't think that you will learn much from our trying to help you.' Andy responded, 'Are you telling me that when I tell you what I honestly believe, you can conclude that I can't learn? How do you arrive at that conclusion?' No response.

The CEOs became increasingly frustrated with Andy. For example:

- We doubt that Andy is genuinely interested in changing.
- Andy says that he wants to learn, but he is closed to learning.
- Andy seeks that advice that will make it possible for him to blame the others.
- Andy seeks absolute control of the situation.

The CEOs were unable to help Andy. They blamed their 'failure' on Andy's behaviour. When asked if they heard his pleas for concrete illustrations, the CEOs said, 'yes'. They added that providing such illustrations would not do much good since Andy was closed. The FM noted that because the CEOs did not test their attributions about Andy, that their logic was self-sealing. Some CEOs agreed, and others disagreed, but they all held Andy responsible for the 'failure'.

Next, FM asked the CEOs how they thought Andy felt about them.

(1) Andy feels he is a victim.
(2) Not understood.
(3) Not helped.

Andy pleads for help. He finds the help unhelpful, and says so. The CEOs conclude that Andy is closed to learning. They predict correctly that Andy feels that he is a victim. The CEOs said that they reached their conclusions about Andy in the first five to ten minutes. Yet, they did not make these attributions public in order to test them. So we have CEOs who advise Andy to be more straightforward and to learn to test the validity of his views, while not behaving consistently with their own advice.

The CEOs were committed to helping Andy to overcome his blindness and to create conditions of trust. Yet the CEOs created behaviours within the educational setting that were similar to the mistrustful and counterproductive ones that Andy had created with the CEO and the Board. The CEOs accomplished this without ever knowing Andy's CEO and Board.

Finally, the CEOs never used their sense of increasing frustration as a platform for learning. For example, FM recalled some of the evaluations and attributions the CEOs developed during the dialogue but kept private. For example, they could have said to Andy:

Andy, we tried to give you helpful advice,
We did it with the best intentions,
We were immediately told it would not work,
We tried to figure out why it would not work,
You told us that you could not trust the CEO,
So Andy, we are left with the feeling that I know of no way
    that we can help you.
So when you ask for help, we say to ourselves, *not me*.

The CEOs agreed that these comments represented their true feelings. 'You said it better than I did', said one CEO, FM asked if some CEOs disagreed. Not one said that they disagreed. These responses indicate that the CEOs were capable of crafting communication that would help Andy to see what he was doing in the room, but they did not do so. I asked the CEOs what led them not to say the above, since it represented their true feelings. Some answered that such candidates might make Andy even more defensive.

Top Financial Officers and Research & Development Executives, and MBA Students

Participants were asked to write a case that focuses on an important problem they want to solve in their organizations. The major feature of the case format is to divide their paper in half. On the right-hand side of the column they write the conversation that went on between the writer and the others involved. On the left-hand column they write any private conversation that they recollected (Argyris and Schön, 1996).

The left-hand column typically includes comments such as:

List 1—Left-Hand Column

---

1. Don't let these guys upset you.
2. Say something positive.
3. This is not going well. Wrap it up and wait for another chance.
4. Remain calm. Stick to the facts.
5. He is clearly defensive.
6. He's playing hardball because he is afraid of losing power.
7. She is over blowing the systems issue to avoid having to change.
8. He is baiting me now.
9. Will he *ever* be able to change?
10. The trouble with you is that you do not really understand accounting as a managerial function.

The session began with the FM distributing the list, telling them that it came from their cases, and asking them, 'What does this list tell you about the individuals who wrote these comments?' They responded:

List 2—Inferences
1.   They were opinionated.
2.   They talk as if they are right.
3.   They are frustrated and angry.
4.   They are entrenched.
5.   They are avoiding conflict.
6.   They are not listening.
9.   They are fearful.
10.   They exhibit lack of empathy.

The FM wrote these responses on the board. He pointed out that their responses were primarily composed of negative evaluations and attributions of defences 'in' others. Moreover, their major conclusion from List 1 about themselves (they knew the wrote these comments) was that they appeared closed to learning.

We see in these reactions the following patterns:

- Evaluations and attributions are made in ways that do not encourage testing. The writers appear to act as if their diagnosis is valid and does not require testing.
- The writers of the cases appear closed to learning or, at least, they see learning as unnecessary. Yet all of them attended the seminar and wrote the case with the expressed purpose of learning how to be more effective in dealing with the human side of enterprise.

The class comments on List 1 led to reflection on a different issue. One participant said that what surprised her was the negativeness of the first list. She recognized her comment in List 1 and it, too, was negative. Yet, she added, she was certain that her intent was to be positive. She guessed that this was probably the intent of others in the class. Several class members responded affirmatively.

The faculty member then asked the executives to analyze List 2, their comments about List 1, as he had written them on the board. The executives responded that these comments, too, were negative. They were evaluations and attributions crafted in ways that did not encourage inquiry. This also surprised them.

Here, we find another general pattern:

- There is a systematic discrepancy between the writers' expressed aspirations to learn and help others to learn and their actual behaviour, which is largely counterproductive for learning. The individuals are systematically unaware of the ways in which they produce their unawareness.

The FM then passed out a third list. It contained examples of the private thoughts and feelings with the actual conversation included in the right-hand column. The conversations were crafted in ways that were diplomatic and smoothed-over. They illustrated skill in spinning.

List 3	*Thoughts and Feelings Unsaid*	*Conversations*
1.	You guys come up with more excuses that make no sense. You do this all the time.	You still have the ability to offer different combinations of products.
2.	If we gave you everything you ask for, we would lose our shirts.	The research we have done shows that there is a consumer movement towards my views. Your sales will not be harmed.

3.	How can I convince the group of the necessity to change while we're on top?	Although we are the leaders, it is becoming more difficult to remain responsive and react quickly enough. Our product development process has to become more effective and efficient.
4.	Winning the Nobel Prize will not help the company. Perhaps it's time to expand development staff and downsize research staff.	I am sure that you all realize that we work in a for-profit industry and must be realistic-oriented. Yet, it should be possible to find commercial value even in basic research.

The next step is for the individuals to learn to craft conversation that would facilitate learning. Often, individuals try to do so and they cannot. This helps us to make the point that they require a new theory-in-use, one that we call Model II.

The governing values of Model II are: produce (1) valid knowledge that is testable, (2) informed choice, and personal responsibility to detect and correct errors. This means that any position taken, any evaluations or attributions made, should be accompanied with illustrations that back up your claims and are crafted in ways that the claims can be tested. Model II is consistent with crafting actions that are based upon productive reasoning. It encourages learning around difficult problems, especially those associated with inner contradiction (Argyris, 1982, 1990, 1993; Argyris *et al.*, 1985; Argyris and Schön, 1996).

Conclusions and Recommendation

There are two strategies to make the productive reasoning mind-set more powerful and to reduce the power of the defensive reasoning mindset. The first strategy focuses primarily on strengthening productive reasoning. Recently, Bossidy and Charan (2002) have presented a perspective of this strategy but, they had little to say about how to reduce directly the defensive reasoning mindset. Apparently, their assumption was that as the effective use of productive reasoning increases, defensive reasoning will decrease. Our observations illustrate a different conclusion. When productive reasoning is used to reduce defensive reasoning, the latter may appear to be reduced. The reality is that defensive reasoning is increased, but it is also driven underground.

A second component of this strategy is to recreate modern organizational structures and learning policies that strengthen the productive reasoning mindset. For example, Ackoff (1999) proposes the concepts of circular organizational and democratic hierarchy. Ackoff is aware of, indeed illustrates with examples, the correct implementation of his ideas requires the reduction of the defensive reasoning mindset. (On a personal note, he and I are exploring opportunities in organizations to produce such change processes.)

The reason why the focus on strengthening only the productive reasoning mindset is likely to have limited effectiveness is illustrated by a recent book. Weick and Sutcliffe (2002) organize their arguments for strengthening the productive reasoning mindset around the concepts of creating high reliability organizations. They recommend the establishment of a collective state of mindfulness. A state of mindfulness is characterized by such features as on-going scrutiny of existing expectations, and by continuous refinement and differentiation based upon newer experiences. Mindfulness is akin to productive reasoning.

There is a puzzle embedded in the analysis presented by the authors. On the one hand, there is direct and indirect acknowledgement that the defensive reasoning mindset exists in organizations. For example, the authors say that they do not see many organizations that approximate the managerial ideal. Organizations are often managed such that decisions are made that justify positions already taken, and where preferences and effectiveness criteria are conflicting, yet they persist. Often the organizations make a series of decisions outcomes by rationalizing what has already happened. Organizations thus exhibit intergroup rivalries and politics.

Moreover, the authors illustrate that organizational cultures can be inflexible and inhibit learning and adaptation. Many organizations assume that a system is not in danger until it is proven to be so. They provide illustrations where inquiry into anomalies was denied because inquiry, doubt, and updating were discouraged. These features are consistent with the defensive reasoning mindset and its accompanying generic counterproductive defensive syndrome. The puzzle is that the underground organization that produces and encourages mindlessness is left alone to continue its counterproductive activities. The assumption appears to be that if the corrective actions strengthen the productive reasoning mindset, defensive reasoning will be reduced, because it will no longer be necessary. Ackoff's work and the case material presented in the article raises questions about this assumption.

What are the challenges faced if there is a desire to enhance mindfulness and to decrease mindlessness in contexts where the participants use Model I theory-in-use, and where organizational defensive routines exist? It is possible to develop some relevant hypotheses by referring to the Andy Case and to the seminars where the left-hand/right-hand case methodologies were used. For example, in the Andy Case, the CEOs exhibited little of what the authors recommended to enhance mindfulness. They exhibited little updating, they did not accept the reality of ignorance, focused primarily upon confirming and not disconfirming, and did so by using self-referential logic, which assured self-fueling and self-sealing processes that inhibited their effectiveness.

In the left-hand/right-hand case material, we saw that the participants did not build capabilities to cope with errors: indeed, they did not see themselves as making errors. Nor did they enhance mindfulness by focusing on, as the authors recommend, a cure rather than a prevention. Their self-censorship strategies (left-hand columns) were primarily preventative. Also, many eased-in to show concern. Unfortunately, the easing-in strategy was interpreted as being a 'lawyering', I-got-you strategy. And, unfortunately, the recipients dealt with their bewilderment and frustration by also easing-in.

The advice offered by the authors to enhance mindfulness was violated continuously by the participants in the cases that they wrote and in their actions in the classrooms where their behaviour was tape-recorded. For example, the authors advise that individuals should carry their labels lightly in order to remain alert and flexible. I believe that it is fair to say that the participants in our sessions would agree with this advice. But they (e.g. the CEOs) would add that the data Andy produced were so overwhelmingly counterproductive that they had to carry over their labels heavily. However, we learned that the categories they carried heavily, they did secretly (e.g. the CEOs never explored their private evaluations of Andy's actions), also the participants who wrote left-hand/right-hand cases crafted them with the intention of not making the others defensive, yet the opposite occurred.

There was little attempt to make underground cover-up strategies discussable. Indeed, striving to do so was seen as foolish, likely to be counterproductive, impractical and, at best, romantic. I believe that it is fair to conclude that the cases written illustrate a mindset of mindlessness. They also illustrated that they were skilfully unaware of acting consistently with mindfulness. The authors define highly reliable organizations as organizations that one can count upon not to fail in doing what is expected of them. The conception of reliability as used in the book was related to the productive reasoning mindset. The underground organizations with its defensive reasoning mindset and the self-fuelling and generic syndrome that inhibits double-loop learning is also a highly reliable organization. It will not fail to produce what is expected of it.

The problems of not addressing directly the defensive reasoning are illustrated by two examples about cultural change. A recent front-page story by Roberts, *et al.* in the *Financial Times* (2002) quotes the present CEO of ABB as saying, 'I really have to sort out what is wishful thinking and what is reality. I have to change the culture, especially to encourage more openness and transparency internally' (p.1). In an article in the *New York Times*, Langley (2002) quotes Mr Dormann as saying that there was a lack of accountability and transparency, and that there were too many turfs.

Mr Dormann is the present Chief Executive Officer and Chairman of ABB. This is the same organization in which Percy Barnevik, a few years earlier, was recognized for transforming ABB's culture so that the organization faced reality, encouraged openness, transparency, initiative, and trust. The question arises: how did ABB lose all these features so quickly, given the laudatory description by many writers about the transformational change championed by Barnevik?

The 3M case also raises some similar questions. 3M is described in the literature for several decades as having a culture that supported innovation, initiative, and trust (Bartlett and Ghoshal, 1995). In a recent article by Hymowitz in the *Wall Street Journal* (2002) the new CEO is cited as saying that he found an organization that lacked a culture that encouraged innovation and initiative.

What are the organizational processes that caused the deterioration of the 3M culture, that produced innovativeness? How aware were the participants that the deterioration was occurring? If they were not, how do we explain that they were producing it? If they were aware, what caused the individuals to go along with it? Also, how did they cover up their collusion, and cover up that they were not covering up? Answers to these questions will help scholars better to understand and explain the nature of organizational culture and how it can be changed in ways that are effective and preservable. The answers will also help the practitioners in disagreeing and producing cultural change. For example, they may be helped to see that the championing processes they use do communicate their commitment, but they do so in ways that strengthen external commitment. External commitment may be necessary in large organizations. Or, it may be necessary at the outset, but internal commitment may be generated as the programme continues. External commitment is not necessarily wrong. What is counterproductive is for the top to champion the changes by championing external commitment, and by making the inconsistency undiscussable.

Changes that genuinely transform organizations are not likely to persevere as long as the defensive mindset is not reduced. Similarly, if scholars are to produce actionable knowledge that goes beyond being the servant of the status quo, they will find it necessary to examine their own defensive reasoning mindset and the norms of their respective communities that support the mindset. This will require research about double-loop learning that appears to produce knowledge that exhibits a high degree of implementable validity.

References

Ackoff, R. L. (1999). *Re-Creating the Corporation*, New York: Oxford University Press.

Argyris, C. (1974). 'Alterative Schools: A Behavioral Analysis.' *Teacher College Record*, 75(4), 429–52.

——(1982). *Reasoning, Learning, and Action: Individual and Organizational*. San Francisco, CA: Jossey-Bass.

——(1990). *Overcoming Organizational Defenses*. Needham, MA: Allyn Bacon.

——(1993). *Knowledge for Action: A Guide to Overcoming Barriers to Organizational Change*. San Francisco, CA: Jossey-Bass.

——(2000). *Flawed Advice and the Management Trap*. New York: Oxford University Press.

——(in preparation). *Productive and Defensive Reasoning in Organizations and Research*.

Argyris, C. (2004). *Reasons and Rationalizations: The Limits of Organizational Knowledge*, Oxford: Oxford University Press.

——Putnam, R., and Smith, D. (1985). *Action Science*. San Francisco, CA: Jossey-Bass.

——and Schön, D. (1996). *Organizational Learning II*. Reading, MA: Addison-Wesley.

Bartlett, C. A. and Ghoshal, S. (1995). 'Changing the Role of Top Management: Beyond Systems to People.' *Harvard Business Review*, May–June, 132–42.

Bossidy, L. and Charan, R. (2002). *Execution*. New York: Crown Business.

Ciampa, D. and Watkins, M. (1999). *Right from the Start*. Boston, MA: Harvard Business School Press.

Goggins, W. C. (1974). 'How the Multidimensional Structure Works at Dow Corning'. *Harvard Business Review*, January–February, 52, 54–65.

Hymowitz, C. (23 April 2002). *Wall Street Journal*, 1.

Langley, A. (9 November 2002). 'ABB to Shed Units and Cut 10,000 Jobs.' *The New York Times*, B3.

Roberts, D., Duyen, A., and Boyre, C. (23 October 2002). *The Financial Times*, 1.

Rogers, William P. *et al.* (1986). *Report of the Presidential Commission on the Space Shuttle Challenger Accident*, 5 vols. Washington, DC: Government Printing Office.

Weick, K. E. and Sutcliffe, K. M. (2002). *Managing the Unexpected*. San Francisco, CA: Jossey-Bass.

Wrong, D. (1961). 'The Over-Socialized Conception of Man in Modern Sociology.' *American Sociological Review*, 26, 183–93.

6

Leadership in a Non-Linear World

Fred E. Fiedler
and
Joseph E. Garcia

How are leaders selected?

In dealing with leaders and managers, our thinking tends to be linear 'The more the better': the more intelligent, the more experienced, the better their education, the more likely we are to hire them. Of course, we know that these linear measures do not necessarily result in better performance. Nonetheless, in selecting candidates for a job, or for admission to a school, the higher their test score, or their grade point average, or the rating of previous performance, the more likely we are to accept the candidate. By and large, this procedure has some merit since it tends to screen out the obviously unfit. But these simple judgements turn out to lead us astray when we attempt to select leaders and managers.

Why is this so? Much of the thinking that underlies assessment programmes, personality tests, and so on, are based on psychological methods, and follows the principle that the better the score, the better will be the person who is a candidate for a job or for promotion. However, when it comes to the selection of leaders, the empirical findings do not support this commonly held assumption. This is clearly shown in Table 6.1 by the results from a wide variety of studies. Leadership performance was measured by the immediate superior in some studies and by panels of experts in others. This table presents the median correlations between the leaders' intelligence scores, their experience in terms of time in service, time on the job or in the organization.

(Incidentally, we shall here use the term leaders and 'managers' interchangeably insofar as managers supervise people and

Table 6.1 Medians and Range of Correlations between Leaders' Intelligence and Experience Measures and Performance

	Median	*Range*	*Number of studies*
Performance and			
intelligence	0.16	0.35--−0.23	13
Performance and the			
following leader			
experience measures			
Time in service	0.10	0.27--−0.28	11
Time in job	0.11	0.38--−0.11	10

Source: Adapted from Fiedler and Garcia, 1987.
Note: The correlations shown in this table indicate the relationship between leadership performance and the leader's intelligence score and experience (time in the organization). The square of the correlation coefficient indicates the degree of the relationship between performance and the various predictor variables. Thus, for example, the median correlation between leader intelligence and performance ($r=0.16$), accounts for approximately 4 per cent of leadership performance. Experience, as measured by time in service, is completely unrelated to leadership performance.

direct their work. Thus, we do not include in our definition managers who have no major responsibilities for supervising subordinates, e.g. a manager of a tool room, or of payroll accounts who has no subordinates other than perhaps a secretary or an assistant.)

A closer look at the assessment of leaders and managers reveals several problems that are often overlooked. Most important, psychologists and personnel officers tend to look principally at the person rather than the effect of the environment in which the person operates. However, a moment's reflection tells us that our behaviour is determined at least as much, if not more, by the environment as by the individual's personality. When we attend a lecture, we sit still and listen. We do not dance, we do not sing, get up and walk around, and we do not talk loudly in contrast to how we behave at an informal party.

The assumption of most assessment programmes is that the way a person behaves in an assessment interview is the way that person will behave in most other situations. Moreover, we tend to assume that such personality attributes as intellectual abilities or creativity are stable and that the individual who is intelligent today will act consistently in an intelligent manner in a variety of other situations (Kelly, 1967). Unfortunately, the results of a large study reviewed in Table 6.2 (Borden, 1980) of an armoured infantry division, in which 327 officers and non-commissioned officers participated, challenge this assumption.

These men were evaluated on their performance by their immediate superiors. Their intelligence scores and experience (commonly defined as time in service) were correlated with performance after standardizing for command level as well as the stress with their superior. The results show that leader intelligence correlated positively with performance when reported stress was low, but not when reported stress was high. Experi-

Table 6.2 Relationship between Leader Intelligence, Experience, and Stress on Performance

Intelligence or experience	Characteristics of the situation	
	Low stress	High stress
Low ability	Average performance	Average performance
High ability	Good performance	Average performance
Experienced	Average performance	Good performance
Inexperienced	Average performance	Average performance

Source: Adapted from Borden 1980.

ence did not correlate with performance when stress was low but positively contributed to performance when stress was high.

Moreover, our studies also show that intellectual abilities and leadership experience interfere with one another. This is especially clear from an experiment by Murphy and Macaulay (Macaulay, 1992; Murphy, 1992). In this experiment, sixty college students were divided into thirds on the basis of their intelligence and previous leadership experience. Those in the upper and lower thirds of the intelligence and experience distribution were used in the experiment. They were given a decision-making task under moderately stressful conditions. The experiment showed that intelligence contributed to task performance when the leader had relatively low experience; experience contributed to performance when the leader had relatively low intelligence. Thus, high intelligence interfered with the use of experience in the performance of the task while high experience interfered with the effective use of intelligence. Yes, these findings are counter-intuitive and fly in the face of the frequent organizational practice of promoting individuals based on their previous accomplishments of technical ability. It is revealing that in professional sports, where the relationship between leadership and team performance is easily scrutinized, that many successful coaches did not have careers as superstar athletes. It is obvious that an understanding of leadership effectiveness depends on knowing how a particular individual will be affected by the situation in which he or she must operate.

What is Leadership?

To understand the role of the leader's immediate work environment, that is, the 'leadership situation', it is worthwhile to review what we mean by leadership. First, leadership is a relationship between an individual and a group of people based on power and influence. Through exerting power and influence, leaders enable a group of people to achieve some predetermined goal. In popular thinking, power and influence derives from the leader's strong personality and charisma. This may be the case in many circumstances, especially in informally organized groups and organizations.

However, real charisma is a relatively uncommon commodity and most groups in formal organizations work under appointed leaders who may not be endowed with charisma. Leaders may be effective but they base their leadership success on factors that do not involve personal charisma. These include two different types of factors. First, these are such personal attributes of the leader as the leader's personality, intelligence, and expertise and second, those that are attributes of the leadership situation. This second set of factors include the structure of the leadership task, the amount of resources over which the leader has discretion, the talent and motivations of group members and the amount of support provided by the formal organization. Leadership situations vary widely with some requiring the leaders to cajole, convince, and entreat their subordinates, while others require leaders to rely on their authority and expertise and to act in a more directive manner. Consequently, situations influence the leadership strategies that will be effective and how power and influence flows in the relationship between the leader and subordinates.

Leadership Situations in the Twenty-First Century

The dominant model of organizations is one important consideration for understanding leadership. While there has been, and will continue to be, great diversity in the types of organizations that exist, broad shifts do occur in terms of the popularity of certain types of organizational form and structure. The dominant organizational form of the twentieth century, especially during the first half of the century, was one of hierarchy and predictability. Largely influenced by the development of the manufacturing sector which was designed for mass production as well as the hierarchical structure in military organizations, organizations were structured around economies of scale, standardization and efficiency. This favoured leadership situations that were stable, predictable, and hierarchical in nature. The technological and demographic changes that marked the end of the twentieth century have produced an environment where many organizations have moved away from the industrial model. Advances in telecommunication, transportation, computing power, and more sophisticated markets have markedly shifted organizations from mechanistic structures to more organic, flexible ways of organizing. Thus, leaders are more likely to find themselves working in self-managed teams that rely upon informal mechanisms of communication and co-ordination, in settings with reduced cycle times where decision making occurs in a real time environment. In these flatter and more flexible organizations, leaders often find themselves without the formal organizational power associated with positions or titles, and relying upon networks across functional and even organizational boundaries to achieve team and organizational goals.

While these changes have not seen their way into every organization, they have shifted the emphasis in most and have certainly influenced the discourse on leadership. More importantly, these changes highlight the dynamics and complexity of leadership and leadership situations and lead us away from unidimensional ways of thinking about leadership and leader selection.

Intelligence, Experience, and Leadership Performance

The counter-intuitive findings of the study on infantry division officers and college students and others serve to highlight how different leadership situations affect the performance of different types of leaders. In reviewing these studies, we note that intellectually demanding tasks such as decision making and creative work require disciplined creativity and deliberate weighing of alternatives. On the other hand, crises, emergencies, and situations of high uncertainty require quick actions that make it difficult to think calmly and logically. Unless covered by extensive prior drill, these situations call for quick and decisive action, based on intuition and hunch, both of which are products of previous experience.

When there is high uncertainty, or little time to think, we generally fall back on what has worked in the past. Leaders with a large repertoire of previously successful behaviours are more likely to perform better than those who lack this fund of experience.

But why is high intelligence detrimental to performance under stressful conditions and experience detrimental under stress-free conditions? To account for these findings, we assume that people seek to capitalize on their strengths. Thus, when faced with a problem, bright people tend to rely on their intellectual abilities (Locklear, 1990) while highly experienced people tend to rely on hunch and intuition that comes from experience rather than on creative and analytical thinking. Unfortunately, the leader cannot simultaneously think in a creative or analytic manner and react automatically on the basis of intuition, hunch, and previously learned behaviour. Thus, under stressful conditions, when an immediate response is called for, intelligent leaders want to delay action in order to weigh all other alternatives (Gibson *et al.*, 1993). This inhibits or interferes with the automatic, experience-based response to the stressful situation and results in a negative correlation between intelligence and performance.

Under low stress, intellectually demanding tasks (e.g. decision making) require deliberation and careful weighing of evidence. In these conditions, the highly experienced leader tends to become impatient with 'all the unnecessary talk' in the belief that 'we already know what to do and we don't need another study'. Hence, the greater the experience, the greater will be the leader's tendency to short-cut or denigrate the needed deliberation, and the more negative will be the correlation between leader experience and group performance. Intelligent leaders tend to brood over problems while leaders with long experience may go ahead based on a past that may not necessarily be applicable to the present.

Personality and Leadership Performance

As with experience and intelligence, leader personality may not have a linear relationship with group performance. A particularly good example of the interaction of leader personality and the leader's environment is exemplified by an extensive research programme on the Contingency Model (See e.g. Fiedler, 1967, and 1978; Fiedler and Garcia, 1987). This leadership theory, here described in oversimplified form, identified two major classes of leaders, those motivated by task accomplishment and those motivated by having successful relationships with others. Both of these types of leaders try to be, and can be, successful.

The leaders' motivations were identified by a simple scale that asks the individual to think of all the persons with whom he or she has ever worked, and then describe the one person with whom the individual found it most difficult to work, that is, their least preferred co-worker (LPC) (See e.g. Fiedler, 1967; Fiedler and Garcia, 1987). Although practically all leaders were motivated to perform well, those who described their 'least preferred co-worker' in very unfavourable terms, tend to be motivated primarily by getting the job done (task-motivated or low LPC) even at the risk of ruining good interpersonal relationships. Those who take a more tempered view of their least preferred co-worker tend to be more concerned with maintaining good and supportive interpersonal relations with those with whom they work (relationship-motivated or high LPC). They give lower priority to task achievement than to supportive interpersonal relations.

The work environment or the immediate 'leadership situation' is classified by how much power and influence it provides the leader. Thus, a leader who is strongly supported by subordinates clearly has more influence than one who is not supported or is distrusted by subordinates. Likewise, a leader who is an expert on the task, who knows exactly what to do and how to do the job, (e.g. a seasoned construction foreman on a building site), will have more power and influence than one who is uncertain about the job and the procedures, or whose job does not provide a clear procedure and clear goals. An example of the latter type is a chairman of a committee whose task may be to have his group write a position paper, or sketch out a plan for the future of the organization. Finally, a leader who has the full support of his or her superior will be more secure and will have more power over the group than one whose superiors do not give this support.

As summarized in Table 6.3 we again see a consistent inter-action between leader personality and the power and influence the organization provides. Leaders who are task-motivated per-form best when they have a great deal of power and influence, but perform relatively poorly when their influence is moderate, and thus depend on the support of their subordinates. Exactly the opposite is the case for leaders who are mostly concerned with interpersonal relations. These individuals perform best when their power and influence are intermediate, because this state of affairs forces them to attend to their interpersonal rela-tions. In low power and influence situations, it is again the task-motivated leader who tends to perform relatively well, while relationship motivated leaders tend to withdraw. (For a more extensive discussion of this point, the reader is referred to such references as Fiedler, 1978; Fiedler and Chemers, 1984; Fielder and Garcia, 1987.) As with experience and intelligence, the situation influences which personality characteristic is likely to determine the leader's effectiveness.

Another manifestation of the leadership situation is stress, and especially stress with the immediate superior or boss. Thus, leaders may report low, moderate, or high stress, especially

Table 6.3 Relationship between Leader Personality and the Leadership Situation on Performance

Leader personality	Characteristics of the leadership situation		
	High influence	Moderate influence	Low influence
Task motivated	Good performance	Poor performance	Good performance
Relationship motivated	Poor performance	Good performance	Poor performance

Source: Adapted from Fiedler and Garcia, 1987.

when this stress emanates from their relationship with their immediate boss. As with power and influence, relationship motivated leaders tend to perform best under conditions of moderate stress. Task-motivated leaders perform best when stress is low or in conditions of high stress. Again, the point we wish to make here is that the organization and the leader's immediate work environment plays a large and critical part in the leader's performance. The main lessons are obvious. First, in order to succeed, the leader's abilities and personality attributes must match the leadership situation. Second, and as we shall illustrate, it is considerably more difficult and often impossible to change the leader's personality and abilities but it is relatively easy to modify the situation so as to match to the situation to the leader (Table 6.3).

The Organization's Role in Promoting Effective Leadership

There is no doubt that the organization plays a major part in the person's career as a leader. Some people are great at starting up a branch office or a new plant or of turning around a failing organization, while others are great administrators of on-going concerns. Few are likely to be good at everything. Those who are good at starting up organizations often turn out to be poor administrators (Bray *et al.*, 1974; Howard and Bray, 1988).

Obviously, by changing the stressfulness of the job, or the stress level with the immediate superior, we can affect the success of the subordinate manager. For example, stress can be a product of poorly trained or unmotivated subordinates, of poor instructions, poor organizational support or inadequately spelled out goals. The point is that the leader's environment, that is, the leader's power and influence, is highly susceptible to change, and with it the level of the leader's performance.

We will illustrate ways in which organizations can assist leaders in changing the power and influence of their leadership situation to match their cognitive abilities, experience, and personality. These illustrations suggest that a high level of power and influence will not necessarily translate into effective leadership. An important reason for this and similar conclusions is that leadership is an interaction between an individual and the leadership environment. We must see to it, therefore, that the leaders we select and train end up in situations that allow them to function well, or that we change the leadership situation so that it fits the leader. Otherwise, selection and training, especially if it is uni-dimensional in orientation, will be largely wasted.

While job descriptions and job analyses contribute to defining one aspect of the leadership situation, they tend to focus on the more rational aspects of the situation. As a rule, they do not tell us anything about the important characteristics of the job that affect power and influence, such as interpersonal stress, member loyalty, subordinates' motivation and abilities, and stress with the immediate superior. While we usually cannot predict future leadership situations, we can teach leaders and their supervisors how they can ameliorate or remove blocks to the effective utilization of cognitive resources and personality that result from the leadership situation. Again, leadership is a social interaction that depends on one individual's ability to exert the right amount of power and influence, that is, 'situational control', over others in order to get the assigned task accomplished.

Matching the Leadership Situation to Fit the Leader

As mentioned earlier, our research has identified four important components of situational control, namely leader–member relations, task structure, position power, and stress. We here illustrate some of the ways to modify each of these to enhance leadership performance. Some suggestions are obvious, others may not be, nor will all of the suggested actions for change be appropriate in all conditions.

To improve leader–member relations you might

- Spend more informal time with subordinates.
- Organize some off-work group activities, for yourself and your subordinates.
- Increase your availability to subordinates.
- Listen to your subordinates' problems.
- Share information 'from above' with your subordinates to make them feel part of the team.
- Obtain rewards for subordinates.

To decrease leader–member relations you could

- Avoid spending informal time with your subordinates.
- See your subordinates by appointment only.
- Keep your contacts with subordinates in a more formal, strictly businesslike manner.
- Avoid becoming involved in subordinates' personal problems.

To increase task structure

- Ask for detailed task instructions and write them down for later reference.
- Seek advice from others who have experience in doing the task.
- Look for information in manuals and books.
- Outline the task and break it down into smaller steps.
- Seek formal training.
- Tell your boss you can do a better job if you have more structured assignments.

To decrease task structure

- Include your group members in planning and decision making.
- Let your boss know you like challenging problems and volunteer your group when these come up.

To increase your position power

- Acquire expertise on the job so you will not have to depend on subordinates for assistance.

- Show your subordinates 'who is boss' by exercising your powers fully.
- Let your subordinates know that your boss is behind you 100 per cent.
- Ask your boss for approval and backing before making questionable decisions.
- Where possible, make sure that information to your group passes through you.

To decrease position power

- Give more responsibility to group members or your assistants.
- Share decision-making powers where possible.
- Do not emphasize that you are the boss.

To reduce stress with your boss

- Avoid eyeball-to-eyeball confrontations with your boss before discussing important issues.
- Rehearse or role-play difficult interviews with someone in your family or a co-worker before taking them up with the boss.
- Communicate by telephone or memorandum rather than in person.
- Praise your boss for not putting you under stress, and compliment your boss for behaviours that lessen stress.

These are guidelines, not iron-clad rules. Note that one situational control factor may affect another. They require that the leader or supervisor use sound judgement. Actions aimed at altering interpersonal relationships with subordinates or one's boss are likely to have the greatest impact, for better or worse, on a leader's power and influence and require special care. As such, changing the situation to match the leader should be done carefully and in incremental steps. Plan the best course of action, consider the effects on other aspects of your job, and then implement. Evaluate your actions frequently so that you can make the necessary adjustments if you have not achieved the desired effect. Among other factors that affect situational control are, for example, transfer, selection, training, and personnel turnover.

Do these 'job-engineering' methods really work? This technique is the essence of the leadership training programme, Leader–Match (Fiedler and Chemers, 1984), which has been validated in more than seventeen different studies (see Fiedler and Garcia, 1987). An extensive review of leadership training by Burke and Day (1986) found only two leadership training programmes they could recommend. These were Sorcher and Goldstein's (1972) behaviour modelling and Leader–Match (Fiedler and Chemers, 1984). A similar review by Wexley and Latham (1981) also noted the extensiveness of empirical support for this training. In addition, several validation studies (e.g. Link, 1992) based on cognitive resource theory, have shown that intellectual performance and experience can be improved by appropriate modifications of the leadership situation.

Non-Linear Thinking about Leadership in the Twenty-First Century

Enhancing leadership performance in the twenty-first century requires a non-linear perspective. Research from the twentieth century has taught us that leadership situations interact with the personal characteristics of leaders in ways that have an important impact on performance. The twenty-first century organization deals with leaders in more complex and fluid situations than characteristic of the past. We offer a view of leadership selection and performance management that takes into account the core element of leadership, namely how personal attributes and situational control interact. While putting this knowledge into action may not always be an easy task, it reflects the reality of a world that looks more like a pretzel than an arrow.

Note

This chapter draws from previously published research.

References

Barnes, V. E., Potter, E. H., and Fiedler, F. E. (1983). 'Effects of Interpersonal Stress on the Prediction of Academic Performance.' *Journal of Applied Psychology*, 68 (4), 686–97.

Borden, D. F. (1980). 'Leader–Boss Stress, Personality, Job Satisfaction and Performance: Another look at the Interrelationship of some old Constructs in the Modern Large Bureaucracy.' Unpublished doctoral dissertation, University of Washington, Seattle.

Bray, D. W., Campbell R. J., and Grant, D. L. (1974). *Formative Years in Business: A Long Term A TandT Study of Managerial Lives*. New York: Wiley.

Burke, M. J., and Day, R. R. (1986). 'A Cumulative Study of the Effectiveness of Managerial Training.' *Journal of Applied Psychology*, 71, 232–46.

Fiedler, F. E. (1967). *A Theory of Leadership Effectiveness*. New York: McGraw-Hill.

——(1978). 'The Contingency Model and the Dynamics of the Leadership Process.' In L. Berkowitz (ed.), *Advances in Experimental Social Psychology* (vol. 11). New York: Academic Press.

Fiedler, F. E. and Chemers, M. M. (1984). *Improving Leadership Effectiveness: The Leader Match Concept* (2nd edn). New York: Wiley.

Fiedler, F. E. and Garcia, J. E. (1987). *New Approaches to Effective Leadership: Cognitive Resources and Organizational Performance*. New York: Wiley.

Gibson, F. W., Fiedler, F. E., and Barrett K. M. (1993). 'Stress, Babble and the Utilization of the Leader's Intellectual Abilities.' *Leadership Quarterly*, 4 (2), 189–208.

Goldstein, A. P. and Sorcher, M. (1974). *Changing Supervisory Behavior*. New York: Pergamon Press.

Howard, A. and Bray, D. W. (1988). *Managerial Lives in Transition: Advancing Age and Changing Times*. New York: Guilford Press.

Kelly, H. H. (1967). 'Attribution theory in social psychology.' In D. Devine (ed.), *Nebraska Symposium on Motivation*, Lincoln, NB: University of Nebraska Press.

Link, T. G. (1992). 'Stress Management Training: An Extension of Cognitive Resource Theory.' Unpublished doctoral dissertation, University of Washington.

Locklear, J. C. (1990). 'The Effects of Individual Intelligence and Organizational Experience on Pre-Decisional Information Acquisition.' Unpublished doctoral dissertation, University of Washington.

Macaulay, J. E. (1992). 'Group Performance: The Effects of Stress and Experience on Leader Use of Fluid and Crystallized Intelligence.' Unpublished doctoral dissertation, University of Washington.

Murphy, S. E. (1992). 'The Contribution of Leadership Experience and Self-Efficacy to Group Performance under Evaluation Apprehension.' Unpublished doctoral dissertation, University of Washington.

Potter, E. H. and Fiedler, F. E. (1981). 'The Utilization of Staff Member Intelligence and Experience under High and Low Stress.' *Academy of Management Journal*, 24 (2), 361–76.

Wexley, K. N. and Latham, G. P. (1981). *Developing and Training Human Resources in Organizations*. Glenview, IL: Scot-Foresman.

7

Leadership in the Private Sector: Yesterday Versus Tomorrow

Gary P. Latham
and
Cynthia D. McCauley

What will 'they' state was important about the role of organizational leaders in the twenty-first century? The pronoun is, of course, the key word in this opening question. 'They' are the behavioural scientists and historians at the end of this millennium. They will be able to explain the type of organizations that leaders led, because they (1) will know how everything turned out, and (2) will have boiled down the story to a manageable length by focusing on a few major themes and trends that turned out to be decisive. The statistics and events that they cite to explain what happened will be only a fraction of the voluminous data that we currently respond to and argue about on an annual (e.g. *Annual Review of Psychology*) if not daily basis. This is the process of distillation, through time, that proves the truth or folly in a forecast.

Futurology is the study of forecasting potential developments based on current conditions. In industrial-organizational psychology it is perhaps explained best by the axiom that among the best predictors of future behaviour is past behaviour. Based on empirical research in the twentieth century, six predictions about the future in private-sector organizations are made in the present chapter. Each prediction points to what will differentiate the effective from the ineffective leader during the coming century. Undoubtedly these predictions will be less than accurate. This is because, as is the case with economists, organizational psychologists have yet to discover which factors are crucial to making a valid forecast. Nevertheless, even oversimplified, unrealistic predictions, including those that are false in some respects, often force people to confront possibilities that would not have occurred to them otherwise. Thus as we stand at the dawn of this new millennium, there is value in examining the background, potential consequences, and future scenarios of the science and practice of leadership in the private sector.

In the twentieth century, at least four events had a major effect on leaders in Euro-American society. The first two profoundly changed the balance of power between leaders and employees, namely employee selection practices and employee participation in the decision-making process. The third event, the economy, provided leaders in the private sector with 'folk hero' status. The fourth factor was technology.

Selection Practices

Yesterday: Tests and Equal Employment Legislation

The First World War ushered in the importance that would be placed on selection throughout the twentieth century. Psychologists were recruited by the US military to develop intelligence tests for the selection of recruits for various military positions. Following the war, Burtt's (1926) comprehensive book, *Employment Psychology*, focused exclusively on the topic of selection with chapter headings that include job analysis, the mental components of the job, types of mental tests, interests in employment psychology, trade tests, the criterion, and rating scales. These scientifically-based selection practices began to make their way into the private sector.

By the latter half of the twentieth century, countries in North America and Europe had passed laws prohibiting employment discrimination on the basis of race, sex, age, religion, and national origin. Unlike their forbears in previous centuries, leaders in the twentieth century were no longer completely free to choose and reject people whom they would lead. Ways of ensuring equal opportunity for people at 'the starting line' so as to avoid costly litigation battles, as well as damaging criticism in the court of public opinion, occupied the attention of organizational decision makers. Their emphasis was primarily on selection and promotion issues with regard to a person's race and sex. With the economic downturn in the latter part of the twentieth century, this emphasis was broadened to that of age, as older people were more likely than their younger colleagues to be singled out for termination. The passage of equal employment legislation resulted in non-whites and women gaining access to meaningful employment in far greater numbers than their grandparents in the first half of the twentieth century, as well as people over the age of forty becoming far less worried than their forbears about losing their job because of age-related reasons. The result is the on-going development of reliable and valid tests for selection and promotion decisions that ensure a demographically heterogeneous workforce in terms of race, sex, and age within such countries as Australia, Canada, the United Kingdom, and the United States (USA).

Tomorrow: Selecting and Developing Leaders for Global Organizations

When something goes on for decades, many people naively come to think that the pattern is relatively permanent. The nineteenth century was Britain's, the twentieth belonged to the USA. The Americans have enjoyed the biggest piece of the production pie since the end of the First World War. During the last decade of the twentieth century, however, the country-by-country slicing of the global economic pie suggested another historical shift. The growth in the US share has stalled, whereas China has been 'eating everybody else's lunch'. Thus, it is increasingly clear that the twenty-first century will belong to East Asia. This means that the US dollar will cease to be the global store of value. Hence organizations will of necessity become increasingly global in their operations. Euro-American nations that inspired the late twentieth-century boom in global trade, and profited most greatly from it, will no longer define the rules. As people in economically poor nations join the international trading game during the first half of the twenty-first century, they will demand and receive a say in the global system.

Social Identity Conflict. Our first major prediction is that there will be a shift in emphasis from the twentieth-century focus on diversity issues within a country regarding the race, sex, and age of employees to tomorrow's organizational leaders having to face differences among countries regarding employee ethnicity, religion, national origin, and political ideology. Just as they are in society at large, these social-identity differences will be a source of conflict in the workplace. This shift will call for the selection and development of leaders who are effective at preventing or managing identity-based conflict within increasingly global organizations (Center for Creative Leadership, 2003).

To select and develop leaders for a more globally diverse organization, what knowledge, skills, and abilities will be predictive of effectiveness? First, in addition to high cognitive ability, these leaders will need high practical intelligence or 'street smarts' (Sternberg, 2003; Sternberg *et al.*, 2003) for working effectively with myriad social identity groups. Social identity conflict is often a battle for hegemony. It represents people's collective need for dignity, recognition, safety, control, purpose, and efficacy (Rothman, 1997). At our most atavistic core, we, as human beings are afraid of 'the other'. To help leaders with the task of working effectively across social identity groups, organizational psychologists need to eliminate the current gap in our literature by building upon and then enhancing the extant work of social psychologists (e.g. Suedfeld, 2000; Dion, 2002) that began immediately after the Second World War on ways of minimizing prejudice, stereotyping, and ethnocentrism (e.g. Adorno *et al.*, 1950; Jones, 1958).

Second, a leader's visionary style in the twenty-first century must be congruent with the heterogeneous culture of a multi-national, multi-ethnic workforce. In the twentieth century, a private-sector leader's vision appealed primarily to cognition.

An example is Henry Ford I, in the early 1900s, predicting with remarkable omniscience the future of the transportation industry. Tomorrow's organizational leaders, in contrast, will formulate a vision that appeals primarily to the employees' affect or emotion—much as twentieth-century social-movement leaders appealed to citizens. The effective leader will make clear that working to attain this vision will not merely enrich one's pocketbook, but more importantly it will directly or indirectly benefit society. Thus, a leader's vision will be expressed in ways that foster unity by creating feelings of cohesion, by giving a multicultural workforce a common cause that it can rally around. The purpose of goal setting (Locke and Latham, 2002) will be to move the vision from affect to behaviour—concrete action steps necessary to attain this superordinate goal.

In addition, private sector leaders in the twenty-first century will be called upon to use the uniting potential of a shared organizational vision, norms, and interdependent tasks to decrease social identity conflict in society at large. The work organization itself will likely be an ideal place to address deep-seated ethnic, religious, and political social identity issues. Because most people must make a living in order to survive, the global organization in the twenty-first century will be one of the few places in society where people will have some contact with people from other social identity groups. Social identity groups tend to seek similar others through religious organizations, schools, neighbourhoods, etc. The twenty-first-century workplace will of necessity be the most heterogeneous institution. Work itself, to the extent that it increases a person's status and self-esteem, may prove to be a precursor to harmonious inter-group performance. The leader of tomorrow will need to discover how to craft a vision, shared organizational norms, and interdependent work that will serve as powerful levers for behaviour change.

Education is a final factor to examine in selecting effective leaders for an increasingly globally diverse organization. The launching of Sputnik by the Soviet Union in 1957 marked the decline in the West of the perceived importance of a university degree in liberal arts. Importance instead was attached to science and business degrees that would enable people to increase the strength of capitalist nations relative to those that were communist. By the end of the twentieth century, most countries had rejected communism as an appropriate ideology by which to be governed.

As the focus on issues regarding an employee's race, sex, and age within a country shift in the twenty-first century to those of ethnicity, religion, and national origin across countries, we predict that there will be a shift back to the importance of a liberal arts degree to enable a leader to foster unity among the differences that exist among employees in a global organization. September 11, 2001 heralded back the value of a leader's fluency in psychology, sociology, world history, political science, religion, and philosophy, in addition to foreign languages— subject matter that is the mainstay of a liberal arts degree, and subject matter that is critical for overcoming cultural ignorance. Think of the hostility that might have been tempered in the twentieth century had we only understood one another better. Ignorance breeds fear, and fear is a powerful motivator but a terrible adviser. People who believe that they are in danger usually think of themselves first, and are prone to seeing threats and conspiracies everywhere. In order to minimize rigidity, insensitivity, and intolerance within a multi-cultural workforce, we predict that demand for an undergraduate business degree will decrease significantly in the twenty-first century as entry into a prestigious MBA programme will require a Bachelor of Arts.

Integrated Decision Making. Our second major prediction is that the complexity of decision making in global organizations will demand a cross-disciplinary perspective, making the functional approach of most business education necessary but not sufficient. Business schools will respond by teaching future business leaders ways to create mental linkages among these disciplines. Leaders will be taught to look beyond functional silos such as finance, marketing, and human resources management, and focus instead on the interrelatedness among functional disciplines. This is because even today problems rarely fall within the boundaries of a specific functional area (e.g. information science) and thus cannot be resolved using the narrow models developed for it. Hence even within a functional boundary (e.g. marketing), tomorrow's organizational problems will undoubtedly sprawl messily across other functions thus creating the need for leaders who can attend simultaneously to a vast array of interconnected variables, and deal effectively with enigmatic choices.

To paraphrase Drucker (2002), there is no such thing as a tax or a marketing decision, there are only business decisions. Yet many people in the twentieth century rarely thought in terms of the organization that employed them; instead they thought primarily in terms of their own specialty. If tomorrow's leaders do not integrate what they are doing with the goals of the organization, they will likely do damage along the way. Thus tomorrow's MBA schools will teach the capacity to think in an integrated multi-disciplinary, cross-functional way (Latham *et al.*, in press). The necessity of doing so is already being contemplated at the University of Toronto (Pfeffer and Fong, 2002).

Employee Involvement

Yesterday: Participation in Decisions

The second major event in the twentieth century that profoundly changed the balance of power between leaders and employees was ushered in by the Second World War. In response to repressive Fascist regimes, behavioural scientists such as McGregor (1960) published seminal articles on the importance of leaders encouraging employee participation in the decision-making process (pdm). In addition to stressing pdm, psychologists, including Likert (1961, 1967), explained ways of designing organizations that facilitate pdm, goal setting, as well as the leader's support for the individual employee. The day of the authoritarian, command and control, unilateral decision-making leader came to an end.

Tomorrow: Shared Responsibility and Accountability

To deal effectively with increasingly complex problems brought on by the accelerating pace of scientific discovery, shifting demographics, de-regulation, new business models, and fluctuating economies, organizations in the twenty-first century will need to draw regularly on the intelligence and experience of the whole organization. Complexity implies unpredictability and unintended consequences. An example of a current complex challenge is the need for a change in culture following a merger or acquisition (Drath, 2001). The challenge is complex because no one can say with any authority or certainty the ways in which things need to change. The leader has no way of being sure of the type of culture that is needed. No one leader who was part of either organization prior to the merger has any kind of gifted insight into the needs of the newly created organization. By virtue of position power, 'the' leader may have the authority to ensure that his or her views are accepted. But, that in itself does not guarantee the effectiveness of these views. Thus many mergers and acquisitions in the twentieth century failed (Marks and Mirvis, 2000).

Facing complex problems requires more than smart leaders and they require more than employee involvement in the decision-making process. To deal with and solve these problems, employees throughout the organization need to be responsible for making sense of the problem, connecting with others to bring multiple experience bases to bear on the problem, and navigating their way to solutions (Palus and Horth, 2004).

Leaders as Facilitators of Shared Work. Our third prediction is that twenty-first-century leaders will not be surrounded with dependent followers looking for someone to show them the way out of a complex challenge, but rather will be expected to facilitate collective efforts to face these challenges. This shift in role will require leaders to focus on asking questions rather than providing answers, making employees face the difficulties that lie ahead rather than painting only positive pictures of the future, and drawing out the strengths that each employee has to contribute rather than dwelling on their shortcomings and flaws. We can actually look to the past to find examples of exercising leadership in this way. In the future, this type of leadership will be the rule rather than the exception.

Why has Socrates been revered century after century when he is the last person with whom any of us would want to have a drink? We believe that the answer is due in part to the fact that he articulated the concept of asking questions rather than providing answers. Socrates believed that 'truth lies within'; the art of leadership is to ask questions that allow for insight and discovery on the part of the person who is being questioned. Replication of Socrates' wisdom regarding empowerment was captured by Drucker at the beginning of the present century: 'In the 1950s great leaders gave great answers; in this new millennium, great leaders will ask great questions' (Drucker, 2002).

Cohen (2002) argued that, on paper, President Lincoln's qualifications in the nineteenth century to serve as commander-in-chief of the union army during the American Civil War paled in comparison to those of his opponent, Jefferson Davis, the President of the Confederacy. Davis had graduated years before from West Point, served with distinction as a soldier in the battle of Monterrey and Buena Vista, and was later appointed in 1853 as Secretary of War for the United States. Lincoln's experience on the other hand, included serving a few months as a junior militia officer. Nevertheless, Lincoln, as President, had behavioural qualities that were as important in the nineteenth century as they will be in the twenty-first, especially for those who must lead in highly difficult circumstances. First, he did not engage in illusions, but rather was clear about the difficulties that lay ahead. History is replete with leaders who, before a clash of arms, had wildly unrealistic images of triumph. One of Lincoln's secretaries observed that: 'He had his hopes and his desires, but he did not commit the strategic sin that Napoleon described of "making pictures" of the world as one wishes it to be, rather than as is' (Cohen, 2002).

A second ability attributed to Lincoln by Cohen was his skill in dealing effectively with flawed, wilful, yet energetic and useful subordinates. This ability was manifested in Lincoln's use of General Hooker, a man who advocated the need for a dictator of both the union army and the US government; it showed in Lincoln's effective use of his wily and manipulative

Secretary of State, William Seward, and it showed in dealings with his abrasive Secretary of War, Edwin Stanton.

Leadership as a Collective Activity. Our fourth prediction is that leadership will come to be understood more as a collective rather than individual activity. Instead of thinking of leadership as being a product of the leader, it will be an outcome of the connections among people who work on leadership tasks. Leadership tasks will remain the same as they were yesterday, namely, setting direction, creating alignment in support of that direction, and gaining people's goal commitment. However, the ways in which these tasks become accomplished will be different tomorrow. They will no longer be carried out by a single leader; they will no longer be coordinated with other organizational leaders through one person who is higher in the authority hierarchy. Rather, these tasks will be carried out by communities of organizational decision makers who think, reflect, discuss, and act together on a day-to-day basis.

This shift in both the understanding and enactment of leadership will be mandated by the increased complexity of leadership work. Tomorrow's organizational environment will be increasingly filled with novel, ill-defined problems—problems that do not lend themselves to rapid solutions by assigning them to a particular leader. Multiple perspectives and expertise will have to be brought to bear, especially due to the multiple groups who will claim a stake in these complex issues. Hence the collective action of multiple individuals will be required. This in itself will become a complex challenge due to the cacophony of differences among employees in the sundry social identity groups. Worse, shared accountability can become the bedrock of social loafing (Latane *et al.*, 1979) or diffused accountability.

Effective collective activity requires more than effective individuals. It requires rich, deep, and varied connections between the various members of the collective. In short, effective leadership in the twenty-first century will require more than psychometrically valid predictors of the individuals who possess specified KSAs identified through job analysis. It will require the development of processes and systems that foster connectivity within an organization. A primary measure of leadership effectiveness will be the degree of an organization's success in anticipating and coping with complex challenges. Adaptivity will differentiate the organization that survives from the organization that becomes extinct in this century.

Our prediction of the necessity to develop leadership as a collective activity requires addressing three interrelated issues:

(1) How will an organization develop its collective capacity for leadership? How will this be different from developing individual leadership capacity? In the past, the focus of leadership development has been the individual, particularly those individuals who were expected to take on key leadership roles in the organization. But, if leadership will occur in the twenty-first century primarily through the connections among individuals working together on leadership tasks, organizational capacity for leadership will also be determined by the strength and richness of these connections. Developing organizational capacity for leadership will likely require developing social as well as human capital (Day, 2000).

(2) How will organizations develop richer forms of connectivity in their organization than they currently have in place? How will this connectivity enable increasingly effective leadership? Perhaps the most promising way of developing connectivity will be to give groups of decision makers a problem or issue that is large in scope, that is too big and

unwieldy for one person, and for which they as a group have shared responsibility and accountability. Connections will be fostered through such shared work. Rich forms of connectivity might also be developed by changing the 'language of the community', that is, by developing ways of talking with one another that demonstrate a commitment to on-going regard, public consensus, and the limits of individual viewpoints (Kegan and Lahey, 2001).

(3) How will organizations recognize their complex challenges? What leadership capabilities will be needed to confront these challenges effectively? Different capabilities will likely be used in recognizing and then solving a problem. Finding solutions to problems will be likely to occur through data gathering and integration, logical analysis, as well as divergent and convergent thinking capabilities. Recognizing yet-unnamed problems and issues will undoubtedly require intuitive sensing, detecting unusual patterns, and synthesis of formerly disconnected information. And to mobilize resources to face complex organizational challenges, individuals across the organization will have to understand or make sense of a challenge in similar ways, thus the capability to make shared sense of complex challenges will certainly become a critical leadership capability (Palus and Horth, 2002).

Public Sector as a Model

Yesterday: Private Sector Economy

A third event that occurred at the beginning and again at the end of the twentieth century had a tremendous effect on the way that the individual leader in the private sector was perceived by the public. This event was the economy. For nations that embraced capitalism, the economy boomed at the beginning and again at the end of the century. Organizations in the private sector, especially those in Euro-Western countries prospered, so much so that their leaders acquired heroic status. This is because the organizations that they led were seen by the ordinary citizen as stores of value for wealth building, as waterfalls of cash.

By the end of the first decade of the twentieth century, however, there was so much trickery and dishonesty on the part of some corporate executives that T. Roosevelt wrote to his brother-in-law that 'the exposures about Harriman, Rockefeller, Heinze, Barney, Morse, Ryan, the insurance men, and others have caused such a genuine shock to people that they have begun to be afraid that every bank really has something rotten in it. In other words, they have passed through the period of unreasoning trust and optimism into unreasoning distrust and pessimism' (Strouse, 1999: 589).

Nevertheless, by the latter two decades of the twentieth century, people once again looked to the private sector for lessons in leadership. This is particularly true in the United States where leaders such as Jack Welch of the General Electric Company and Lee Iaccoca of the Chrysler Corporation achieved folk-hero status as their organizations repeatedly broke profit records. Their every opinion was treated as a gem, their every whim as reasonable. But, at the dawn of the twenty-first century, the mythology that the 'private sector knows best' once again came to an abrupt halt with the revelations of stock-price manipulations and the subsequent collapses of American corporate giants (e.g. Enron). 'From heroes to goats' proclaimed a special issue of the often fawning *Fortune* magazine in the USA. A national poll in Canada revealed that corporate executives in

2002 had taken on the status of villains because of lack of business ethics. 'Business leader' was viewed as an oxymoron. It would appear that there are few if any new lies or truths, just different cycles.

Tomorrow: From Melting Pot to Mosaic

Our fifth prediction is that in the twenty-first century, leadership in the private sector will look to their counterparts in the public sector, especially those in countries such as Canada and Singapore, on ways to develop norms regarding ethics, tolerance, and appreciation for diverse ways of thinking and behaving in a multinational organization. The government of Singapore has passed legislation to foster 'living across differences' (Latham and Napier, 1989). The religious holidays of Buddhists, Christians, Hindus, Muslims, and Taoists are officially observed by the nation. Eighty-four per cent of the Singaporeans live in public housing. The Housing and Development Board has an integration policy resulting in Chinese, Malays, and Indians living side by side.

American idealism of a 'melting pot' whereby immigrants are pressured to let go of their respective cultural heritages so as to assimilate with the norms of their newly adopted country (Blair *et al.*, 1998) will give way to the historical emphasis in Canada on a 'mosaic' (Burton, 1982). The Canadian mosaic emphasizes the preservation and enhancement of diversity rather than assimilation. The focus is on the positive connections among multicultural heritages of Canadians.

We predict that tomorrow's organizational citizens will demand a global governance system that models Canadian norms regarding peace, order, and good government. Leaders in the private sector will have to lead by consensus as do their counterparts in the political arena (e.g. European Union; United Nations). Leadership will be defined in terms of the ability to discover the connections within a mosaic that foster harmonization. Organization norms will make a virtue of a culture that fosters tolerance of ethnic diversity. An unintended consequence of continuing to emphasize a 'melting pot' will be heightened resentment among social identity groups within the organization toward the organization, dramatically worsening the ability to 'lead across differences' and enrich 'connections'.

Given that cultural differences regarding perceived fairness already exist between the Canadian and American workforce (Seijts *et al.*, 2002), two countries that have been heretofore described as indistinguishable in terms of values (Hofstede, 1980), one can barely imagine the differences that will exist tomorrow among Eastern and Western cultures. Canada, for example, already has stronger social democratic and trade union movements than the USA (Rose and Chaison, 1996). Americans on average tend to be more supportive of management's prerogative to do what is necessary to attain an organization's goals, while Canadians are more inclined to focus on the concerns of employees for quality and fairness than employers' demands of organizational efficiency (Lipset and Meltz, 1999). Americans tend to focus on their own personal rights in contrast to Canadians who focus more on the rights of others (Evans *et al.*, 1992).

Taken together, these findings suggest that tomorrow's leadership will have to understand historical, social, and political issues among cultures in order to forge a mosaic. Again, this is why obtaining a liberal arts degree rather than an undergraduate degree in business will be so important. Tomorrow's leadership will have to be aware of potential differences in reactions to various organizational practices (e.g. drug testing, promotability criteria, layoffs) in order to avoid misunderstandings in the workplace, and to be sensitive to the various human resource management policies that affect perceptions of fairness in the workforce and in the surrounding local communities. Because individuals draw inferences quickly about unknown or poorly understood aspects of the organization on the basis of whatever partial knowledge they have, the leadership of tomorrow must communicate clear, credible justifications for the actions that are taken.

Science and Technology: Quantum Leaps Forward

Yesterday: Who Could Have Predicted?

Who in 1900 would have foreseen the effect of the light bulb on the ability of organizations to employ people in the workplace twenty-four hours a day? Who would have predicted the speed, ease, and comfort with which leaders would travel via car and aeroplane to visit employees in widely dispersed geographical areas? Who would have anticipated the use of the telephone, fax machines, and video conferences to facilitate communication between leaders and their employees around the world? And who in psychology in 1900 would have foreseen that the subject of leadership would occupy the attention of behavioural scientists throughout the last three decades of the twentieth century, continuing unabated into the twenty-first century? How many psychologists in 1900 foresaw the development of computer hardware and statistical software to instantly analyze data on leadership and employee effectiveness? In 1990, only a decade ago, how many people predicted how e-mail would bring about pigeon-like behaviour in a Skinner Box on the part of leaders – leaders who peck on variable interval, if not continuous re-inforcement schedules for morsels of information?

Tomorrow: Without Predictability, Be Optimistic!

No chapter on futurology can be written without reference to the impact of science and technology on leadership behaviour. Because we do not know the answers to yesterday's questions posed above, we find this subject matter regarding tomorrow overwhelmingly impossible for us to speculate meaningfully. Thus our sixth and final prediction in this chapter is based solely on optimism. Within this century, science and technology will make us literally a global village (McLuhan and Power, 1989), a virtual community (Rheingold, 1993). As Taylor (2003) has noted, large geographically dispersed groups, connected only by thin threads of communication technology such as mobile phones, text messaging, two way pagers, and e-mail can already be drawn together at a moment's notice, like schools of fish, to perform some collective action.

Summary

Psychometric findings in the twentieth century showed that most of the variance in a criterion could be explained by three to five predictors. Armed with this knowledge, we predicted tomorrow's leadership behaviour based on four events that occurred yesterday, namely, the emphasis that was placed on selection following the First World War, the importance given to employee participation in decision making following the

Second World War, the effect of the economy on the way leaders in the private sector were perceived by the public at the beginning and again at the end of the twentieth century, and the quantum leaps forward in science and technology that affected the quality of working life of leaders and the employees whom they led. Consequently, the following six predictions were made regarding the leadership context in the twenty-first century. Each change in context will put new demands on organizational leaders:

(1) The emphasis given in the twentieth century to developing reliable and valid measures of cognitive intelligence for selecting people will shift in the twenty-first century to measures of practical intelligence. The emphasis given to eliminating prejudice based on race, sex, and age will shift to ways of eliminating ethnocentrism. Social identity groups in which ethnocentrism is imbedded will result in the spill-over of religious, political, and ideological conflict into the workplace. Effective leaders will (a) possess practical intelligence for working effectively with different identity groups; (b) convey a vision that appeals primarily to employees' emotions and makes clear that what they are doing benefits society; and (c) have the ability to craft and foster shared norms, and interdependent work that unites employees. A liberal arts education will better prepare leaders for this new context than a science or business degree.

(2) The complexity of decision making in global organizations will demand a cross-discipline perspective. The problems organizational leaders face will rarely fall within the boundaries of a specific functional area. Effective leaders will understand the interrelatedness among functional

disciplines, and they will attend simultaneously to a vast array of interconnected variables.

(3) Organizations will not be populated with dependent followers looking for someone to show them the way out of a complex challenge; instead they will be made up of employees who are well educated and self motivated, with high expectations of working with others to solve problems. To capitalize on the knowledge and experience across the organization, effective leaders will excel at asking questions, providing realistic pictures of the future and its challenges, and seeing and drawing out the strengths of each employee.

(4) Leadership will come to be understood more as a collective rather than individual activity. Global organizations will be confronted with complex and ill-defined challenges—challenges that will be faced by a community of leaders working in interconnected ways. Effective leaders will engage in shared sense-making, in holding conflicting views in productive tension, and in developing connections throughout the organization.

(5) The private sector will look to the public arena for lessons on ethics as well as an appreciation for ways of working effectively with diverse social identity groups. American idealism for a 'melting pot' will be replaced by the Canadian emphasis on a 'mosaic'. Effective leaders will discover connections within a mosaic that fosters harmonization without losing important differences across groups.

(6) Advances in science and technology will allow the global organization to become a virtual community. Communities foster connections, and connections build trust. Perhaps, just perhaps, differences among people will be embraced rather than shunned.

Note

1. The authors thank Wilfred Drath, Soosan Latham, and Melvin Sorcher for their helpful comments in preparing this chapter.

References

Adorno, T. W., Frenkel-Brunswick, E., Levinson, D. J., and Sanford, R.N. (1950). *The Authoritarian Personality*. New York: Harper.

Blair, J., Overland, O., and Winkler, A. (1998). 'From Melting Pot to Mosaic: The Changing Role of Immigration in American Life.' Retrieved 24 January 2003 from Salzburg Seminar, American Studies Center, *www.salzburgseminar.org/sessions.cfm?core_id=68and core_group=asc*.

Burton, P. (1982). *Why we Act like Canadians*. Toronto: McClelland and Stewart.

Center for Creative Leadership. (2003). 'Description of the Leadership Across Differences Project.' Greensboro, NC: Author.

Cohen, E. A. (2002). *Supreme Command: Soldiers, Statesmen, and Leadership in Wartime*. New York: Free Press.

Day, D. V. (2000). 'Leadership Development: A Review in Context.' *Leadership Quarterly*, 11, 581–613.

Dion, K. L. (2002). 'The Social Psychology of Perceived Prejudice and Discrimination.' *Canadian Psychology*, 43, 1–10.

Drath, W. H. (2001). *The Deep Blue Sea: Rethinking the Source of Leadership*. San Francisco, CA: Jossey-Bass.

Drucker, P. (2002). 'Integrated Thinking.' Invited Address to the Joseph Rotman School of Management, University of Toronto. June.

Evans, W., Lane, H., and O'Grady, S. (1992). *Border Crossings: Doing Business in the US*. Scarborough, Ontario: Prentice-Hall Canada, Inc.

Hofstede, G. (1980). *Culture's Consequences: International Differences in Work-Related Values*. Beverly Hills, CA: Sage Publications.

Jones, M. B. (1958). 'Religious Values and Authoritarian Tendency.' *Journal of Social Psychology*, 48, 83–9.

Kegan, R. and Lahey, L. L. (2001). *How the Way we Talk can Change the Way we Work: Seven Languages for Transformation*. San Francisco, CA: Jossey-Bass.

Latane, B., Williams, K., and Harkins, S. (1979). 'Many Hands make Light the Work: The Causes and Consequences of Social Loafing.' *Journal of Personality and Social Psychology*, 37, 822–32.

Latham, G. P., Latham, S. D., and Whyte, G. (in press). 'Fostering Integrative Thinking: Adapting the Executive Education Model to the MBA program.' *Journal of Management Education*.

Latham, G. P. and Napier, N. (1989). 'Chinese Human Resource Practices in Hong Kong and Singapore.' In K. Rowland and J. Ferris (eds.), *International Human Resources Management*, pp. 173–99. Greenwich, CT: JAI Press.

Likert, R. (1961). *New Patterns of Management*. New York: McGraw-Hill.

——(1967). *The Human Organization*. New York: McGraw-Hill.

Lipset, S. M. and Meltz, N. M. (1999). 'Canadian and American Attitudes toward Work and Institutions.' *Perspectives on Work*, 1, 14–19.

Locke, E. A. and Latham, G. P. (2002). 'Building a Practically Useful Theory of Goal Setting and Task Motivation: A 35-Year Odyssey.' *American Psychologist*, 57, 705–17.

Marks, M. L. and Mirvis, P. (2000). 'Managing Mergers, Acquisitions, and Alliances: Creating an Effective Transition Structure.' *Organizational Dynamics*, 28, 35–47.

McGregor, D. (1960). *The Human Side of Enterprise*. New York: McGraw-Hill.

McLuhan, M. and Power, B. R. (1989). *The Global Village: Transformations in World Life and Media in the 21st Century*. New York: Oxford University Press.

Palus, C. J. and Horth, D. M. (2002). *The Leader's Edge: Six Creative Competencies for Navigating Complex Challenges*. San Francisco, CA: Jossey-Bass.

——(2004). 'Exploration for development.' In C. D. McCauley and E. Van Velsor (eds.), *The Center for Creative Leadership Handbook of Leadership Development* (2nd edn). pp. 438–64 San Francisco: Jossey-Bass.

Pfeffer, J. and Fong, C. T. (2002). 'The End of Business schools? Less Success than Meets the Eye. *Academy of Management Learning and Education*, 1, 78–95.

Rheingold, H. (1993). *The Virtual Community: Homesteading on the Electronic Frontier*. Reading, MA: Addison-Wesley Publishing Company.

Rose, J. B. and Chaison, G. N. (1996). 'Linking Union Density and Union Effectiveness. The North American Experience.' *Industrial Relations*, 35, 78–105.

Rothman, J. (1997). *Resolving Identity-Based Conflict in Nations, Organizations, and Communities*. San Francisco, CA: Jossey-Bass.

Seijts, G. H., Skarlicki, D. P., and Gilliland, S. W. (2002). 'Reactions to Managing Counterproductive Behavior through the Implementation of a Drug and Alcohol Testing Program: American and Canadians are more different than you Might Expect. *International Journal of Selection and Assessment*, 10, 135–42.

Sternberg, R. J. (2003). 'Construct Validity of the Theory of Special Intelligence.' In R. J. Sternberg, J. Lautrey, and T. I. Lubart (eds.), *Models of Intelligence: International Perspectives*, pp. 55–77. Washington, DC: American Psychological Association.

Sternberg, R. J., Lautrey, J., and Lubart, T. I. (2003). 'Where are we in the Field of Intelligence, How did we get here, and Where are we Going?' In R. J. Sternberg, J. Lautrey, and T. I. Lubart, T. I. (eds.), *Models of Intelligence: International Perspectives*, pp. 3–25. Washington, DC: American Psychological Association.

Strouse, J. (1999). *Morgan: American Financier*. Random House, New York.

Suedfeld, P. (2000). 'Reverberations of the Holocaust Fifty Years Later: Psychology's Contributions to Understanding Persecution and Genocide.' *Canadian Psychology*, 41, 1–9.

Taylor, C. (2003). 'Day of the Smart Mobs.' *Time*. 10 March 35.

8

Twenty-First-Century Leadership—The God of Small Things; or Putting the 'Ship' back into 'Leadership'

Keith Grint

What twenty-first-century leadership will look like is often derived from some configuration of the kind of organization that such leadership 'requires'. Since we will allegedly have flatter organizations (less hierarchical), more sophisticated technologies making virtual organizations viable, a more educated and culturally less quiescent workforce, all set within an ever-more competitive global environment that makes long-term careers irrelevant, then future leaders will need to reflect this brave new world. In other words, for all that leaders are held to be important, they are actually relegated to the role of a dependent variable, a functional requisite of the situation, configured in line with the 'logic of the context'. But even assuming that we can agree on what the context will look like, there are major differences in the way we construct this configuration that need to be assessed before we can even begin to answer the question: what will twenty-first-century leadership look like? In what follows, let us first approach the topic by considering the two variables that tend to figure highly in most treatments of leadership: space and time. And upon these two variables hang diametrically opposed interpretations of the answer: eternal and contingent models of leadership. I then focus on a philosophical critique of these models before returning to the possibility that there are eternal requirements—but these do not support traditional ideas of leadership.

Modelling Leadership Requirements: Eternal and Contingent

If the assumption is that space and time are irrelevant to modelling leadership, then it does not matter what the twenty-first-century organization or business will look like, because the leadership format will remain stable: leadership requirements are eternal. Thus the question is not what leadership model is most suitable for the future but what kind of leadership model is best, period. This kind of model has been associated with a wide number of leadership theories, including Carlyle's 'Heroic Man' and some trait theories that suggest certain traits are both essential to leadership and essentially unchanging across space and time. Some form of charisma, the ability to envision a radically different solution to an aged problem, the ability to mobilize followers and so on are, in this approach, just a few of these universal requirements because the future is just a reflection of the past. The most radical version of this approach relates to the 'hard-wiring' model of evolutionary psychology. In this perspective, leadership is something that we have always had and something that some of us are born with. This genetic make-up tends to propel 'alpha-males'—those with high levels of testosterone—into positions of leadership where—if successful—they then generate high levels of serotonin, a hormone associated with happiness. The subsequent forms of natural selection eliminate all but the strongest, or rather all but the most appropriate for leadership positions (Nicholson, 2000: 97–125). In effect the requirements of leadership are hard-wired into humans and remain relatively stable across space and time. Or as Nicholson (2000: 1) puts it: 'We may have taken ourselves out of the Stone Age but we haven't taken the Stone Age out of ourselves.'

Under these circumstances we might, perhaps, follow Plato in concentrating on the question: 'Who should rule us?', even if his answer—the wisest rather than the most popular—runs contrary to our current democratic trend. But if leadership is hard-wired then simply facilitating the process of natural selection should be sufficient to resolve the problem because the kind of leadership is unlikely to change in the near or distant future. The persistence of this selection model is evident in the large number of TV programmes that operate on precisely this philosophical basis, such as Big Brother, Popstars, Fame Academy, and so on. We might then ask whether all the concern for different leadership styles is mere propaganda, a shifting debate about morality generated by the chattering classes or by those who believe history is on their side but ultimately deployed by those with

ship in the twentieth century than in any other, there are many examples of decentralized leadership in previous centuries, and the growth of fundamentalist religious governments in the last two decades do not bode well for a continuously enlightening leadership style.

Perhaps, then, if space and time are important in generating radically different organizations that demand significantly variable leadership forms then a contingency-based approach would be better (Fiedler, 1997). These suggest that once we have established the context and format of such organizations then, and only then, can we begin to decipher the 'needs' for leadership. This form of reasoning, often nestling within a functionalist philosophy, usually implies some form of materialist determinism; in effect the future material world will determine the cultural context that supports leadership. So, for example, if our future world is very dynamic, competitive and unstable, then we 'need' to provide flexible and decentralized leadership systems. On the other hand, if the future returns to the more stable global system that we allegedly experienced just after the Second World War, or if the future that we were allegedly about to enter resembles 'the end of history' that was almost upon us after the collapse of communism, then we can return to the stable hierarchies and centralized administrative leadership that dominated the 1950s and 1960s. For instance, it may be that 'crisis' situations require authoritarian or at least decisive leadership, while more stable periods facilitate the development of more liberal models.

A third take on time is in a circular format. Here the fashions of leadership revolve across time and space so that authoritarian and liberal leaders displace each other in sequences that may last some time. There is no essential 'end point' in this model, just a sequence of revolutions but these changes can be related to the differing contexts within which they occur. In Barley and

Kunda's (2000) version of this, the endless cycle of management styles relates directly to periods within the economic 'long wave'. Hence, expansionary periods are associated with 'rational' or scientific forms of management, such as Scientific Management or Systems Theory approaches, while contracting economic periods are associated with more 'normative' management styles, such as Industrial Betterment, Human Relations, Organizational Cultures, and so on. Here the future leadership style will depend upon the point of the next cycle so the trick is to predict the cycle and then derive the appropriate leadership style. Elitist models of leadership, such as Pareto's (1997), also tend to adopt the cyclical approach but lock them into the oscillating forms of elites rather than cycles of the economy.

The final variant on temporal change is that there is no pattern here, just a sequence of changes that have no 'destination' and thus no prediction is possible: the future may be an extrapolation of past trends or it may reveal a cyclical return to 'old-fashioned virtues' or it may simply be completely novel, something beyond our current comprehension. If this is true then the chances of anyone predicting entirely novel developments are remote and we shall simply have to wait and see. Of course, this then returns us to the possibility of an eternal leadership style: it doesn't matter what the future holds, 'traditional' leaders will still lead. But there is a different 'take' on the requirements of leadership that needs further exploration here: the very idea of 'requirements' legitimizes rather than simply explains the role of leaders.

The Construction of Leadership

It could be argued that the causal direction of the question should be reversed—thus the question should not be what kind of leader will the future organization need but what kind of future organizations will the current crop of leaders construct? This 'construction' can itself be of two variants.

First, leaders 'build' the future context—in the sense that Hitler laid the foundations for the Nazi State, or Roosevelt laid the foundations for the USA to enter the Second World War or Mao Tse-tung constructed the ideological basis for Communist China, and so on. Of course, this leader-focused approach assumes that individuals rather than collectives are responsible for the construction of the future—in much the same way that Carlyle suggested, or in one of Napoleon's favourite examples 'The Gauls were not conquered by the Roman legions but by Caesar' (quoted in Goldsworthy, 2003: 377). Tolstoy believed the opposite—that leaders were merely propelled by their organizations as a bow-wave is propelled by a boat, but it can still be argued that the future is constructed by contemporary leadership even if that leadership has a collective form (Ackerman and Duvall, 2000).

Second, we need to consider whether we can ever secure a transparent rendition of the context without reference to the relationship between leaders and organizations. In other words, are leaders neutral in the interpretations of contexts and organizations or are they deeply implicated in those renditions—to the point where no 'objective' analysis is available? In effect, who says what the context is (usually a crisis) and that we therefore need leaders of a particular kind (usually 'decisive')? Usually the answer is: the existing leaders or their ardent detractors and competitors for power. If, for instance, we are to believe Prime Minister Blair and President Bush, the situation just prior to the second Gulf War was perilous—Saddam Hussein's weapons of mass destruction were on the verge of being mobilized and could be deployed within forty-five minutes. This 'objective situation' clearly required leadership that was decisive and effective—hence the war against Iraq. But it is no longer clear precisely what this military threat actually was: it may be that there was no threat, so the situation did not require military conflict because the policy of containment was working and had done so since the end of the first Gulf War. Now the point is not whether there ever were weapons of mass destruction but that the situation is *constructed* by those with control over the information. Thus the anti-war campaigns tried—and failed—to construct an account of the situation that downplayed the threat. What remains, therefore is not a true and a false account of the situation because we will probably never know what that actually was. Instead we have contending accounts, some of which are perceived as more powerful than others and thus are able to mobilize support for particular actions. It is often very difficult, then, to establish what the context actually is and what the requirements of the situation are, and quite different forms of leadership have succeeded in markedly similar circumstances to bedevil our attempts to link the situation to the 'required' leadership (Grint, 2000). This seems to leave us bereft of ideas but I want to suggest a way around the apparent dead-end that will suggest why both the universal and contingent approaches to leadership are problematic and what we can do about it. The two primary problems of leadership are omniscience and omnipotence and both are fatal to trait and contingency approaches. In what follows I want to suggest that their limitations provide a key to understanding how we might, after all, consider what kind of leadership might be preferable in the future.

Omniscience and Omnipotence:
Putting the 'ship' back into 'Leader-ship'

Let us consider omniscience first. When listing the traits required by formal leaders, it is usual for any number of characteristics to emerge: charisma, energy, vision, confidence, tolerance, communication skills, 'presence', the ability to multitask, listening skills, decisiveness, team building, 'distance', strategic skills, and so on and so forth. No two lists constructed by leadership students or leaders ever seem to be the same and no consensus exists as to which traits or characteristics or competences are essential or optional. Indeed, the most interesting aspect of list-making is that by the time the list is complete the only plausible description of the owner of such a skill base is 'God'. Irrespective of whether the traits are contradictory it is usually impossible for anyone to name leaders who have all these traits, at least to any significant degree; yet it seems clear that all these traits are necessary to a successful organization. Thus we are left with a paradox: the leaders who have all of these—the omniscient leaders—do not exist, but we seem to need them.

One resolution of this paradox is that the focus should be shifted from the leader to leadership—such that as a social phenomenon the leadership characteristics may well be present within the leadership team or the followers even if no individual possesses them all. Thus it is the crew of the metaphorical 'ship' not the literal ship's 'captain' that has the requirements to construct and maintain an organization; hence the need to put the 'ship' back into 'the leadership'. In other words, rather than leadership being restricted to the gods it might instead be associated with the opposite. As Arundhati (Roy 1998) remarks about her own novel, 'To me the god of small things is the inversion of God. God's a big thing and god's in control. The god of small things . . . '[2] Here I want to suggest that leadership is better configured as *The God of Small Things*.

The Big Idea, then, is that there isn't one; there are only lots of small actions taken by followers that combine to make a difference. This is not the same as saying that small actions operate as 'Tipping Points' (Gladwell, 2002), though they might, but rather that big things are the consequence of an accumulation of small things. An organization is not an oil tanker which goes where the captain steers it, but a living and disparate organism, a network of individuals—its direction and speed is thus a consequence of many small decisions and acts (Barabási, 2003; Kilduff and Tsai, 2003). Or, as William Lowndes (1652–1724) [Auditor of the Land Revenue under Queen Anne] suggested, 'Take care of the pence and the pounds will take care of themselves.' This has been liberally translated as 'Take care of the small things and the big things will take care of themselves,' but the important thing here is to note the shift from individual heroes to multiple heroics. This doesn't mean that CEOs, Head Teachers, Chief Constables, Generals, and so on, are irrelevant; their role is critical but limited and dependent upon the actions of subordinates. Because of this, success and failure are often dependent upon small decisions and small acts—both by leaders and 'followers' who also 'lead'. Hence The Big Idea is that Leadership is the God of Small Things. This implies that we should abandon Plato's question: 'Who should rule us?' and focus instead on Popper's question: 'How can we stop our rulers ruining us?'[3] In effect, we cannot secure omniscient leaders but because we concentrate on the selection mechanism those that become formal leaders often assume they are omniscient and are therefore very likely to make mistakes that may affect all of us mere followers and undermine our organizations.

The effects of this are clear in a comparison between Stalin and Hitler. During the invasion of Poland, Hitler allowed his generals to take the necessary military decisions and only intervened once, to be overruled by Von Rundstead. However the success of the invasion, plus the collapse of France and Western Europe then tempted Hitler to believe himself as unnaturally gifted as a military strategist—to the point where he intervened more and more in military decisions from 1941. And, contrary to his self-perception, since he was not omniscient, he committed more and more mistakes, allowing the Soviet and Allied armies to prevail. In contrast, Stalin began the Winter War against Finland, assuming himself to be the only one capable of driving the strategy forward. Yet the problems in the Finnish debacle and the catastrophic period during the beginning of the German invasion of the Soviet Union in 1941 eventually forced him to recognize his own limitations and to transfer authority to Soviet generals like Zukhov and Antonov, who were prepared to face Stalin down. Indeed, one could well argue that it was this 'Constructive Dissent' between all the Allied political and military leaders (Churchill and Brooke, and Marshall and Roosevelt included) that enabled the Allies to destroy the German political system of 'Destructive Consent' in which few military or political leaders dared to provide Hitler with the information he needed, rather than wanted.

Similarly, at the battles of Lodi (1796), Marengo (1800), and Austerlitz (1805), Napoleon listened to his generals and engaged in conversations about strategy, but by the time of his later defeats at Moscow (1812) and Waterloo (1815) he had all but abandoned any thoughts of taking advice from subordinates and insisted that only his personal planning and direction could achieve victory. As Marshal Ségur's diary noted in Russia, 'His pride, his policies and perhaps his health gave him the worst advice of all, which was to take no-one's advice' (Weider and Guegen, 2000: 139). As Chandler (1966: 161) insists, at Waterloo: Napoleon was 'discouraging even his ablest generals from indulging in original thought'.

Nor are attributions of omniscience limited to national military or political leaders alone. For example, when the Air Florida 90 ('Palm 90'), flight crashed on 13 January 1982 in poor weather conditions, it is apparent from the conversation between Captain Larry Wheaton and the 1st Officer Roger Pettit that the latter was unconvinced that the plane was ready for lift off, yet his inability to stop Wheaton from going ahead inadvertently led to the crash.[4] A similar level of 'inappropriate subordination' seems to have occurred in Marks and Spencer. According to Judy Bevan, Richard Greenbury, having achieved significant successes became more and more isolated from his subordinate board members to the point where they only engaged in destructive consent and not in constructive dissent. As she remarks about one of the final board meetings through the words of a board member:

The thing about Rick is that he never understood the impact he had on people—people were just too scared to say what they thought. I remember one meeting we had to discuss a new policy and two or three directors got me on one side beforehand and said they were really unhappy about it. Then Rick made his presentation and asked for views. There was total silence until one said, 'Chairman we are all 100% behind you on this one.' And that was the end of the meeting.

(Bevan, 2002: 3)

Alfred Sloan, according to Drucker (2003) faced a similar problem with his board but was able to recognize the manifestations of Destructive Consent, 'Gentlemen, I take it we are all in complete agreement on the decision here?' [Consensus of nodding heads.] 'Then I propose we postpone further discussion of this matter until our next meeting to give ourselves time to develop disagreement and perhaps gain some understanding of what the decision is all about.'

Finally, take the case of Wayne Jowett who was erroneously injected with Vincristine, by the intrathecal route on 4 January 2001, under the supervision of the Specialist Registrar Dr Mulhem, by Dr Morton, a Senior House Officer at the Queen's Medical Centre Nottingham (QMC).[5] Such a procedure almost always results in death but the issue here is not that a mistake was made. According to the BBC version of events:

Dr Mulhem read out the name and dose of the drug, but he did not say how it should be administered and said that when he saw the Vincristine that he was thinking of another drug which is administered spinally. Dr Morton asked whether the Vincristine should be given spinally and said Dr Mulhem had told him yes. *He said he was surprised by this, but had not felt he could challenge a superior.*

(my emphasis)[6]

Note here how the subordinate is, once again, concerned about the veracity of the decision made by the superordinate but unable or unwilling to challenge that decision.

Nor is the problem of knowledge limited to individuals. In September 1998 Long Term Capital Management (LTCM), a Hedge Fund, was in debt to the tune of \$4.6 billion and was only bailed out by the intervention of the US Federal Reserve organized by Greenspan.[7] LTCM included two Nobel Economics Prize winners and an ex-VP of the American Federal Reserve. It used complex math formulas to spread risk across a range of stocks, bonds, etc. and its sophistication encouraged Robert Merton (one of the Nobel Prize winners) to claim that the model 'would provide the perfect hedge'; it obviously did not (Stein, 2003: HR 56:5).

It should be clear from these examples that assumptions of omnipotence are unfortunately likely and likely to be unfortunate in their consequences. But even if we could find omniscient leaders to solve our twenty-first-century leadership problems, would they have the necessary power to ensure their ideal solutions were executed—in effect can we secure omnipotent leaders?

Perhaps the first thing to note is that attributing god-like qualities to leaders does not result in god-like qualities—but it might encourage us to think of leaders as gods and take 'appropriate action'. For example, during the last Football World Cup I asked my MBA class what kind of leader the English coach, Sven Goran Eriksson, was? The immediate answer from one English student was that since England had just beaten Argentina 'Sven must be a god!' But when I then asked what would happen if England lost their next game against Brazil the same student responded, 'We will crucify him!' Here is an intriguing dialogue for it exposes the attributions of saint and sinner, saviour and scapegoat, that hoists leaders onto pedestals that cannot support them and then ensures those same leaders are hoist by their own petard.

What this also reveals is the consequence of attributing omnipotence to leaders—we, the followers, are rendered irresponsible by our own action, for when the gods of leadership fail their impossible task—as fail they must—we followers have a scapegoat to take all the blame for what is, in reality, our own failure to accept responsibility.[8] On the one hand our response to such 'failure' is indicative of the spread of a philosophy of 'zero-tolerance' towards mistakes, despite the inevitability of error in a world of imperfect knowledge and imperfect control. On the other hand the yearning for perfection in leaders perhaps reflects our collective dissatisfaction with the lives of unacknowledged followers—the gods of small things. As Albert Schweitzer (1998) in his autobiography *Out of My Life and Thought* remarked

Of all the will toward the ideal in mankind only a small part can manifest itself in public action. All the rest of this force must be content with small and obscure deeds. The sum of these, however, is a thousand times stronger than the acts of those who receive wide public recognition. The latter, compared to the former, are like the foam on the waves of a deep ocean.

Thus although it is the collective followers that move the wheel of history along it is their formal leaders who claim the responsibility, leaving most people to sink unacknowledged by history, nameless but not pointless. George Eliot (1965: 896) makes this poignantly clear at the end of *Middlemarch* in her description of Dorothea:

Her full nature, like that river of which Cyrus broke the strength, spent itself in channels which had no great name on the earth. But the effect of her being on those around her was incalculably diffusive: for the growing good of the world is partly dependent on unhistoric acts; and that things are not so ill with you and me as they might have been, is half owing to the number who lived faithfully a hidden life, and rest in unvisited tombs.

A useful way to consider the all too easily overlooked role of followers in the construction of a leader's power is to envisage the difference between a domino-run and a Mexican wave. In the former all the power resides in the first movement that stimulates the dominoes to fall in sequence, generating a 'run'. Thus power lies with the pusher, the leader. But a Mexican wave that runs around a sports stadium does not depend on an individual leader to make it work—it works without apparent leadership and it 'dies' when the collective decide not to engage in further 'waves'. In effect, power is a consequence as much as a cause of followership: if—and only if—followers follow then leaders become powerful, but that act remains contingent not determined, and certainly not determined by any future imaginings because acts are quintessentially indeterminate: followers always have the choice not to act, and though they may pay the consequences of not acting the point is that no leader or situation can guarantee followership—leaders are neither omnipotent nor omniscient.

Conclusion

I began by asking what kind of leadership might be appropriate for the twenty-first century but I suggested that this was a difficult question to answer until we had established what kind of model was being used: if we assume an eternal model of leadership then the question becomes irrelevant—what ever worked in the past will work in the future. If this is not acceptable then we need to configure the future through some configuration of the role of space and time and four were briefly addressed with their different future leadership demands: linear models often adopt 'whig' historicist perspectives that talk of ever-more progressive leaders; contingent models demand that we establish what the context might be and then derive the functional needs for leadership from a rigorous review of the leadership requirements from this; circular models often oscillate between authoritarian and progressive leaders depending on the 'needs' of the period, while patternless approaches, by definition, are the most obscure in their prescriptive consequences. However, I suggested that we might need to reconsider the relationship between context and leader either by reversing it—what context do leaders create?—

or by examining the extent to which the situation is whatever the persuasive leaders can persuade us it is. That might seem to lead us into a blind alley but I then suggested that the weaknesses of the eternal and the contingent models offer us a way out of the problem of leadership. In short, that because leaders are neither omniscient nor omnipotent the only mechanism for configuring organizational leadership with at least some chance of long-term success would be to shift from Destructive Consent to Constructive Dissent and to abandon the idea that the individual leader can resolve all organizational problems. On the contrary only when organizations are awash with deep or distributed leadership and responsible followers, rather than beached by isolated leaders cast adrift from their irresponsible followers, will organizations succeed in the long term. This surely is the lesson for the future: leaders have never been, nor will they ever be, omnipotent or omniscient and we should organize on that basis. We need to put the ship back into leadership because organizations—like ships—are not run by individual captains but by a complete crew, not by leaders who are gods of great things but by people who are the gods of small things.

Notes

1. See Hassard (1996) for a review of the importance of Time in organizations.
2. See *www.eng.fju.edu.tw/worldlit/lecture/Roy.ppt*
3. Thanks to Jack Nasher-Awakemian for reminding me of this distinction.
4. See *http://pw1.netcom.com/~asapilot/p90.html*
5. 'Provided Vincristine is administered intravenously (IV), it is a powerful and useful drug in the fight against leukaemia. However,

if the drug is administered, in error, through an intrathecal injection (IT) the result is usually the death of the patient or if the patient does survive, then they typically suffer from severe neurological trauma.' *External Inquiry into the adverse incident that occurred at Queen's Medical Centre, Nottingham, 4th January 2001* by Professor Brian Toft. *www.doh.gov.uk/qmcinquiry/*

6. See *http://news.bbc.co.uk/1/hi/health/1284244.stm*

7. Hedge Funds (started with LTCM in 1994) are limited partnerships, with a maximum of 99 partners and are almost unregulated. Around 4,000 exist, supported only by very wealthy institutions and individuals. They have very high leverage/gearing (debt to equity/capital). At LTCM it was 50/250–1 (mostly it is about 2–1)).

8. See Heifetz (1994) on the issue of follower responsibility.

References

Ackerman, P. and Duvall, J. (2000). *A Force More Powerful*. London: Palgrave.

Barabási, A. L. (2003). *Linked*. London: Plume.

Barley, S. R. and Kunda, G. (2000). 'Design and Devotion.' In K. Grint (ed.), *Work and Society*. Cambridge: Polity Press.

Bevan, J. (2002). *The Rise and Fall of Marks and Spencer*. London: Profile Books.

Chandler, D. (1966). *The Campaigns of Napoleon*. London: Macmillan.

Drucker, H. (2003). *Effective Management*. London: HarperCollins.

Elliot, G. (1965). *Middlemarch*. Harmondsworth: Penguin.

Fiedler, F. (1997). 'Situational Control and a Dynamic Theory of Leadership.' In K. Grint (ed.), *Leadership: Classical, Contemporary and Critical Approaches*. Oxford: Oxford University Press.

Gladwell, M. (2002). *The Tipping Point*. London: Abacus.

Goldsworthy, A. (2003). *In the Name of Rome: The Men who Won the Roman Empire*. London: Weidenfeld and Nicolson.

Grint, K. (2000). *The Arts of Leadership*. Oxford: Oxford University Press.

Hassard, J. (1996). 'Images of Time in Work and Organization.' In Sr Clegg, C. Hardy, and W. R. Nord (eds.), *Handbook of Organization Studies*. London: Sage.

Heifetz, R. A. (1994). *Leadership Without Easy Answers*. Cambridge, MA.: Harvard University Press.

Kilduff, M. and Tsai, W. (2003). *Social Networks and Organizations*. London: Sage.

Krulak, C. C. (1999). 'The Strategic Corporal: Leadership in the Three Block War.' *Marines Magazine*, January 1999.

Nasher-Awakemian, J. (2003). Private communication.

Nicholson, N. (2000). *Managing the Human Animal*. London: Texere.

Pareto, V. (1997). 'The Treatise on General Sociology.' In K. Grint (ed.), *Leadership: Classical, Contemporary and Critical Approaches*. Oxford: Oxford University Press.

Roy, A. (1998). *The God of Small Things*. London: Flamingo.

Stein, M. (2003). 'Unbounded Irrationality: Risk and Organizational Narcissism at Long Term Capital Management.' *Human Relations* 56(5), 523–40.

Schweitzer, A. (1998). *Out of My Life and Thought*. Baltimore, MA: Johns Hopkins University Press.

Weider, B. and Guegen, E. (2000). *Napoleon: The Man Who Shaped Europe*. Staplehurst: Spellmount.

9

An Agenda for Understanding Individual Leadership in Corporate Leadership Systems

Anne Sigismund Huff
and
Kathrin Moeslein

This chapter argues that a better bridge is needed between the needs and challenges of individual leaders and the practices of large corporations trying to select, support, measure, motivate, and develop very large numbers of leaders around the world. In proposing a theoretic and empirical agenda that takes into account the corporate need to devise leadership *systems*, we draw on observations from a study conducted with corporate partners at the Technical University of Munich (TUM). Our desire is to find ways to understand more about how the 'art' required from individual leaders interacts with the 'science' offered by the kind of corporate leadership systems observed in this study of large and 'super-large' (over 100,000 employees) companies. A key idea for future work is that simplicity is critical for both effective corporate systems and the necessary sensemaking of individual leaders, but that simplicity must facilitate improvization and other more complex exchanges between individuals and corporate systems if it is to be effective.

The Changing Face of Leadership Studies

'Leadership is one of the most observed and least understood phenomena on earth', J. M. Burns wrote in 1978. At about the same time, Ralph Stogdill evaluated more than 3,000 studies of leadership research and came to similar conclusions: 'Four decades of research on leadership have produced a bewildering mass of findings . . . the endless accumulation of empirical data has not produced an integrated understanding of leadership' (1974, vii).

Thirty years later, we believe the leadership field is in a somewhat similar condition. Empirical studies continue to use a broad range of approaches and yield disparate findings, with perhaps even more white spots in the overall conceptual landscape than in previous decades. However, there appears to be a clearer agenda for moving forward, with recent authors identifying a difficult but more integrated set of issues for research and practice. This agenda includes:

- The challenge of moving from traditional 'leader research' to a more organization orientated *'leadership research'* (e.g. Yukl, 1989; Day, 2000; Lowe and Gardner, 2000);
- The challenge of moving from the traditional focus on 'leadership in organizations' towards a research focus that is more orientated towards *'leadership of organizations'* (e.g. Boal and Hooijberg, 2000; Yukl, 2001; Daft, 2002);
- The need to take into account emerging forms of *'distributed leadership'* (delegated leadership, co-leadership, peer-leadership or shared leadership) to assure organizational *innovation and change* (e.g. House and Aditya, 1997; Gronn, 2002; Hiller, 2002).

These challenges for future leadership research respond to the increased demands and capabilities of individuals in organizations (Gratton, 2004); they emphasize a need for leaders to be more flexible and more responsive to local circumstances, and to recognize the importance of micro-processes in achieving organizational outcomes (Johnson and Huff, 1998). Table 9.1 summarizes the subsequent and significant change in the leadership field in terms of evolving models of leadership over time.

In our view this is a useful overview of the range of leadership behaviours discussed over the long history of the field. While leaders still adopt older 'command and control' techniques, and occasionally these are effective and appropriate, the primary challenges for both research and practice lie to the right of the figure. But this focus of attention, which seems so appropriate when leadership is seen as a field concerned only with the individual, raises a dilemma that is the point of departure for this chapter. There is another set of shaping factors affecting how leadership must be understood. More specifically, the increasing scale, speed, and globalizing complexities of

Table 9.1 Evolving Models of Leadership

	Ancient	Traditional	Modern	Future
Idea of Leadership	Domination	Influence	Common goals	Reciprocal relations
Action of Leadership	Commanding followers	Motivating followers	Creating inner commitment	Mutual meaning making
Focus of Leadership Development	Power of the leader	Interpersonal skills of the leader	Self-knowledge of the leader	Interactions of the group

Source: Drath, 1998: 408.

organizational life raise additional challenges for leadership research. An extended agenda for research must respond to:

- The need to pay more attention to *communication* in a way that takes into account the increasing scale of coordination required in large organizations, as well as the potentials and pitfalls of modern information and communication technology (e.g. Daft, 1999, 2002; Lowe and Gardner, 2000);
- The need to include issues of *strategy* (e.g. Cannella and Monroe, 1997; House and Aditya, 1997; Boal and Hooijberg, 2000; Lowe and Gardner, 2000);
- The need for research on the *leadership systems* increasingly used by large organizations (Conger 1998; Lowe and Gardner 2000).

Our point is that most leadership research has been 'terribly interested in individuals' (Goffee 2003), with most researchers completely neglecting the corporate context. Yet, 'Leadership Is More Than One Person!' claims James O'Toole (2000): 'We have been wrong for a long time. And I mean all of us in business, academia, consulting, and journalism...Businesses dependent on a single great leader run a terrible risk.'

While many leadership researchers, who often depend upon psychological theories, are guilty as charged, there is an interesting exception to this observation of neglect. Driven by engineering research and corporate practice, more structured approaches to leadership research are emerging. They focus not on leadership itself, but on *managing leaders*. In the next few pages we summarize this very different way of thinking about leadership, at a different level of analysis, before addressing the question of how the two foci of attention might be brought together.

Leadership with an Engineering Flavour: The Move from Art to Science

When Donald E. Knuth published the first edition of his seminal book *The Art of Computer Programming* in 1968, programming was still a talent understood by few. In 1981, however, when David Gries published his major book *The Science of Programming*, the landscape of the software development profession had already fundamentally changed. Gries summarized how software engineering approaches were able to achieve overwhelming success for large-scale programming, with major consequences for corporate life. Subsequently, large corporations have moved from process engineering, through service engineering to knowledge engineering, innovation engineering, community engineering, and even trust engineering. The Capability Maturity Models (CMMs) of Carnegie Mellon's Software Engineering Institute (SEI) have been particularly influential. Originally developed for the improvement of software development processes, the approach has been translated to many fields of organizational activity and the process oriented improvement of management practices in general. Adopted by many organizations worldwide, CMM frameworks claim to 'help organizations increase the maturity of their human resources, process, and technology assets to improve long-term business performance' (*www.sei.cmu.edu/managing/managing.html*). With 'People CMM', corporate human resource management should follow the same rules and concepts that were originally designed to improve software development processes (Curtis *et al.*, 1995, 2002). 'Participatory Culture', for instance, is seen as 'a process area at maturity level 3' that is clearly defined and described in the process engineering handbook.

Leadership systems following this engineering mindset are now well established in many large corporations. They provide a broad range of tools, instruments, mechanisms, and rules for the management of leaders at a meta-level that has been largely neglected by leadership research. The systems try to bring order to (a) the identification of leadership talents, (b) the way specific leadership tasks are carried out, (c) the assessment of performance, (d) the translation of assessment results into system wide implications, and (e) the use of the data collected in development programmes. This is the context for understanding leadership at a corporate level. One important implication is that the 'art of leadership' often praised by those who study individual leaders is more and more subject to relatively rigid management processes. More and more often leadership takes place in an institutional context of enablers and constraints that are overtly established with the best intent—to improve the company's 'leadership capital' more systematically, or scientifically.

There is, however, an apparent contradiction between many descriptions of effective individual leadership (and its need sometimes to break rules, initiate change, and provoke innovations) and descriptions of effective corporate leadership from a systems perspective (and its need to set boundaries, exclude possibilities, and provide coherence). We are interested in this intersection as a fascinating field for future research. How does individual and corporate leadership interact? Can corporate leadership systems leverage individual sensemaking or are they more likely to structure, restrict, and restrain the individual leader's efforts? We believe there are more negative than positive answers to these questions, but that there are examples of successful interaction between corporate systems and individual agency that deserve further inquiry. In this brief chapter we offer an example from a recent study of corporate systems, and draw on the literature of sense-making to outline the beginning of a research agenda.

The TUM Leadership Systems Study

Our observations on corporate leadership systems are drawn from a two-year study of thirty-seven large multinationals in Germany, Great Britain, the USA, and the Netherlands, carried out by the second author and her associates (see Reichwald *et al.*, 2003). Between October 2001 and September 2003 more than 110 executives were included in the investigation. The study consisted of in-depth interviews, review of confidential corporate documents and collection of published information on the leadership systems of the involved corporations. The companies included came from a broad range of industries, including automobile (e.g. BMW, DaimlerChrysler), IT, electronics, and software (e.g. Cisco Systems, HP, IBM, Philips, SAP), telecommunications services (e.g. BT, Deutsche Telekom), energy (e.g. Chevron Texaco, E.On), risk, insurance, and financial services (e.g. Allianz, Deutsche Bank, JP Morgan Chase, Liberty Mutual, Marsh, Munich Re), systems and solutions (e.g. BAE Systems, Siemens), and travel/tourism (e.g. Lufthansa, TUI).

The focus of the study was on the instruments, concepts, and strategies used to develop corporate leadership capital. All companies included in the research used a broad range of tools and processes to support the management of their leaders. They differed, however, in the extent to which these practices were implemented and integrated. Almost always, the purpose and underlying assumptions of the corporate systems studied could be described in terms of their association with different disciplines. For example:

- *Personnel management:* e.g. leadership-assessment centres, executive surveys and performance reviews, management training.

- *Controlling:* e.g. shareholder value management, economic value added (EVA), Balanced Scorecard (BSC).
- *Corporate communication:* e.g. vision and mission statements, corporate culture and value management, open-door policies, multimedia and event communication, external marketing.
- *Organization:* e.g. differentiated leadership hierarchies, incentive systems, profit centre structures, implementation of trust-based organization structures.
- *Strategic management:* e.g. strategic competence planning, strengths–weaknesses–portfolios, business impact initiatives, integrated business planning processes.

All of these practices, and many others, were described by interviewees as supporting leaders with their everyday workload, making their performance measurable, promoting good leadership skills, identifying leadership deficiencies and helping eliminate them, creating incentives for good leadership, facilitating and improving the selection of leadership talents, selectively developing leaders, and making the corporate build-up of leadership capital possible.

To proceed, this complex landscape had to be simplified. That was accomplished in discussion with a nucleus of interview partners from seven core companies in the study, with further inputs from workshops with experts from research and practice, and a survey of current organization, communication, and leadership research. The result of this complex dialogue was the identification of four action fields representing key questions addressed by corporate leadership systems:

- How can leadership talents be identified and promoted to excellency? (*Selection of Leaders and Leadership Development*)

- How can executives be supported by leadership systems that are useful in everyday tasks? (*Leadership as a Day-to-day Interactive Process*)
- How is leadership performance evaluated and measured? (*Leadership Metrics*)
- How are evaluation results used to more broadly develop leadership capacity in the organisation? (*Leadership Deployment*)

These action fields covering processes of selection, support, measurement, capacity expansion, and development were described as the logically interacting generic building blocks of leadership systems, as shown in Fig. 9.1.

An important purpose of the TUM study was to evaluate activities as well as supporting tools and instruments in each area, trying to understand the way they interacted from a systems perspective. A primary outcome of this evaluation was the importance of simplicity. The systems that were judged most effective focused their instrument landscape and linked the

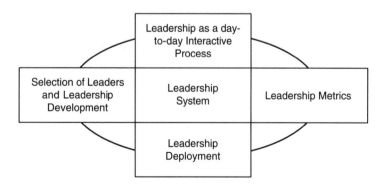

Figure 9.1 *The Generic Leadership System.*
Source: **Reichwald et al., 2003).**

results to structure, strategy, and culture within the company. They not only integrated applications, but built in communication processes between leaders at all levels of the corporate hierarchy to increase the chances that they were understood and applied in similar ways. In contrast, the systems that were judged less effective included a larger variety of smaller tools and procedures, operating in relative isolation. Many of these appeared to be useful enough when judged individually, but they were difficult for participants to understand as a group because they were not linked together in any transparent way.

An Example from the TUM Study

A brief summary from one of the 'super-large' players in the TUM study that was judged to have an effective leadership system may prove instructive. While leadership systems in many companies are seen as a subset of the overall human resource management system and are given relatively little attention by people outside of HRM, this company's leadership system manages to reach widespread acknowledgement—comparable to their financial management system—by linking both together. Both adopt equally rigid timetables and strict deadlines. Both are seen as delivering value to the corporation.

The leadership system in our example is described by managers and external observers as web-based and easy to use, transparent, consequential, and integrated across the four generic fields summarized in Fig. 9.1. Tools and instruments falling within each of the four categories of Fig. 9.1 are closely integrated with the overall business processes of the company, and there is a synchronized timeline between the critical activities of leadership selection, support, measurement, expansion, and development on the one hand, and the milestones of the company's financial processes on the other. Perhaps most importantly, several observers reported that this company's leadership system has a significant impact on the overall success of the company. As one manager noted: 'Leadership and business are interlinked—they challenge each other!'

As with several other highly ranked corporate leadership systems in this study, many of the tools used are based on widely available concepts or even commercial products, but these are tailored to the company's specific needs. Measurement of leadership performance, for example, builds upon company designed peer reviews, partner and customer feedback. These often use but extend concepts from the Balanced Scorecard (Kaplan and Norton, 1996). Observers know limitations of this approach, and can be somewhat cynical. As one observer put it—'The Balanced Scorecard is like Harry Potter! Suddenly, everyone talks about the same thing and all have the impression that they understand each other.' Despite the jokes, this approach is widely used and its use is seen as supporting company-wide integration.

Tools and instruments that link leadership performance with the selection of leaders and their development are rare in the companies studied in the TUM project; usually monetary incentives like salary are linked to performance measurement, non-monetary incentives are not. In our example company, however, 360-degree feedback (e.g. Ward, 1997; Toegel and Conger, 2003) is used to draw strengths–weaknesses–profiles for each individual leader, and these feed into performance evaluation and feedback sessions. The result of the performance evaluation forms a rigid ranking of the 'Top 5 per cent', the 'Best 20 per cent;', the 'Majority of 66 per cent;' and the 'Bottom 9 per cent'. (One manager noted that 'There is a fixed number of the bottom

9 per cent—in that way you can't cheat on the evaluation.') For all those measured, performance evaluation also forms the basis for career and development planning. Again, while aware of the problems that may arise when linking 360-degree feedback to performance evaluation and development plans, the integration of these concepts is widely accepted in this example company. The use of linked tools is seen as a positive and unifying aspect of the company's leadership systems by executives at different levels in different units of the corporation.

The basis for leadership development in this company is a 'Management Resource Review' that compares and manages the top-leadership talents of the company. A virtual corporate university has been established as a centre of excellence for all forms of leadership (leading markets, innovations, technology, and people). The widely understood goal of this corporate university is to establish a joint understanding of leadership and culture for the company as a whole. It is thus basically a communication channel that tries to connect leaders at all levels but also aims to connect with partners outside the company through partnering with research institutions, business schools, or selected customers.

Leadership System Components as Useful Inputs to Improvization by Individuals

It is commonplace in the strategy literature to observe that success at one point in time, such as we have just described, can lead to later stagnation and decline. We began this chapter with two relatively straightforward ideas that relate to this problem. First, the desirability of simplicity from a systems point of view has an interesting counterpart in the necessity of simplification from the perspective of individual cognitive processes (Walsh, 1995). We thought the storyline of the paper would develop a subsequent idea, something like 'Simplicity is necessary both for leadership systems and for the sensemaking of individual leaders, but somehow the system has to allow, even encourage, individual improvisation in response to varied local conditions or else simplicity on both sides becomes increasingly risky.' Improvisation seemed a particularly good metaphor to link to emerging forms of leadership, backed by a small but significant literature (e.g. Mangham and Pye, 1991).

However, when we looked more closely at the various articles and working papers we had on improvisation, we had to admit that we didn't know as much about the central metaphor of improvisation as we thought. In this short chapter we will draw on a powerful piece by Karl Weick (1998), who over the years has written a number of influential articles on jazz, to develop a more complicated storyline that we are eager to develop into a more complete agenda for empirical research.

Weick uses Berliner's (1994: 241) somewhat complicated but evocative definition: 'Improvisation involves reworking precomposed material and designs in relation to unanticipated ideas conceived, shaped, and transformed under the special conditions of performance, thereby adding unique features to every creation.' It is the focus on 'precomposed material' that gave us pause. That idea becomes even more interesting as Weick draws on Berliner (1994: 66–71) to suggest 'degrees of improvisation' from 'interpretation' through 'embellishment' and 'variation' before reaching what might be more accurately called improvisation itself. As one might expect, 'activities toward the "interpretation" end of the continuum are more dependent on the models they start with than are activities toward the improvisation end' (Weick, 1998: 545). However, subsequent discussion of the source material of different forms of improvisation departed from some of our expectations, and deserves fuller explication:

> as modifications become more like improvisations and less like interpretations, their content is more heavily influenced by past experience, dispositions, and local conditions...Thus, interpretation and embellishment should be initiated more quickly under time pressure than is true for variation and improvisation. Deliberate injunctions to be radically different may falter if they fail to specify precisely what the original model is, in what sense it is to remain a constraint, and which of its properties are constants and which are variables. These questions don't arise in the three approximations to improvisation represented by interpretation, embellishment, and variation. The point is, deliberate improvisation is much tougher, much more time consuming, and places higher demands on resources, than does deliberate interpretation. If deliberateness is a key requirement for something to qualify as organisational improvisation...then full-scale improvisation should be rare in time-pressured settings. But, if it could be accomplished despite these hurdles, then it should be a substantial, sustainable, competitive advantage.

(1998: 545)

Thus we have to add to our original thoughts about leadership systems that they may (and sometimes should) provide the 'kernel' around which a useful improvisation works. Weick quotes the musician Charles Mingus, who says 'you can't improvise on nothing; you've gotta improvise on something'.

This leads us back to the Balanced Score Card—a 'theme' described as 'like Harry Potter' in that 'everyone' within our example firm at least 'thought' they knew what it meant. The interface of interest is precisely this: how is the leadership system used (or, 'played' in a jazz metaphor) within the organization? How can those at the top of the organization, who are ultimately responsible for managing managers, help individuals employ required systems to innovate within specific subunits? Innovation often has been seen as antithetical to system requirements. We want to explore systems as potentially providing critical components for innovation—'critical' in the sense that improvisation around the same theme facilitates communication and coordination in very large companies.

A Preliminary Agenda for Leadership Studies

The brief description of a leadership system judged especially effective in the TUM study with the more discursive discussion of improvisation offered by Karl Weick, suggests just one approach to understanding the complex and often contradictory requirements of selecting, supporting, measuring, motivating, and developing individual leaders. Other options for further research can be linked to the suggestions reviewed in the introduction of this chapter:

(1) *Grapple with the language and logic of systems.* If leadership research is to have an organizational focus, as recommended in the literature, we believe it must give greater attention to the engineering-tradition of leadership systems. This is the overarching point of our chapter, and is especially important if the context of study is to be the world's largest organizations.

One way to study the adoption, implementation, and impact of systems thinking may be to examine the more mature and well-tested systemic efforts in fields like quality management, process management, or innovation management. For example, it is hard to over-emphasize the importance and impact of Six Sigma on many large multinationals over the last two decades. Pioneered by Motorola in the 1980s, this approach to improving profitability by reducing defects in manufactured components subsequently has been shown to generate significant performance improvements in a number of organizations, of varied sizes, not only in manufacturing but in contexts as varied as healthcare and financial services (Harry and Schroeder, 2000). It has also influenced the design and implementation of leadership systems (Tichy and Cardwell, 2002).

TQM, in its many guises, is seen as a fad by many academics. Although it certainly has its faddish aspects, we would observe that it both signified and helped embed systems thinking in corporations, including companies without manufacturing or tangible product sales. Our basic point is that leadership research (and training) must directly address and learn from the applications of this distinctive mindset in order to avoid overly simplistic approaches to leadership in the future. 'Banner fatigue' is evident in many organizations that have been the subject of too many systems quickly replaced by alternatives. The agenda for research and practice is to avoid cynicism by designing systems that genuinely support (and do not hinder) individual leadership efforts.

(2) *Explore the philosophical disconnects between different leadership functions.* If we are to study the leadership *of* organizations, as recommended (e.g. Boal and Hooijberg, 2000), one obvious agenda is to consider the impediments to co-ordination that arise from the different disciplinary homes of leadership systems in organizations, with their accompanying philosophical differences (e.g. Bass, 1990). Most

notably, there is a significant difference in monitoring, evaluation, and other governance efforts, often rooted in an agency perspective, and development and support efforts that depend on assumptions from more positive views of human behaviour.

(3) *Focus on the interface between systems requirements and the demands of distributed leadership.* One of the largest challenges for leadership systems would appear to be accommodating the requirements of innovation and change in many, varied settings. While variety and flexibility are essential to distributed leadership (e.g. House and Aditya, 1997), systems thinking tends to seek integration and routinization. We have explored some ideas about improvisation in this brief chapter; many more avenues to improving innovation are available.

(4) *Understand the impact of changing communication technologies and new organizational forms.* Communication has always been seen as part—and perhaps even the core (see Mintzberg, 1973)—of the leadership picture, but significant changes in information and communication technology, along with increasing demands of a globalizing economy, suggest new items on the research agenda (e.g. Avolio *et al.*, 2000). The advent of new ICT does not seem to have changed the key role of personal face-to-face communication in the daily work of leaders, but the overall workload of each individual leader has risen, tasks have further fragmented and travel has increased (Pribilla *et al.*, 1997). More systemic support for meeting these challenges is needed.

(5) *Study content to improve understanding of process.* Content issues need to be put to the forefront of leadership research, if it is to connect with the primary, strategic concerns of organizations (e.g. Cannella and Monroe, 1997; Lowe and

Gardner, 2000). As one example, we have a particular interest in the effective leadership of international teams. The subject of individual and cultural difference has always been on the leadership agenda, often with the observation that 'requisite variety' is needed to match complex environments (Beer, 1967). Several of the corporations studied at TUM see this issue as a major agenda item, and leadership studies needs to provide additional insight.

(6) *Explore the strengths and weaknesses of specific leadership systems.* If leadership research is to grapple with issues of leadership systems, as has been recommended (e.g. Conger, 1998; Lowe and Gardner, 2000), they must be investigated in detail. Popular management tools and practices like Balanced Scorecard deserve greater attention because of their pervasive use and influence. A particularly interesting outcome of the TUM study was the large number of such tools and practices in simultaneous use within the same company, despite some apparent contradictions. In many instances they were significantly modified in use. One of our agenda items for the future is to look at local adaptation of leadership practices and central response to such adaptations. Ideally, as briefly outlined above, modification can become a strength of the leadership system in use, but this certainly is not easy to accommodate at scale.

Conclusion

Perhaps readers will wonder if we are saying anything new in this chapter. Indeed this is a question we have asked and will continue to ask ourselves, because management and leadership have long been described as requiring a balance between inspiration and control, and between creative interpretation and simplifying rationality. We have drawn attention to scale in this chapter, but major military and religious efforts have acted at astonishing scale for many centuries.

The most obvious changes in today's conditions are not just the significant increase in the number of such macro efforts, but the technologies available to support them. Indeed, the empirical study we have briefly described is built on a ten-year research cooperation between Peter Pribilla, member of the Corporate Executive Committee of Siemens AG until his untimely death in 2003, and Ralf Reichwald, Dean of the TUM Business School. Their collaboration focused on the nature of leadership, leadership communication, and institutional support structures in large multinationals. As briefly cited above, their first joint study, in 1993/4, was a twenty-year follow-up of Henry Mintzberg's study of the *Nature of Managerial Work*. Modern information and communication technology (facsimile, e-mail, voice mail, video conferencing, and so on) were not available in the world Mintzberg studied in the early 1970s. The special focus of the Pribilla and Reichwald study was the impact of these forms of media on leadership communication and the daily work of leaders and their followers (Pribilla *et al.*, 1997). Their early observations lead to an increasing interest in the shaping influence of leadership systems, and the study described above.

In the past, the options for operating at scale have been largely confined to messianic vision and/or command and control. One question in this chapter is whether the newer, much more distributed forms of leadership outlined by Drath (1998) in Table 9.1 can operate within very large organizations. That seems new to us.

References

Avolio, B. J., Kahai, S., and Dodge, G. (2000). 'E-leading in Organizations and its Implications for Theory, Research, and Practice.' *Leadership Quarterly*, 11 (4), 615–68.

Bass, B. M. (1990). In Bass and Stogdill's *Handbook of Leadership: Theory, Research, and Managerial Applications*, 3rd edn. New York: The Free Press.

Beer, S. (1967). *Management Science*. London: Aldus Books.

Berliner, P. F. (1994). *Thinking in Jazz: The Infinite Art of Improvisation*. Chicago, IL: University of Chicago Press.

Boal, K. B. and Hooijberg, R. (2000). 'Strategic Leadership Research. Moving On.' *Leadership Quarterly*, 11 (4), 515–49.

Burns, J. M. (1978). *Leadership*. New York: Harper and Row.

Cannella, A. A. Jr and Monroe, M. J. (1997). 'Contrasting Perspectives on Strategic Leaders: Toward a More Realistic View of Top Managers.' *Journal of Management*, 23, (3), 213–37.

Conger, J. A. (1998). 'Qualitative Research as the Cornerstone Methodology for Understanding Leadership.' *Leadership Quarterly*, 9 (1), 107–22.

Curtis, B., Hefley, W. E., and Miller, S. A. (1995). 'People Capability Maturity Model, Version 1, CMU/SEI-95-MM-002.' Software Engineering Institute, Carnegie Mellon University, Pittsburgh, PA, September.

Curtis, B., Hefley, W. E., and Miller, S. A. (2002). *The People Capability Model. Guidelines for Improving the Workforce*. Boston, MA: Addison-Wesley.

Daft, R. L. (1999). *Leadership. Theory and Practice*. Fort Worth, TX: Dryden Press.

—— (2002). *The Leadership Experience*, 2nd edn. Orlando, FL: Harcourt.

Day, D. V. (2000). 'Leadership Development: A Review in Context' *Leadership Quarterly*, 11 (4), 581–613.

Drath, W. H. (1998). 'Approaching the Future of Leadership Development.' In: C. D. McCauley, R. S. Moxley, and E. Van Velsor (eds.),

The Center for Creative Leadership: Handbook of Leadership Development, 403–432. San Francisco, CA, Jossey-Bass.

Goffee, R. (2003). 'Leadership, Creativity and Innovation.' Presentation Given at the 3rd Annual Innovation Exchange Conference, London Business School, London, 4 December 2003.

Gratton, L. (2004). *The Democratic Enterprise: Liberating Your Business with Individual Freedom and Shared Purpose.* London: FT Prentice Hall.

Gries, D. (1981). *The Science of Programming.* Berlin: Springer.

Gronn, P. (2002). 'Distributed Leadership as a Unit of Analysis.' *Leadership Quarterly*, 13 (4), August, 423–52.

Harry, M. and Schroeder, R. (2000). *SIX Sigma. The Breakthrough Management Strategy Revolutionizing the World's Top Corporations.* New York: Doubleday.

Hiller, N. J. (2002). 'Understanding and Measuring Shared Leadership in Work Teams.' Working paper, The Pennsylvania State University, September (*www.ccl.org/pdf/general/CCL_kenclark_hiller.pdf*).

House, R. J. and Aditya, R. N. (1997). 'The Social Scientific Study of Leadership: Quo Vadis?' *Journal of Management*, 23 (3), 409–73.

Johnson, G, and Huff, A. S. (1998). 'Everyday Innovation / Everyday Strategy.' In G. Hamel, C. K. Prahalad, H. Thomas, and D. O'Neal (eds.), *Strategic Flexibility: Managing in a Turbulent Environment*, pp. 13–27, Chichester, John Wiley and Sons.

Kaplan, R. S. and Norton, D. P. (1996). *The Balanced Scorecard: Translating Strategy into Action.* Boston, MA: Harvard Business School Press.

Knuth, D. E. (1968). *The Art of Computer Programming*, vol. 1. Reading, MA: Addison-Wesley.

Lowe, K. B. and Gardner, W. L. (2000). 'Ten Years of The Leadership Quarterly: Contributions and Challenges for the Future.' *Leadership Quarterly*, 11 (4), 459–514.

Mangham, I. and Pye, A. (1991). *The Doing of Managing.* Oxford: Blackwell.

Mintzberg, H. (1973). *The Nature of Managerial Work*. New York: Harper and Row.

O'Toole, J. (2000). 'Leadership is More than One Person!' MG Newsletter. *Management General 2003* (*www.mgeneral.com*).

Pribilla, P., Reichwald, R., and Goecke, R. (1997). 'Companies and Markets in Transition—Communication Strategies for the Manager of the Future.' TUM Business School, Working Paper WP 010697, Munich, June 1997 (*www.leadership-research.org*).

Reichwald, R., Moeslein, K., and Siebert, J. (2003). 'Leadership Excellence—Comparing Leadership Systems.' Final Report, TUM Business School, IWP-250603, June (*www.leadership-research.org*).

Stogdill, R. M. (1974). *Handbook of Leadership: A Survey of the Literature*. New York: Free Press.

Tichy, N. M. and Cardwell, N. (2002). *The Cycle of Leadership. How Great Leaders Teach their Companies to Win*. New York: Harper Business.

Toegel, G. and Conger, J. A. (2003). '360-Degree Feedback—Time for Reinvention.' *Academy of Management Learning and Education*, 2 (3), 297–311.

Walsh, J. P. (1995). 'Managerial and Organizational Cognition: Notes from a Trip down Memory Lane.' *Organization Science*, 6 (3), 280–321.

Ward, P. (1997). *360-Degree Feedback*. London: Institute of Personnel Development.

Weick, K. E. (1998). 'Improvisation as a Mindset for Organisational Analysis.' *Organization Science*, 9 (5), 543–55.

Yukl, G. (1989). 'Managerial Leadership: A Review of Theory and Research.' *Journal of Management*, 15 (2), 251–89.

——(2001). *Leadership in Organizations*, 5th edn. Upper Saddle River, NJ: Prentice-Hall.

Part III

The Practitioners' View

10

Leading Human Capital and the Global Economy

Hamish McRae

The key theme over the next generation will be variety. There will be no preferred models of corporate organization, no single route to assured success. But all forms of organization in the developed world will have to focus on developing one particular resource: human capital. There will be more pressure than ever before on attracting skilled and creative people, and identifying and enhancing those special qualities.

Unless there is some global catastrophe, the next generation will see the further advance of globalization. In shorthand, more and more of the world's manufacturing output will be located in China and more and more of its service capacity in India. The question for the developed world—or rather the present developed world, for many more countries will make the leap to developed status in the next thirty years—will be to find ways of justifying its high wage levels. The ageing of the population of Europe will put particular pressures on management to get the maximum productivity out of a shrinking workforce.

Of course some industries will be more affected than others. Public utilities will remain located in the regions they serve. Many government services will remain 'on-shore'. Boom industries like health care and education will still serve their local populations and much of their workforce will remain locally employed. Specialist or 'craft' manufacturing will remain and in many places expand. But other industries, such as IT services and mass-manufacturing, will continue to move offshore to lower-waged communities. The front end, the face to the customer, will stay; but the back end, where the goods are manufactured and services generated, will tend to move away.

These changes will complicate management in three separate but interconnected ways.

- First, companies will find in their international relationships that they are managing complex supply chains, often with organizations in different continents and with a workforce with different cultural norms.
- Second, at home they will find that they are managing a much more diversified group of people: more self-employed, more part-timers, more students, more semi-retired.
- Third, as noted above, they will have to make the very best use of their scarcest resource: the human capital of their staff.

Some thoughts about each:

There are a host of different models for outsourcing internationally, from the wholly owned overseas subsidiary, through various forms of joint venture, to the arms-length contract with an independent supplier. The legal structures will not change, or at least not in any significant way. But there will be new forms of partnership which recognize changes in the nature of out-sourcing and the increasing intellectual contribution made by these new partners.

For example, many new ventures will be with suppliers of services rather than goods. The shift of manufacturing jobs from the USA to China has attracted wide attention, but the shift of service sector jobs to India has hardly begun. But not only do Western managers have much more experience of outsourcing manufacturing; the nature of most service transactions is more complex, requires more human interaction, and is accordingly harder to manage.

In addition, as education levels in China and India ap-proach—maybe surpass—those in the USA and Western Europe, Western managers will find that the process of manage-ment becomes much more of a two-way street. This is already happening at a technical level; expect it to occur at a manage-ment level too. So Western companies will become importers of ideas about the appropriate way to run an enterprise and how best to manage the people within it.

Meanwhile within the developed world, management will self-evidently have to adapt to a more diversified workforce, but also to customers who will reflect that diversity. The changing workforce will not just reflect known changes in dem-ography: more older workers, more part-timers, more self-employed, and so on. Companies can adapt to that. It will also have to cope with more diversified attitudes. There will be some careerists, of course. But the proportion of the workforce that is seeking a career will decline. At the other extreme, there will be rather more workers who will simply want to be paid for piecework. They too can be accommodated; indeed, as it becomes easier to measure output in service industries as well as in manufacturing, we can expect the shift towards piecework to spread.

The difficult part will be managing what might be called 'intellectual piecework'. Many of the most talented people will hardly to want to work for salaries, however large. They will want to work for their own ventures, perhaps teach at a university, though perhaps also have some long-term relationship with a large corporation. To what extent can companies safely buy in the skills they need to run their business? How do they craft relationships that satisfy both parties? Here, some different forms of corporate organization may be needed. There are at least three potential models that may be adapted to new needs. One is the university model—where academics are given a platform and a basis for study, while being expected to develop money-making ventures too. Another is the Hollywood model—where a group of self-employed professionals come together for a specific film, depart at the end of it, but then come together again for the next project. Still another is the investment trust—where the management simply makes investments in other corporations, in effect choosing managements rather than running anything itself. Expect the growth of private equity funds to grow rapidly because they have greater freedom to invest widely than conventional investment trusts.

The common theme in all of the above is the need to attract, nurture, and retain human capital. The communications revolution levels the global playing field. The globalization of finance means that capital will flow to the place where it achieves its highest return. Knowledge transfers across continents and between corporations faster than ever before, also flowing to the places where it generates the highest return. Clever people move around both to study and to work. Just as Western countries as a whole have to find ways of justifying the high wages of their people, so individual companies have to justify their continued existence by using available knowledge more cleverly than their rivals—and by nurturing and applying the embedded knowledge of their people.

In one sense this is not new. Competition has always levelled playing fields. But the task has become much tougher and will become tougher still. But that is surely an extraordinarily exciting challenge, for one simple reason. While knowledge has become ever more widespread, wisdom has not. Companies, countries, and individuals all have one feature in common— they all make mistakes. That is the core of the challenge to management: to be wise in the quest to manage clever, thoughtful, decent human beings.

11

The Twenty-First Century Manager Book: Working on (and on and on...)

Sir Howard Davies

When I first became a Chief Executive, in 1987, the most racy telecommunications technology available was the fax. The internet, and the e-mail were distant fantasies. And the principal health hazard from mobile phones, far from cancer-inducing microwaves, was the risk of muscular strain from carrying a hefty brick around London.

Yet, even then, fashionable forecasters predicted the end of organizational life as they knew it. Traditional corporate structures, whether in the public or private sector, would quickly become atomized as individuals chose homeworking, or teleworking, or just not working in preference to life as an indentured commuter. We would quickly move to a model in which organizations had a small quorum permanent staff, and bought in other services by the yard to fulfil their corporate mission. Hierarchies would be flattened; indeed the favoured model would soon become a kind of solar system, with moons and planets circling at varying distances from the core.

Perhaps I have missed something, but looking back after sixteen years in the corner office, I find that rather less has changed than was then widely predicted. True, the corner office itself is on the way out. For the last five years I have been at a common-or-garden desk—still in the corner, but open to the elements and to the importunate. But it seems to me that the traditional organizational model has proved surprisingly robust to technological change and that rumours of its death have, to coin a phrase, been greatly exaggerated. The number of people using London's underground and commuter rail system tells its own story. After a recession-induced decline in the early 1990s, commuting numbers have been relentlessly rising for over a decade, with the results in terms of slower traffic speed and increased congestion being visible to anyone. Reversion to a bourgeois idyll, with mums and dads working from home in semi-detached metroland seems as far away as ever.

Yet it would be idle to pretend that nothing has changed. And the task of a senior manager in the 2000s is significantly different from what it was in the 1980s. But how do those differences manifest themselves? If we have not seen a wholesale reconstruction of organizational models, what trends have we seen, and how might we expect them to develop further in the 2010s and 2020s?

I identify five significant trends which, taken together, are likely to have a significant impact on organization shape, and indeed on the demands placed on senior managers.

First, it is undoubtedly true that the British workplace is becoming more diverse. There are more women at all levels, and more members of the ethnic communities, though the speed and scale of their progress up the organizational hierarchies is somewhat mixed, to a large extent reflecting the different educational attainments in those communities. In London, too, a striking trend in recent years has been an influx of foreigners of all kinds, from the 'old commonwealth', of course, but also increasingly from Continental Europe. That is particularly noticeable in the financial City. I took a team of regulatory staff off to Germany recently for an important negotiation with our opposite numbers there. It wasn't until we sat around the table that I realized my team consisted of two Americans, a German woman, a Dane, and a Frenchwoman. I was the token Brit.

In my view this has been entirely positive. And in the places I have worked it has not been necessary to preach the advantages of cultural diversity. They are obvious to everyone. That trend will continue, I am quite sure. But we should not forget that, in terms of equality of outcome, the toughest nuts still remain to be cracked: the pockets of high unemployment in some inner-city ethnic communities, and the problems of low expectations and aspirations which are characteristic of those pockets. While a good number of employers have attempted outreach programmes to access those communities, they have been greeted so far with mixed success.

Second, it is also true that there are more flexible working patterns today than there were twenty years ago. There are more people working on contracts. There are more part-timers, more career breaks, more attention is paid to family friendly working. But this is not all going in one direction. For example, it became a fad to remove as many people as possible from 'the staff' and put them on rolling short-term contracts. Legal changes driven by European directives have made this meaningless in terms of cost saving or reduction of redundancy obligations. My own organization has switched policy, as a result. We are only interested in putting people on short-term contracts if the need for their skills is genuinely short term itself. So, in fact, the proportion of our staff who are full-time and permanent, is slightly rising—something that would not have been forecast a few years ago.

I also notice some potentially difficult signs of pushback from employees who are not benefiting from flexible working. They point out that while it is possible to organize part-time contracts and flexible work patterns, it is typically only possible to do that if there is a core management team which provides the continuity, and accepts overall responsibility for the output. Are reward structures recognizing the obligations on the smaller core of full-timers? Are some employees abusing the flexibilities available? They may be delivering the basic output required of their job, but we all know that in most organizations the difficult parts of working life are those demands which arise unpredictably. They are typically dealt with by those who are in the office full-time, and it is hard to share them out among the cohorts of part-timers. I suspect this problem may become more difficult to handle as time goes by.

It is closely linked to a *third* trend. Hierarchies have indeed been flattened in many organizations. That is, overall, a positive development, both in terms of individual job satisfaction and in terms of efficiency and effectiveness for the customer. But my own perception is that this flattening has had an uncomfortable side effect. The responsibilities on the most senior managers have increased, as intermediate tiers of management control have been removed. While it is conventional to ridicule the efforts of intermediate management layers, in many organizations they did do something, which was typically the mediation of disputes, and some element of quality control over awkward decisions. Those awkward decisions, and that quality control responsibility has drifted upwards. This has resulted in a more uneven distribution of responsibilities. It is perhaps one of the forces which have driven growing income inequality in many firms, and higher and higher awards for people at the top. Some of these excessive rewards have been driven by greed, I am quite sure. But they may also have had some of their roots in the perception among senior executives that their own lives have become nastier, more brutish, and shorter.

The *fourth* trend is towards a more market-based approach to career planning. My first employer, the Foreign Office, then operated a grid system. A new employee could be given an outline of the way his (and in the early 1970s the recruits were almost exclusively male) career would be likely to develop over the succeeding thirty-five years, sometimes even including projected postings a decade or more away. It was possible to play a joker, as an individual, and occasionally to refuse a posting which was particularly unappealing, but the notion of upward career planning was unknown.

Now, I imagine the FSA is not unusual in operating a very different set of processes. There is a graduate programme, which organizes careers for the first two or three years, but thereafter employees are 'on the market'. Jobs are advertised, and individuals apply for them, through a rigorous interviewing process. It would be honest to acknowledge that not everybody is comfortable with this market system, and there are some significant drawbacks. Most organizations do have jobs which are less desirable than others, but which need to be done. It is also the case that junior staff may not have the information they require on which to make good decisions about their future careers, and indeed some would positively prefer to be moved around, at least for a few years. (Some would even prefer that throughout their careers, though it is not fashionable to acknowledge it.) I suspect that the purely market-based approach to career development has reached its high point, and that many organizations may retreat from it, in the interests of satisfying individuals' aspirations, and of getting the job done. But moving back is not straightforward. Doing so can easily look reactionary and paternalistic.

My *fifth* and final trend is, I suspect, the most difficult to handle. Up till now, the decision on when an individual's career should end has been rendered entirely straightforward by mandatory retirement ages, buttressed by pension schemes which create powerful incentives to leave at one's highest salary level. Those incentives have frequently been further reinforced by early retirement bonuses, enabling management to ease out staff and create upward mobility. This is all about to change.

In the first place, there will be new legislation outlawing age discrimination, and perhaps making managing retirement a thing of the past. But probably just as important is the carnage inflicted on occupational pension schemes by a combination of falling stock markets and increased longevity. Most companies now have a deficit on their pension schemes. They have responded predictably, by closing defined benefit schemes and shifting to a defined contribution arrangement which has the effect of switching risk from the employer to the employee. That, combined with lower annuity rates, has caused individuals to realize that their pension provision is by no means as secure or as generous as they once thought. The option of retiring in the early fifties, which was widely available in the 1980s and 1990s, is now a luxury which few people can afford. So employers will need to deal with demands from staff to continue in work, rather than demands to be released. The underlying causes of this change—we are living longer and healthier—are positive. But it will put significant strain on current working practices, and will require a radical change of mindset in senior management. I suspect it is the most significant trend which managers face, far more important than any individual technological innovation.

I am quite sure that, in practice, the twenty-first-century manager will face other challenges we cannot now easily predict. That is part of the fun of corporate life. But these five trends will keep them busy for the foreseeable future.

12

Managing Performance through People—the Challenge for Tomorrow's Organization

Geoff Armstrong

To say that the role of management in today's world is to deliver business performance seems self-evident. And yet, as we progress through the next twenty years and beyond, it is clear that delivering sustainable performance is and will be the *only* game in town. It is also clear, however, that managing performance will become more complex and not the preserve of a few at the senior levels of the organization simply focused on achieving financial results.

There are signs already that this new reality is dawning. Organizations and investors increasingly see intangible assets such as research, brands, customer relationships, and capabilities such as organizational flexibility, as key sources of competitive advantage. But few organizations are currently managing these as assets and realizing the benefits on the performance of their businesses. Nowhere is this more apparent than in the management of people. That is nothing new, but the impact of this failure will be increasingly catastrophic as we move through the twenty-first century.

A new perspective on business performance is the foundation for meeting that challenge—one that puts the effective management of people at the heart of the business and measures success by:

- People's views about the way they are managed, their trust in management and their willingness to work with colleagues to raise the collective performance of the organization that employs them.
- People's contributions to shaping and delivering strategies which go beyond those that are just good enough today.
- The people assets available to the business, particularly the diversity of the knowledge, skill, and experience base of the workforce continually updated by learning.

We start by exploring why people management is a critical driver of performance in tomorrow's organization and then set out four legacies of management culture that, until examined, explored, and turned upside down, will continue to hinder performance in the new world. We end by looking ahead to some of the critical features that will underpin effective management capability in the twenty-first century.

People and organization in the twenty-first century—the performance challenge

With increasingly sophisticated consumers demanding high quality and efficient service rather than just low-priced standardized goods, the challenge to all organizations, in the public and private sectors, is to compete on the basis of quality, design, personalized service, and efficiency of delivery. It will be customer delight, not just satisfaction, that drives their choice of where to spend their money. This means creating, anticipating, and responding to customer demand and innovating in both product and service development to keep ahead of the game. Moreover, with intensifying competition—increasingly from economies such as China and India and from non-traditional competitors—fragmenting global markets, continual advances in technology, and changing customer tastes, organizations must be prepared to change constantly and fast. They must create the capability and capacity to continually reinvent business strategies and models. This is not about change at the margins but about the capacity for continuous and fundamental change that goes to the heart of the organization.

Performance in this environment can no longer be only about achieving financial results. Innovation, speed, flexibility, and intangible assets will become more vital to differentiating between success and failure. And understanding how a much more complex choice of drivers can create or destroy value will become the focus for management action.

Creating the capacity and capability for continuous change requires three fundamental shifts in current business organization and management practice:

- First, creating and sustaining an 'adaptive organization' capable of reinventing and delivering new strategies.

- Second, acquiring and developing people's competence. High-quality customized products and services are rich in inputs of knowledge. What people at work do really is the primary driver of value, not the capital, technology, or systems they are able to call upon.

- Third, mobilizing the people contribution alongside changes in technology and business processes will increasingly be key to creating unique relationships with customers. At work the relationships between people and their managers will cause discretionary contribution to be given or withheld.

It is the ability to align organization and management systems and employee behaviour in ways that support strategy that becomes the 'invisible asset' that is particular to a company and not easily imitated by competitors.

Employee Behaviours: The holy Grail

The touchstone of success in making these shifts will be the contributions of everyone who works for the business. And the value added by these contributions will depend fundamentally on people's behaviour, their knowledge and competence. Even today, organizations can no longer rely merely on people turning up for work on time and carrying out instructions correctly. In addition, they are seeking people who are willing and able to take responsibility for their own performance in achieving business objectives, for satisfying customers, and for keeping themselves up to date in their own competence and experience through continuous learning. But, as turbulence and competition intensify, businesses will increasingly need the whole workforce to take responsibility for meeting business imperatives by:

- managing relationships with a growing range of stakeholders
- initiating and managing change and innovation
- enabling their own and others' teams to improve their added value.

Central questions for managers then become 'how do we get people to perform beyond better, to go the extra mile?' 'And what will persuade people to use their discretion to improve their performance?' Ability, motivation, and space, both to use and hone their skills and to contribute to collective efforts, are critical ingredients for eliciting this discretionary behaviour (Purcell *et al.*, 2002). The key challenge for managers today is to create the organization (relationships, processes, and practices) that will develop and sustain this behaviour tomorrow. Evidence of change is already apparent. Organizations no longer rely solely on hierarchy as the prime source of control. They are establishing cross-functional teams, outsourcing non-core functions and focusing on processes rather than product lines (Pettigrew *et al.*, 2000). They are managing more interdependent units to exploit opportunities for value creation.

In consequence, new kinds of business relationships are emerging—networks of suppliers—built on enduring connections through joint venture agreements, formal alliances, interlocking shareholdings, or long-standing contracts. Boundaries between an organization and its external partners are becoming highly permeable; internal networks increasingly go across functions or divisions, for example with project teams.

Moving through the twenty-first century however, it is increasingly evident that it will not be enough simply to build and manage networks of relationships. With the scale and pace of reorganization (organizations are now undergoing major change once every three years; Whittington and Mayer, 2002), real performance gains will be from delivering, at speed, *repeated shifts* in the nature of these networks and relationships—a capability for 'adaptive organizing'.

Before we explore some of the cornerstones of management capability that will underpin adaptive organization, we look at some of the legacies of management culture that unless acted on will continue to dog the step-changes required.

Four legacies of management culture

Many of the management cultures that exist in our organizations are a considerable obstacle to managing the performance of the 'adaptive organization'. Through our research work involving large numbers of organizations in the private and public sectors, some of the obstacles we have found are:

Legacy no. 1: Management is only about Top Management

Many senior level executives and investors think this way. Evidence of this mindset at work is demonstrated by a recent survey by CIPD that found two-thirds of organizations had a defined strategy that involved board members in its development. But fewer than half of the organizations surveyed involved line managers and less than 10 per cent involved other employees. Other studies similarly show the persistence of top-down management cultures that do not involve people beyond the top team in decisions about the nature and implementation of organizational change (Whittington and Mayer, 2002). And yet we know that the role of line managers, and front-line leadership in particular, is pivotal to bringing to life organizational practices that foster the employee behaviour required to implement strategy (Purcell *et al.*, 2002).

Legacy no. 2: Management is about Ownership and Power

In many organizations, older ways of managing are colliding with new realities about what makes organizations tick. Traditional ways of managing centring on a constant series of battles for resources, turf, and ideology, and assigning ownership to particular groups are no longer appropriate and will undoubtedly carry less significance in the future. Buying and selling assets, hiring a few and firing many are decisions that can be made by individual leaders protecting their 'turf'. But to deliver durable and radical innovation and performance requires an interconnected management capability that can mobilize the knowledge and expertise of the wider organization. Moreover, it is based on shared values, common understanding and acceptance of accountability for the performance of the business as a whole.

Legacy no. 3: Management is about Controlling Tasks

Throughout a typical company, managers make daily decisions to anticipate and respond to customer requirements; to plan and design products and processes; to acquire materials; to build products; and to market and provide services. Historical approaches to management have seen these activities as a series of tasks and the role of managers as maximizing the efficient delivery of these separate tasks—through planning, controlling,

co-ordinating, and so on. The limitations of scientific management in knowledge-based and service-based economies is recognized, but the legacy of 'management by tasks' remains deeply
embedded in organizations.

Delivering the kind of performance required for the twenty-
first century will require managers to be responsible for creating
contexts which both challenge and support people to deliver
business outcomes and results. Shifting mindsets and behaviours
from *doing* tasks to delivering business outcomes implies a fundamental shift in how the business and managers are managed.
Nowhere will there need to be a more fundamental shift than in
the management of people.

Legacy no. 4: Management is only about Business Decisions

This is a management culture that sees the focus of management
action as being purely about analysis and factually rational
decisions. Conventional executive education programmes
often typify this kind of focus where the emphasis is on the
'hard skills' in areas of marketing and finance, for example,
and little attention is paid to people management skills, such as
how to make things happen or manage change. When discussions about organizational and people capabilities command the
same order of importance as the budget or latest acquisition
strategy on board agendas, we will know that organizations
are making progress towards a more rounded view of what
delivers performance. So what does the management challenge
look like beyond these legacies and what are some of the critical
features that will underpin adaptive organization and management?

Putting People Management at the Heart of 'Adaptive Organization'

We offer three cornerstones for creating and sustaining adaptive organization over the next twenty years:

Strategies for Agility

Leading in the unknown and in times of ambiguity requires a radical shift in the process for developing new business models and strategies and business planning. Management theory about the role of strategy has seen the pendulum swing from detailed long-term incremental planning developed by a small coterie of 'experts' around the boardroom table, which managers were expected to stick to rigidly, to urging them instead to 'thrive on chaos' and reject strategic planning systems entirely. Neither approach will work in creating sustainable performance in the new world. What is clear is that business strategies will continue to have a shorter and shorter shelf-life. Managers will have to demonstrate leadership in both leading the creation of new strategies and managing the implementation of rapid shifts in strategic priorities. The value of business planning will be in a more dynamic process for 'strategizing' (Whittington and Mayer, 1999), where it will be the robustness and flexibility of the strategy development process itself that will be key to enabling opportunities for reinvention and value-creation.

Delivering strategies for agility will require managers at all levels to:

- work with colleagues throughout the organization in order to understand and develop its direction and performance drivers, and use networks and relationships for acquiring and sharing knowledge about what is happening in the outside world

- identify and develop the core capabilities for creating value for customers and other stakeholders and develop a shared clarity about meaning and direction.

Internal Business, Organization, and Management Coherence

To deliver agile strategies, however, requires more than having the 'right' strategy. Without the internal organization, management, and people capabilities to deliver it, opportunities for delivering value to customers are compromised. Those who exploit the connections between strategy, organization, management systems, and employee behaviour will outwit competitors. But the quality of the connection between business strategy, organization, and management depends on the quality of the strategic management process in the organization.

At the heart of making that connection must be a process that makes explicit the preconditions for business success and a plan for change—a process that regularly reviews the business, organization, and management requirements. Many organizations have a form of review process in place but evidence demonstrates the quality is often patchy (*Developing Managers for Business Performance*, CIPD, 2002).

The overall aim of the review process is to explore first the connections between different business models that will enable the enterprise to succeed and the distinctive competencies that will support them. And second, the gap between performance goals and actual performance and the required characteristics and capabilities of the organization.

The important thing here is that the process is strong on dialogue (not paper or the mechanics of the process); that it is likely to be bottom-up—initiated at the business unit level but to a framework of questioning that may be corporately provided. Management competencies underpinning success in this will rely increasingly on the ability to read and evaluate the business environment. Success will depend on the ability to create compelling stories for change and engage with a range of stakeholders to harness opportunities for value-creation. This goes beyond what we know as 'communication' and taps into the motivations that make us go beyond the business plan and job description. It is through building such a 'connected' leadership extending throughout the organization that the people management sources of value will be maximized.

Execution Excellence

The third core management capability in an 'adaptive' organization is getting the implementation right and at the speed required to deliver business results.

So what turns strategy into action and impact?

- a people management 'architecture' that makes explicit the links between the business strategy, management practice, and employee behaviours required to deliver it.
- Core components in the architecture that can drive change in employee behaviours are building challenge and influence into how results are achieved, training, performance appraisal, teamworking, and involvement in decision making. (Purcell *et al.*, 2002)

However, simply putting in place a number of management practices is not enough. The important thing here is that practices are designed to support the employee behaviour that will create and drive successful change. Shifting management responsibility and accountability from administering processes to achieving changes in employee behaviour is fundamental to delivering execution excellence in the twenty-first century and it represents a marked difference from where we are currently.

- Front-line management and leadership

But an architecture for guiding people management practice is only part of the mix for success—other competitor organizations can copy particular practices. What makes the difference is how these practices 'come alive'. This is where line managers and team leaders play a pivotal role in making the relationship between employees and the organization work—in motivating and empowering employees to respond to the challenges required by the business. In creating and maintaining trusted relationships with employees, we will see managers moving from supervisors and controllers to coaches and facilitators.

It is not just about getting good managers but about establishing the context in which they can be good managers and providing them with the skills, tools, and so on to manage effectively (Purcell *et al.*, 2002). Here we come back to the importance of a rigorous business, organization, and management review process—essential to identifying the capabilities required of managers to deliver the business strategy and the range of organization and development interventions that will drive and support their action. However good the execution is, value will be created or destroyed by how well your strategy is responding to shifts in the market and how well you make the connections with all the internal capabilities that can drive value.

Where is this Leading us?

We have argued that the big question for management in the twenty-first century is not about more or less management but 'what kind of management', as we attempt to build organizations capable of enduring performance. Increasingly today we see two quite distinct streams of top management behaviour. The first might be characterized as the 'transactional' school, where the main emphasis is on trading and reducing costs to the bone. The second stream is characterized by a focus on the business process and on developing organizational capacity and capability for managing ever-higher value through continuous change. Delivering performance in the future will be for those who can skilfully combine a blend of both—a focus on the quality of organization and management with, for example, making and assimilating strategic acquisitions and building effective networks of suppliers.

Enduring and unique sources of competitive advantage will come through an adaptive organization—capable of continuously and consistently organizing relationships, processes, and management practices to create, anticipate, and respond to change; the knowledge and talent of people and mobilizing people's behaviour to support the delivery of fast-changing strategies. Managing across these dimensions in alignment is the challenge ahead and this new perspective on management is the foundation for meeting that challenge.

The big question is how to ensure we have the 'right' contexts and robust processes that will guide management action through the chaos. We have asserted that processes and competence for sustaining agile strategies, internal coherence across all potential drivers of value, and execution excellence are essential. To reap the benefits requires changes in the relationship between managers and employees and shared accountability and responsibility for performance. When people are your greatest asset, effective people management *really* is the only game in town.

References

Developing Managers For Business Performance (2002). CIPD Executive Briefing.

Pettigrew, A. and Fenton, E. (2000). *The Innovating Organisation*. London: Sage.

Purcell, J., Kinnie, N., Hutchinson, S., Rayton, B., Swart, J. (2002). *Understanding the People and Performance Link: Unlocking the Black Box*. CIPD Research Report.

Whittington, R. and Mayer (1999). 'Change and Complementarities in the New Competitive Landscape.' *Organisation Science*, 10 (5), 519–50.

Whittington, R. and Mayer, M. (2000). *The European Corporation: Strategy, Structure and Social Science*. Oxford: Oxford University Press.

———(2002). *Organising For Success in the Twenty-First Century*. CIPD Research Report.

13

Managing for Creativity

Sir Michael Bichard

It is always exciting to be able to predict major changes to the look of organizations. But, in truth, I doubt that the next two decades will bring transformational change. Yes, there will be more SMEs, more niche companies and more virtual organizations. And yes, in the remaining large, often public sector corporates there will be an increase in devolution. But organizations are by nature conservative and it is sobering to reflect how in the public sector, for example, the devolution/modernization rhetoric of the last decade has not been matched by the reality of central targets and central control.

For me, the more interesting question is not how managers will need to adjust their skills and style to adapt to organizational change—but what capabilities organizations will need to develop in order to succeed, and what consequences this will have for managers. And if there is one thing which will distinguish the great twenty-first century organizations from the rest, it will be their creativity.

In the private sector, growth and profitability will be fuelled by the innovation required for new products, new services, and new design. In the public sector, resolving complex social problems with perpetually limited resources will demand creativity even more than improved management—contrary to current accepted wisdom. So perhaps *the* key characteristic of the successful twenty-first-century leader will be the ability to build cultures where creativity is valued and can thrive. The very best leaders will find ways of actively enhancing their people's creativity.

Of course, there is a tendency to believe that creativity is a given—in the sense that it is either inherited or the equivalent of intellect as in 'I am clever therefore I must be creative'. But creativity is not a given. Some leaders enhance it by the way they behave, the way they structure their organization, the skills they help develop, and the rewards and incentives they put in place. And some leaders do not.

Take behaviour: the best creative leaders will first ensure that they stay fresh themselves. How many of us as we grow older narrow our field of friends, gradually excluding those who don't agree with our prejudices or who make us feel uncomfortable? How many of us listen to the same music, read the same authors, watch the same programmes? In truth, how many of us mellow, conform, and become the very antipathy of creative thinking, just at the time of life when we should be stretching our comfort zones.

We can also become increasingly skilled at inhibiting the creativity of others. A few years ago I worked with a company called 'What If' on how to increase levels of creativity in a government department. Memorably they described the ten best ways to kill an idea. Tell someone for example that 'it's been tried before and it didn't work' or 'I'm just too busy.' And contrast that with the leaders who respond by saying 'that's interesting tell me more!'

Many leaders ensure that good ideas never see the light of day simply because they do not allow them to be developed to the point where they can be properly assessed. That may be because we have encouraged leaders to think that effectiveness is evidenced by fast decisions. But the best leaders will sometimes make sure that quick judgements are *not* made.

The most effective creative leaders will challenge hierarchies and abhor status. All the evidence suggests that hierarchical, status conscious organizations are not creative but, even now, too many leaders take comfort in both. Some still seem to believe that an idea can only be a good idea if it comes from a senior grade in the organization. Others still take refuge in the hierarchies, which prevent the free flow of ideas necessary for creativity. They show by their behaviour that they find it difficult to cope with challenge—but creativity often flows directly from junior staff feeling able not only to challenge accepted wisdom but also the organization's senior personnel. Of course, to feel comfortable when being challenged, you've got to be confident in your role and too many people in leadership positions don't look confident. They struggle to survive and hierarchies help inadequate leaders to survive because they protect them. The problem is that in hierarchical organizations leaders are valued for past achievements because that's how they got where they are. In creative organizations people are valued for the contribution they are making today and will make tomorrow.

To be creative, organizations need *energy*—more energy than is necessary merely to survive. And the best leaders have the ability to create energy or, in the words of Gary Hamel, 'they can harness the passion of their employees to succeed'. How do they do it?

For a start, they instill belief. I've never yet met a successful leader who did not believe in what they were doing, in their product, or their service. And they find ways of communicating that belief and their passion. In the public sector the task is sometimes to legitimize the passion, to make it acceptable to believe because there is so much scepticism and intellectual detachment. It's cool, too often, not to commit, and sarcasm has become an art form. In reality little is achieved without passion, although it's a lot easier to be a spectator. But leaders who value more the people who critique ideas rather than those who produce them will always lead sterile organizations.

Leaders who create energy surround themselves with other people who create energy. They know that people either create energy or consume it and that you can't afford too many consumers if energy levels are to stay high. But tomorrow's leaders will also need to tackle the ways in which the organization loses energy. Stanton Marris, the consultants, recently described how energy is lost because of friction between parts—between head office and the field, marketing and finance, or education and social services. They explained how energy is lost because of activity that adds no value: the meetings no one wants, the reports no one needs, and the unclear roles which create friction and require energy to make them work. And they reflected on how much time is spent managing upwards, playing politics, and watching your back.

The twenty-first-century leader will need to get their people to focus energy on the things that will help the organization perform better—rather than on the things that will further their careers. And they set an example by clearing away some of the obstacles which frustrate people and prevent them from delivering a good service.

Creativity and innovation often result from making the unexpected connections. But every organization I have worked for has had a tendency to work in silos failing as a result to tackle effectively those complex social issues which do not conform to bureaucratic boundaries. The twenty-first-century leader will place a premium on making new connections, joining up policy *and* delivery. They will see that a key part of their role is to develop collaborations outside with partner organizations and with clients, who can so often provide the spark to ignite creative thinking. They will also understand the importance of diversity to creativity and will unequivocally champion equality of opportunity as a precondition of diversity.

New connections are made when new people bring with them different ways of doing things and creative leaders will ensure that their organization imports enough new talent to renew itself. Arie de Geus has said that organizations need to ask themselves regularly whether they are fast flowing streams—with new people constantly bringing new ideas—or stagnant puddles. If you engineer a stagnant puddle it won't create much that doesn't smell.

Risk will continue to be a big issue for creative leaders. It is fashionable at the moment to encourage people to take more risks but the twenty-first-century challenge will be to *manage* risk effectively. Successful creative leaders will not just understand risk management, they will practise it. They will help people to define whether the risk is financial, political, or reputational. They will help their people to minimize risk and have in place contingency plans to deal with unexpected problems. Creativity will always involve risk, because it is about trying new things. The successful leader will be prepared to confront that. He or she will deal with the risk that goes wrong in a way that encourages further innovation; will not look first for someone to blame; and, if the risk was reasonable and well managed, will provide support and share the responsibility.

The truth is that creativity and innovation are much more likely where the leader has built a culture of trust. People will not take risks or use their initiative when they are not confident that support will be available when they need it. Nor will they share new, maybe surprising ideas with colleagues they do not trust. So, perhaps more than anything else the new creative leader will have the ability to develop climates of trust where people feel safe to experiment.

So where does this all leave us? PwC did some work a while ago on the differences between creative and non-creative organizations. They concluded that the least creative organizations were prescriptive, centralist, risk averse, hierarchical, status conscious, and introspective with vertical communications. Such organizations tend to be grey places and creativity does not thrive in grey places. The creative leaders of the twenty-first century will understand that. They will develop cultures where fun is acceptable even though the intent is serious, where trust is endemic, where energy levels are high, and recognition pervasive. But, how much fun are *you* to work with?

14

Herding Cats or Luxuriating in Talent? Leadership and Management of Universities

David Rhind

Universities are complex organizations which pose quite demanding leadership challenges. In many respects they are prototypes of twenty-first-century enterprises. They create little by way of physical goods, have traditionally (at least in the UK) been substantially self-governing and are populated by clever, creative, and independent individuals, some of whom are antipathetic to traditional line management approaches. Many of their successes arise from the endeavours of individuals or groups deep within the organization, often initially unknown to senior management.

This chapter describes some of the influences on Higher Education Institutions and some of the drivers for enhancement of leadership and management in universities. These drivers include demands for greater direct accountability to (multiple) funders, global competition (most recently from for-profit organizations), plus the need to attract top talent and to burnish brand image.

There are many requirements of successful leaders in academia similar to those in other sectors. But the web of complexities, the multiplicities of targets to meet sometimes conflicting requirements, the factors which motivate individual academics, and the ambiguities involved in management in the sector are distinctive. Brutal, full-frontal commercial approaches to leadership do not work except where severe financial stringency makes threats to jobs immediate. More subtle approaches—in which the two most important elements are the ability to recruit and retain superb staff and the willingness and ability to persuade and communicate the need for changes—are required. Successful leadership also requires recognition of achievement by staff as crucial to their esteem. And it involves skills in enhancing brand image, fund-raising, and in making periodic changes of approach to refresh universities.

The University World

The university world as presently understood dates back over 900 years and has apparently been very stable (until recently):

Taking as a starting point, 1520, when the Lutheran Church was founded, some 66 institutions that existed then still exist today in the Western world in recognizable forms: the Catholic Church, the

Lutheran Church, the parliaments of Iceland and the Isle of Man, and 62 universities...They have experienced wars, revolutions, depressions, and industrial transformations, and have come out less changed than almost any other segment of their societies.

(Carnegie Commission on Higher Education, 1968)

Moreover, universities have been central to national success:

Colleges and universities are wonderful places. They sustain a culture—one of inquiry and skepticism—that is essential not only to the intellectual life but also to the democratic and economic ideals of the United States. Who can question that our success as a nation is closely tied to the fact that we have created in this country the most successful system of higher education in the world?

(Frye, 2002: 9–14)

Yet, despite this picture of stability and a ready acceptance of the value of universities, higher education is almost everywhere in turmoil, with change being desired or urged by many stakeholders. Such views are not generally shared by many practising academics. This chapter begins by setting the contemporary scene in Higher Education (HE), then addresses the leadership qualities required to succeed in it.

Higher Education as a Boom Industry—and more

Even at present, HE is a hugely significant enterprise, especially in economic development. For instance, the structure of employment in Britain has changed greatly since the 1970s towards 'knowledge working'. The massive restructuring of employment to such industries, notably in the service sector and away from manufacturing, is manifested in major cities such as Newcastle, which have changed from substantial reliance on heavy industries to becoming 'Knowledge Centres', boasting multiple universities with strong local as well as international linkages. In the USA, the 100 or so universities in the Boston area are key players in local, regional, and national success—as are those in many other parts of that country and most others.

The beneficial impact of universities is on both the individual and society as a whole. For these reasons, HE has become a growth business worldwide. Figure 14.1 illustrates the situation so far as migration of students to the educational market leaders is concerned. Each overseas undergraduate student typically pays fees much higher than the government-controlled fees for home students.

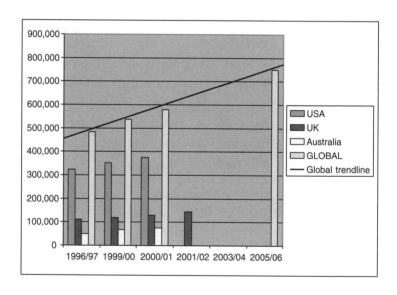

Figure 14.1 *Increase and Projected Increases in the Number of Overseas Students, Broken down by the Major Educational Suppliers.*
Source: Higher Education Statistics Agency (HESA), Fulbright Commission and IDP Education Australia.

In Britain, some 6 per cent of the populace went to universities in the mid 1960s; the equivalent figure is now over 40 per cent and is higher still in many other OECD countries. There is still potential for growth in these countries through more flexible learning forms than the traditional honours course and at post-graduate level. In many other countries, such as China and other countries in South East Asia, the growth of HE has scarcely begun by Western standards. Daniel (1996) claimed that, on average, one university a week was being created worldwide.

In some respects, then, the HE sector is a precursor of others in the twenty-first century. Universities were engaged in know-ledge creation, testing, and management long before govern-ments and commerce discovered the term. The best of them have provided an environment in which highly self-motivated, intelligent (and often lowly paid) individuals have made new discoveries that have changed the world, both in peace and war, for ever.

But HE in general and universities in particular are not simply a major service industry. They exist—with different emphases in different countries and in different places therein—with a multi-plicity of purposes. These can be summarized as:

- Enhancing the skills sets and competences of those in the populace who will later become leaders of businesses, gov-ernments, not-for-profit and educational organizations.
- Creating wealth or providing the underpinning of future wealth for the country or their supporting organization through new inventions or discoveries.
- Creating new knowledge for the sake of it.
- Enhancing public understanding and challenging ortho-doxy wherever that can be shown to be flawed—both vital ingredients for a democratic society.

- Fostering social cohesion by bringing together people from different backgrounds.

It will be obvious that several of these interact or even overlap. Moreover, the nature of universities varies worldwide. In mainland Europe, most are manifestations of the state, with staff on public service contracts. In the USA, there is a variety of different models including major and minor private universities, the land-grant universities and community colleges. For many of them—but especially the private ones—the philanthropy of alumni is crucial to their success. In Britain, universities are autonomous bodies with an independent governing body. Few have any significant endowment funds. All bar one of them is in receipt of public funds and—irrespective of how small these funds are—each university is subject to a high level of oversight and inspection (see below).

Finally, universities have one unusual characteristic. So far as teaching is concerned, their obvious stock of products consists of courses which are periodically up-dated or replaced. But their students are all-important, migrating from being 'customers' to 'products' (conveying new knowledge and skills into employment) to 'ambassadors' for their university. In regard to both students and staff, universities constitute the ultimate 'people business'.

The Impact of New Technologies

Technological change has played a considerable role in universities, as in all other enterprises. One aspect of this, the density of storage of information and our ability to access it from anywhere, is graphically illustrated in Fig. 14.2; the implications for university libraries alone are obvious. Beyond its capacity for storage

Figure 14.2a *The Entirety of the 'Geographical Framework' of Britain in the 1960s.*
Information was stored as 40 million copies of (240,000 different) maps in Ordnance Survey's West Building (tall building in centre foreground). Photograph kindly supplied by Ordnance Survey.

and sifting of information, Information and Communications Technology (ICT) has revolutionized our ability to deliver education at a distance. Daniel (1996) argued that it has the capacity to change university teaching fundamentally, both enriching it and providing the economies of scale necessary for the move from elite to mass higher education. He identified eleven mega-univer-

Figure 14.2b *The equivalent information can now be held in Compact Disk format in one hand and copied in a few minutes.*
Photograph courtesy of Landmark Information Group.
Copyright © **Prodat Systems Plc 2002.** © **Crown copyright 2002. All rights reserved. Licence number 1000240449.**

sities, each of which enrols over 100,000 students and all of which use distance learning methods, increasingly based on ICT. The largest of these have over half a million students.

What has become clear however is that education lacking face-to-face contact is rarely successful, so hybrid models are evolving. ICT has certainly facilitated the safe (replicated) storage of coursework and worked exercises, enabled sharing of the material so as to reduce duplication of course creation and has fostered common and explicit standards of coursework. But it has also triggered much debate on the Intellectual Property Rights in such coursework and the ability of staff to take copies with them when they change jobs—in a way which rarely occurred before widespread use of material in computer form. And its use has in some cases raised student expectations to the level that staff are actually more burdened than hitherto with answering e-mailed questions, etc.

The contemporary university leader is thus faced with a revolution in how the university could work. But he or she is also faced with a new set of challenges alongside old ones partially resolved, alongside a clamour for new 'investment'.

Money and Values

Bok (2003: 9) explained the incessant need for more resources in universities thus:

Universities share one characteristic with compulsive gamblers and exiled royalty: there is never enough money to satisfy their desires. Faculty and students are forever developing new interests and ambitions, most of which cost money. The prices of books and journals rise relentlessly. Better and more costly technology and scientific apparatus constantly appear and must be acquired to stay at the cutting edge.

Universities are certainly not unique in such a characteristic. Moreover, there are other, good rationales for increasing revenues—one of which is to generate the wherewithal to fund competitive staff salaries (see below). Bok has argued that the consequence of a drive to increase revenues has been an over-commercialization of university activities in the USA and elsewhere which is undermining core academic values. He cites examples of increased secrecy in corporate-funded research, the proliferation of for-profit internet companies initiated by university staff and supported by venture capitalists, industry-sponsored educational programmes for doctors and conflicts of interest in research on human subjects as examples which he sees as questionable given the traditional values of a university. Bok stressed the importance of public trust in the university and its staff as sources of disinterested research, teaching, and advice.

Complexity and Ambiguity are the Norm in HE

The admixture of different governance arrangements, different missions, differential impacts of government involvement, current brand image, financial status, and legacy effects in HE ensure that leadership and management of universities is not simply a matter for prescription. Since the size range of British HEIs exceeds 200 (Fig. 14.3), leaders face rather different challenges. Allied to this is the rapid change now underway in many countries in their HE. The change is driven by state and public concerns over cost, a search for new sources of revenue, by a desire to widen access to universities beyond the traditional beneficiaries, by global competition, and by the hunt for more and manifest outputs and demonstrable benefits from engagement with the university. Manifestations of responses to these drivers have included mergers of institutions and the appearance of radically new approaches to running Higher Education organizations, such as for-profit enterprises like the University of Phoenix.

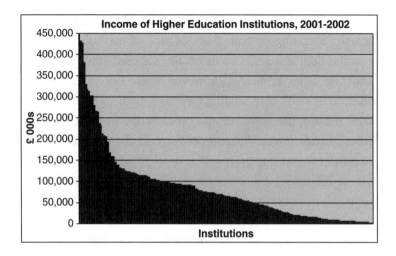

Figure 14.3 *Graph of 170 British HEIs Ranked by Size of Total Income.*
Source: **HESA**

The reality then is that university leaders exist—even more perhaps than those in many businesses and governments—in a world of ambiguity, uncertainty, multiple conflicting objectives, and change. Many have to straddle the public and private sector divides in all of their activities. In short, leadership and management of universities is not trivial, whatever it may have been in the 1970s when such institutions were populated by small elites and consumed modest proportions of GDP, mostly provided by government.

The UK Higher Education Context

Given the diversity described above, this chapter will concentrate particularly on the British university sector—not least because it has been demonstrably successful on teaching, research, attracting students from outside of the UK, and other criteria, despite a series of externally imposed challenges. The situation is far from ideal however: while British universities seem to be more than holding their own against those on mainland Europe, the resources and organization of top US universities provide formidable competition and the UK share of the 'top prizes'—an imperfect indicator of merit—shows how the UK is falling behind, even standardizing by national populations. Thus, between 1980 and 2002, US universities won thirty-four Nobel prizes in physics to the UK's none; in chemistry, the ratio was thirty-one to four; in medicine, it was thirty-five to six; in economics it was twenty-eight to three. In recent years, many UK winners have actually worked in the USA.

This section outlines the main characteristics of the UK HE system. For our present purposes, these are:

- Diversity, with some 170 HEIs in receipt of some measure of central government funding, ranging in size from those with a total turnover of £447m to under £2m, many with different foci or combination of them (e.g. international research-intensive universities, to those focused on education for a local populace, to specialist bodies such as conservatoires); see Fig. 14.3. This diversity has increased since the early 1990s.
- A status which in practice spans the public and private sectors. Though largely autonomous organizations by charter and eligible to go bankrupt, British universities are treated by government as being part of the public sector whenever this is convenient and that is how many citizens perceive them.

- Diversified sources of funding which are in totality inadequate for the range of activities chosen by or wished upon universities. Many have diverted available funds to support the core activities of teaching and research. Areas of under-investment include infrastructure such as buildings, management information systems, and human resource development.

- Few reserves or endowments exist as compared to major US universities. 'Either Oxford or Cambridge (with endowments of £2 billion each) would come 15th in the US list, while no other UK university would come in the top 150' (Sutton Trust, 2003). Moreover, about half of the English universities are trading at a deficit: the median trading surplus is about 1.5 per cent (Ramsden, 2003) while the overall sector surplus on income in 2001 was 0.44 per cent.

- A catastrophic overall decline in salaries of many staff relative to other groups—see Fig. 14.4—such that differentiation is occurring rapidly between subject areas and different regions but lower-paid staff (including young academics) are very poorly paid. Problems of recruitment and retention are rife in some subject and geographical areas and will get worse as present staff with equity in housing retire. In some subjects, staff are drawn in from Eastern Europe or the developing world (draining those areas of some of their most talented people). High financial and prestige rewards to the institution for doing well in national assessments of research have led to much more overt competition for staff with high reputations.

- An internal organization such as that the strategic direction, content, delivery, and quality assurance of much of the core business of teaching and research are at least

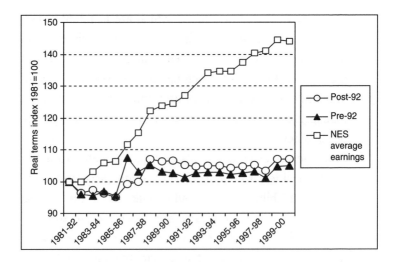

Figure 14.4 *Average Academic and Academic-Related Pay and Average Earnings 1981–2001 (in real terms): subdivided by pre- and post-1992 universities and compared to average earnings derived from the National Earnings Survey (NES).*
Source: **AUT.**

heavily influenced by a hugely diverse set of individuals and where traditional line management is relatively weak. In the best situations, this has a huge advantage because it fosters commitment, innovation, competition, and the exercise of professionalism. In worse circumstances, it can result in an inchoate and unpredictable organization with no focus, no obvious legitimation other than what suits individual staff members, lacking obvious synergies and proneness to financial failure.

- Volatile student demand. There is now much greater consumer interest in employability arising from different courses (and institutions); perceptions of reality do not always match reality, however, and other factors come into play (e.g. prior competence in mathematics). As one example, home student applications to media studies have boomed and those in engineering have declined sharply in the UK.

- The internationalization of universities manifested most clearly through recruitment of students from outside the UK studying there. Figure 14.1 shows how numbers have grown sharply; the extreme example (ignoring very small institutions and those with headquarters outside the UK) is the London School of Economics (LSE) which has over 60 per cent of its students and a higher proportion of its revenues from outside of Britain.

- Many universities—especially those created prior to the 1992 Higher Education Act—have only recently begun to embrace marketing on a major scale. This is in contrast to advertising by the University of Chicago and the formation of a Bureau of Publicity by the University of Pennsylvania in the early 1900s, according to Bok, 2003; some US universities however have only led UK ones by a decade or so (see Pulley, 2003).

- Hugely intrusive requirements by government in the name of accountability in relation to teaching quality and research (where both periodic national reviews of both in every department take place, leading to league tables of performance in the press). In addition, the government's funding bodies annually require compliance with a large number of 'top down' initiatives. The government's White Paper of January 2003 reinforced this 'top down' approach while avowedly encouraging diversity and autonomy of universities.

- As in almost every other organization, internal communications are typically held by the staff to be deficient and responsible for many problems. This is despite vast efforts often being made through provision of paper documents in committees or newsletters, extensive use of web-based news and e-mail services and 'state of the union' talks by the CEO. Typically, staff views of others are often jaundiced or incomplete: in one study in The City University, staff believed they provided good service for their colleagues and students on 95 per cent of occasions but only received it half of the time!.

Leadership and Management

It is widely accepted that different styles of leadership can succeed and what succeeds in one place may not succeed in apparently similar situations elsewhere or at a later date. The Jack Welch style of leadership, as exemplified in General Electric, is constrained in British universities by employment legislation and university charters. The clearest manifestation of industrial-style leadership was the attempt to merge two of the largest UK HEIs—Imperial College (IC) and University College London (UCL)—by their two leaders in 2002. Both individuals were from an industrial background, one having led the merger of the pharmaceutical giants Glaxo Welcome and SmithKline-Beecham. The merger of IC and UCL failed because the academic staff were unconvinced of the likely benefits of the union. Two other major and contemporaneous mergers of HE institutions led by academics came to fruition.

So how can we know what will be effective in any given situation? Much of what is published on leadership and management in the world outside academia is either blindingly obvious, suffused with superficial platitudes, or so generic as to be of little practical help. Thus Heifertz and Laurie (1997) opining in the *Harvard Business Review* on the work of leadership in a time of change argued:

Adaptive work is required when our deeply held beliefs are challenged, when the values that made us successful become less relevant, and when legitimate yet competing perspectives emerge...adaptive change is distressing for the people going through it. They need to take on new roles, new relationships, new values, new behaviours and new approaches to work...leaders must disorient them [staff] so that new relationships can develop.

They offered six principles for leading adaptive work: ' "getting on the balcony" [taking a "helicopter view"], identifying the adaptive challenge, regulating distress, maintaining disciplined attention, giving the work back to the people, and protecting voices of leadership from below'. They illustrate these breathtaking insights with a single case study. In many other fields of academia such material would be regarded as unsubstantiated *ex cathedra* statements with a wholly inadequate evidence base. Yet academia is in no position to feel superior. Astonishingly, the volume and quality of research specifically in universities on how successful universities work has been small: the bulk of the publications seems to arise from former (often US) university presidents who may not be disinterested investigators and reporters.

The need for greater understanding of what constitutes good leadership and management and the dissemination of good practice has long been recognized in the UK. The Higher Education Staff Development Agency has sought to enhance staff competences for over fifteen years, notably through its Top Management Programme; its services are voluntarily subscribed to by virtually all HEIs, covering 97 per cent of the sector workforce. In early 2003, however, the Secretary of State for Education and Skills argued that the sector needed much enhanced leadership skills. His White Paper proposed the creation and funding of a Leadership and Management Foundation to be launched in 2004. The realization of the government plans should expand the budgets allocated to such development by a factor of three or more.

In summary, then, leadership and management in universities has little to draw upon given the complexities of the issues that have to be faced and the particularities involved. What follows in this chapter is merely based upon personal reflections and experience as a CEO of two £100 million turnover enterprises, one of which is an HEI. Readers will judge whether it should be accorded any more respect than the Heifertz and Laurie (1997) study.

Some Principles of Good Leadership in HE

Ensuring good performance of an institution on a small number of criteria—attracting enough good calibre students and teaching them well, the carrying out of research of international quality and applicability, and remaining solvent—is a necessary but not sufficient condition for overall success as a university leader. There are a large number of Critical Success Factors whose achievement underpins sustainable HE leadership success. Some of these are common to all organizations. They include:

- Good strategic vision and awareness of the operating environment, knowledge of what the competition is doing (in products, processes, and systems), the ability to anticipate problems and the skills to see opportunities in chaos or change. These abilities need not of course be the preserve of one individual leader but must be strongly present in the 'top team'.

- Self-awareness, the ability to identify and act upon the niche strengths and the weaknesses of the organization, and the antennae to assess its capacity and appetite for change and risk.

- Skills adequate to ensure that the organization identifies its core values and that these are manifested throughout the organization (e.g. in denying access to those students qualified mainly through sports skills or parental wealth). Sound processes (e.g. for risk identification and management) must be embedded across the HEI.

- Marketing and sales skills, exercised so as to enhance the brand image of the organization, attract more high calibre students and attract development funding from alumni and others—thereby creating a virtuous spiral (see below).

- The ability and willingness to forge partnerships, even with competitors, where mutual benefit exists—irrespective of where the partners are domiciled.

- Ensuring that the physical infrastructure is at least adequate for the required purposes (students paying high fees for certain postgraduate courses have higher expectations than those on standard undergraduate courses) and that the trade-offs adopted between investing in human and physical capital are sound.

- An awareness of the influence of different governments (e.g. through new legislation or financial inducements) and its agencies on operations—but a healthy disregard for some at least of these bodies where their (sometimes transitory) views will undermine the success of the enterprise.

- Setting clear domains of activity, creating personal responsibility for success in meeting targets within them, minimizing central interference and creating the will to cut costs wherever possible—while ensuring quality meets the customer needs.
- An ability to recover quickly and learn from disasters.
- Recognizing that much effective change occurs 'bottom-up' and seeking ideas from small, often 'free-wheeling', groups—especially those not already socialized into respect for the senior management.
- Visibility of the CEO and the top team to staff, plus an ability to enthuse and motivate them and earn their respect.
- Recognition that some at least of the work must be highly enjoyable to those involved if dedication is to be maintained; success must be publicly celebrated.

Leading the Staff

It is obvious that no one of these factors is sufficient to bring success. But the one that comes nearest to it revolves around the recruitment, retention, and enthusing of the right staff. Universities are the extreme case of networking organizations at almost all levels. A study carried out in The City University identified many hundreds of real partnerships arising from individual, departmental, school, or corporate initiative—but even in the three last cases the role of particular individuals was crucial. Power and authority in universities are generally more diffuse than in some other organizations. This can be inconvenient to managers but permits extraordinary 'bottom up' innovation and rapid adjustments and anticipations of problems if the culture is appropriate.

It follows that, more even than elsewhere, the selection, retention, nurturing, and rewarding of staff is crucial. 'Rewards packages' need to be based upon what the staff members value, not just more money (even when that is affordable). With the exception of some staff in business schools and in areas such as economics, monetary reward is rarely more than the fourth most significant driver for staff. Encouragement and saying 'thank you' is a crucial part of management's role as well as dealing effectively with poor performance. Since success often originates deep within an HEI, it requires engagement with all levels of the organization and high visibility of the CEO and the top team to be truly effective.

There is one generic problem that is sometimes difficult to resolve. This arises from the widespread internal belief that universities are (or used to be and need to be again) collegiate organizations. By this is usually meant self-governing (by the academic staff) and where decisions taken by one group of staff are respected and supported by others. All of this was historically operated within a UK context where national pay scales and terms and conditions were in operation and where universities were broadly similar in their aspirant culture, values, curriculum, and outlook—even if not all succeeded to the same extent. The demise of the 'we think of ourselves as mini-Oxbridges' largely began in the 1960s but accelerated in the 1990s after the doubling of the number of universities by the Conservative government through the awarding of university status to the former polytechnics. Today the real collegiality in most universities is often less than that in a business where at least the goals are relatively simple and clear to all staff. In a university, the prime driver for an individual academic is often how his or her research is rated by worldwide peers and the success of their group or department.

Yet the department or individual is rarely able to prosper on its own. Minor perturbations (such as illness of a key staff member, often on the support staff) can negate success. Inter-actions between groups or individuals can lead to huge tensions and spectacular bust-ups. All this is becoming more likely in a world where differentiation of rewards according to the capacity to attract income and with the disintegration of the old 'nation-alized industry model' of staff employment are proceeding apace. The clear implication for the leaders and senior managers is that they must become adept in what the private sector has always done—accept diversity in how staff are treated (within frameworks set by legislation and good practice guidance). However if the university is to be anything other than a firm it has to have one other crucial element. This is the ability of academic, academic-related and at least some other staff to have significant free time for thinking, exploring new ideas and challenging the *status quo*. The treadmill of teaching and administration in most British universities is now undermining their creative capacity. Under all plausible financial scenarios, the need to free up time for thinking cannot be a right of everyone. Only some staff will be able to make demonstrably good use of this, the most precious of resources. An under-valued role of senior management is to ensure that everyone relevant on the staff who can create real benefits from such thinking time gets it, even if that makes still more difficult the work of others.

Leadership and Structural Change

Many universities have engaged in structural change in recent years but many others are recognizably similar to what they were during the 1970s. In one sense their success is testimony to the flexibility and adaptability of the management and staff concerned. But, while structures are rarely catastrophic, they can inhibit new developments. Purposeful change of them can be a valuable management tool for modernization and a trigger for fundamental re-thinking on a broad front.

The classical Oxbridge model of central university and its discipline-based departments with an orthogonal set of colleges did not become commonplace in the rest of British universities. Many universities in the 1970s became somewhat centralized providers of services and the setters of detailed rules within which departments operated. Intermediate structures such as faculties rarely had executive responsibility. The university finances were typically a 'black box'; attempts to obtain income and expenditure accounts by departments which saw themselves as successful (and cross-subsidizing others) were normally resisted by the central bureaucracy.

In the last decade or so there has grown up a spectrum of devolution. Some universities still operate a largely command economy. But the 'formularization' of external funding and a recognition of the importance of signals that can be sent by transparency have led some universities to become essentially holding companies in which functioning academic (or business) units have profit and loss responsibility. Once finance has been devolved it is commonplace for some aspects of other functions such as Human Resources and staff promotions to follow. This has posed new challenges for leaders and senior managers. It has made cross-subsidy between the units evident, encouraged complaints about the level of central overheads from highly articulate staff, necessitated larger units if functions are to be devolved, and required different sorts of academic leaders to be groomed (and additional training). On the plus side it has (where done well) incentivized units to generate additional resource and take responsibility for key functions such as health and safety, rather than relying on 'the university's expert'.

But none of this is inherently stable. Re-centralization of such functions may be necessary in whole or in part: financial exigency for the whole organization may well require renewed close central control over all expenditure and income. The changes in ICT which led away from centralized IT functions to highly devolved ones are now being reversed, at least so far as inter-operative financial, student record, assessment, and many other functions are concerned. The need for consistent, institution-wide management information is growing: for instance, it is increasingly incumbent on university leaders and managers to know levels of student and other stakeholder satisfaction across all parts of the enterprise. Inability to address inadequate performance (e.g. as measured in student satisfaction) in one part of the university may well lead to reputational damage or even litigation for the whole institution.

All this leads to the one inescapable conclusion about leadership in universities. As a result of the plethora of change drivers, good universities are in constant change (though change is not of course an invariant indicator on its own of a good university). Much of this change imposes some cost on all staff. Academic and research staff in particular often do not always see the benefits from such change though they often do experience the costs. Such staff cannot generally be instructed simply to break the very rationale of their existence and the basis of all their academic training—to analyze and criticize (hopefully constructively) the way the world works or plans for its improvement. Their up-bringing, reinforced by the direct effects of change on themselves, can make them extremely vocal critics and some university structures provide vehicles for unconvinced staff blocking proposed changes.

Effecting significant structural change in any organization is often painful but relatively straightforward where severe financial exigency exists. To effect change—especially which requires change of culture—in a university where this driver is absent requires determination, 'big picture vision', a commitment to the long term, and the willingness and ability to persuade the staff. Next to the ability to recruit and retain superb staff, communications skills are perhaps the most important characteristics of any university leader. Staff in universities are infinitely supportive when persuaded of the logic of change. They are frequently congenitally obstructive when told that something simply must happen.

Brand Image and Enhancement

The quality of a university's brand is now every bit as important to its success as those of commercial enterprises. Excellent brands—such as those of Cambridge, Harvard, LSE, MIT, Oxford, and Stanford—attract top quality students from across the world. They facilitate gifts from alumni and foundations. They give credence to the opinions and work of staff and ensure that, other things being equal, their research is influential in shaping government and other policies. In short, good brands help create a virtuous spiral.

Yet there are many examples of excellence in British universities at least which are not manifested in the brand of the institution. For example, many of the post-1992 universities have been independently assessed as providing teaching of very high quality. Well over half of British universities have been independently peer-assessed as having at least one department operating at truly world-class levels in their research. Yet the way in which newspaper league tables of British universities have been assembled has ensured that such factors have not materialized in brand image.

Daniel (1996: 8) has claimed that the reputation that the public accords to a particular university combines various factors:

First, in most countries, there is a strong correlation between the reputation of an institution and its age. Second, people tend to equate quality with exclusivity of access. Third, universities with lavish resources are assumed to be better. Fourth, educational systems with small classes and plenty of human interaction are well regarded.

There is not much a university leader of a recently established university can do about the first. To establish a good brand image took at least twenty-five (and more normally fifty) years in the late twentieth century in Britain. Given this, what is the way forward for aspiring HEIs presently lacking an appropriately exalted brand image? Being good is not enough if you are a relatively recent arrival in the business. The solution seems to be to focus activity on certain distinctive niche strengths, ensure high quality of both teaching and research—and to proselytize relentlessly about these through every possible channel. Many senior figures in business, government, and the media are astonishingly ignorant of what has happened in universities in recent years, being strongly influenced by their own student experience in those universities then existing. The engagement of senior university leaders in such promotional and awareness-raising activities is therefore not optional. Many key influencers take their cue from the confidence and 'salesmanship' of the leader as much as from impressive (and accurate) statistics.

Conclusions

Leading universities successfully is manifestly not impossible but it is non-trivial. Fortunately, leaders and managers in the sector do not have to be as awesomely accomplished as Caesar to be successful:

> Julius Caesar was able to write, dictate and read at the same time, simultaneously dictating to his secretaries four letters on the most important subjects or, if he had nothing else to do, as many as seven.
>
> (Suetonius)

As indicated throughout this chapter, many competences of successful leaders in this sector are common to those elsewhere, such as making trade-offs between property development and investing in staff when resources are inadequate for both. But the ability to make 'good hires' and the ability and willingness to debate and discuss with staff—especially academic staff—in a language they recognize are perhaps the two most crucial success factors. The latter is particularly crucial in fostering inter- or multi-disciplinary work and assessing the merits of investing in the same. Based on all that has been said earlier, the qualities of a successful leader in the university sector can be summarized as in Table 14.1.

Lest the reader see all that has been written about the challenges of leadership in universities as being somehow negative, this is not so. It is certainly challenging—but it is also deeply creative and exciting. To be head of a higher education institution is a privilege since you are helping to shape the futures of many people. Leadership has its rewards.

Table 14.1 The Qualities and Characteristics of a Successful Leader in the HE Sector (the priority of each will change with circumstance)

Making good 'hires'	Excellent communication skills
Appreciation and knowledge of the university world and its values (but without slavish adherence to them)	Strategic vision, combined with an analytical ability to 'drill down' into selected areas of detail as required
Understanding the workings of the university, including finance, human resources, and university processes	Sound judgement, e.g. in recognizing potential and in assessing risk
Having good contacts outside the university among gatekeepers and key influencers in the business, government, media, and other stakeholder communities	Good team-building skills
Ambition, determination, energy, and stamina to overcome the constant—and often unexpected—challenges and the capacity to initiate and complete change successfully	Global awareness of what is going on in the relevant national and global, as well as local, communities and some ability to influence the agendas. Increasingly this is being obtained by working for a period outside the sector, perhaps overseas
A personality which is capable of interacting with many different stakeholders and, at the same time, able to inspire staff and others	ICT literacy and use; it is impossible to understand the potential without such familiarity
A willingness to engage and skills in fund-raising	Being lucky and having a sense of humour

Note

Thanks are due to Ian Creagh, Jason Dykes, Chris Morris, and Brian Ramsden for supplying some of the information used in this chapter.

References

Bok, D. (2003). *Universities in the Marketplace: The Commercialization of Higher Education*. Princeton, Princeton University Press.

Carnegie Commission on Higher Education (1968). *Quality and Equality: New Levels of Federal Responsibility for Higher Education*. New York, McGraw-Hill.

Daniel, J. S. (1996). *Mega-Universities and Knowledge Media: Technology Strategies for Higher Education*. London, Kogan Page.

Frye, B. E. (2002). 'Reflections.' *EDUCAUSE Review*, January 2002, 9–14.

Heifetz, R. A. and Laurie, D. (1997). 'The Work of Leadership.' *Harvard Business Review*, 75(1): 124–34. January–February.

Pulley, J. L. (2003). 'Romancing the brand.' *The Chronicle of Higher Education*, 24 October 2003.

Ramsden, B. (2003). *Patterns in Higher Education Institutions in the UK: Third Report*. London, Universities UK and SCOP.

Sutton Trust (2003). 'University Endowments—A US/UK Comparison.' Discussion Paper, March 2003.

15

Management Education and Leadership

Sue Cox
and
Steve Fox

Interest in leadership development has grown substantially over the past decade. Organizations increasingly see leadership capability as a source of competitive advantage. However, the UK evidence on the state of the current management and leadership capability (and its relation to performance) reported by the Council for Excellence in Management and Leadership (CEML) suggests that there is much dissatisfaction from managers, at all levels, with the quality of leadership within their organization. There is also agreement that professional associations should incorporate leadership development as a vital part of their pre-qualification and CPD programmes (Fox *et al.*, 2001). In the light of these findings, it is not surprising that leadership development and leadership studies have become big business for management educators in the UK. In this section of the book, we reflect on the changing nature of management education within business schools and highlight the importance of effective partnerships in leadership development. We will cover the main criticisms of management education and the two major reform movements which have addressed these, which set the scene for the recent renaissance in leadership development. We will conclude by discussing what leadership development shares with the reform movements.

We will argue that leadership development is a valuable corrective to a dangerous imbalance in the nature of management education. Management education has its long-standing critics on both sides of the Atlantic. Very early on, Henry Mintzberg (1976) argued that it was too 'analytical', emphasizing quantitative analysis at the expense of softer skills—narrow left-brain analysis more than holistic right-brain creativity. More recently, Grey and Mitev (1995) have argued that management education is too 'technocratic'. It simply buys into the existing technical specialisms and professional silos of management without addressing (a) how they should be integrated in a real organizational context and (b) the social and ethical consequences of technocracy. In between these two sets of criticisms, Hayes and Abernathy (1980) took Mintzberg's view further, laying the relative decline of the 1970s US economy at the overly quantitative, overly specialized, doors of management education. They blame economists and accountants for the short-term thinking in Western developed countries, which reduces investment in necessary long-term research and development and long-term international marketing strategies which are sensitive to non-Western cultures and their very different business systems. This is a technocratic argument to defeat a technocratic bias in management education: it claims that if Western management education encourages a longer-term view of investment and a wider, deeper appreciation of other cultures, their values, and strategic business development, then Western countries will halt economic decline and head towards sustainable growth.

Criticisms, like those discussed above, have been consistent over the last three decades and there have been periodic attempts to reform management education, the latest of which involves the recent renaissance in leadership research and development. We would argue that these reform movements have been partial and have sometimes even perpetuated or intensified the very forms of analytical technocracy they were intended to change. We will conclude by suggesting ways in which the leadership reform movement can avoid these pitfalls and draw lessons from the past.

The 1980s' Reform Movement 1: The Turn to Competency

The 1980s were a period in which reformers of management education began to emphasize the idea of 'competency'. Rather than analytical skills and techniques, they wanted to develop managers' actual ability to do things and to do them to certain standards of performance. The emphasis was on 'softer skills' such as interpersonal influencing, networking, agenda-shaping, negotiating—the kinds of skills that researchers like Henry Mintzberg had seen managers doing in the workplace. These skills could not be seen in the traditional academic forms of assessment, such as exams, tests, essays. And they could not necessarily be seen by academics who were divorced from the real world but could be seen by managers who lived in the real world, trading on their tacit knowledge and know-how.

The competency movement generated new ways of thinking about management, not simply emphasizing what an individual *knew*—subject specialist 'head knowledge' such as quantitative technique, legal knowledge, historical knowledge—but emphasizing what an individual was competent to *do*. Competence was not just knowledge about something, but knowledge of how to do something to a certain standard of performance in the workplace, recognized by others who could do that too. This engaging idea added a focus within management education upon the outcomes achieved by applying knowledge in practice. It emphasized that the ability to put knowledge to work depended upon soft skills—influencing, persuading, networking—which were not officially taught in business schools but were only an incidental by-product in some cases.

This then encouraged educators and developers to produce classifications of competencies through the application of occupational psychology's techniques, which became widely used in the 1980s to disseminate the competency idea through management education and development systems. However, critics of the competency movement have pointed out that the psychometric instruments on which such classifications were based, tended to be just as individualizing and technocratic as previous approaches. In effect they substituted one form of technocracy with another, arguably even more pernicious form. The net result was that the 'competent manager' was viewed as an identikit individual, whose competence at specific performative tasks could be easily assessed by trained psychologists. What was missing was any sense of how such managers could and should work together in teams, or collectively run a company, or deal with the moral and cultural challenges of management and the huge orchestral work of pulling many disparate contributions together into effective streams of organizational action and achievement (Burgoyne, 1989).

The 1990s' Reform Movement 2: The Practical Turn

Exponents of the competency movement sought to place new emphasis upon the *practice* of management. This theme, which has continued into the 1990s, connects to socially situated learning theory and community of practice theory. However, unlike the competency movement's reliance on psychology's techniques for producing classifications of individual competency against which to assess individual standards of competence, socially situated learning theory emphasized the real working contexts in which people practised their skills. This approach drew upon anthropology rather than psychology, and produced many detailed case studies of people learning in concert with each other, ranging from how a team of US naval quartermasters navigated ship to how Xerox photocopier technicians shared their tacit knowledge of the machines they had to service. In our own work (Fox *et al.*, 2001) we heard how junior lawyers learned from experienced case lawyers and senior partners in the firm; how architects 'graduated' from designing parts of building to designing whole buildings and how clergymen and women moved from running a small parish to co-ordinating a whole diocese.

Alternative forms of management education became increasingly popular which drew upon the detailed analysis of how communities of working people learn in practice with each other. For example, 'practice-based education' as it is found at Northeastern University and 'learning community' approaches as they have been developed at Lancaster and MIT.

Like the competency movement, the turn to practice responded to the criticisms of management education; that it was too abstract, too analytical, too technocratic, and like all formal education, *decontextualized* from the concrete material and social situations in which managers and other practical people have to live and act (Fox, 1997). It was pointed out that formal management education and development was merely the tip of a learning iceberg. Most learning takes place in the occupational world, in practical circumstances, hidden from the bright lights of the classroom and the rational debate of teachers and their students. The competency classifications developed by occupational psychologists were now seen as being themselves too abstract and insufficiently sensitive to infinitely varied, practical social contexts.

The *practical turn* is driven less by new psychometrics of individual competence or skill, and more by a new respect for the messy, confusing, morally challenging, practical world of management. Its consequence for management researchers and teachers is that they should spend more time out 'in the field' studying and understanding management practices in context (Fox, 1997). As a consequence their educational philosophies and designs are beginning to take management action and practices as the starting point of the educational process, rather than the end point.

New Century: New Learning—The Leadership Renaissance

Nowhere is managerial work more technically complex and morally challenging and contextually bound than it is for those in leadership positions at various levels within organizations. It is in these management positions that 'soft skills' are arguably most needed and that the challenge of enhancing performance is most keenly felt. The growing literature on leadership, discussed elsewhere within this text, has focused on the interactions of individual leaders within their organizations and social contexts. This notion of context could be said to differentiate 'leadership' from 'management' development and provide the focus for effective organizational capacity building.

Within the organizational context effective development has the potential to expand the collective capacity of organizational members to engage in leadership roles and processes. Peter Drucker (1995), in his text *Managing in Times of Great Change*, has highlighted the stark nature of organizational change that is all pervasive:

In the traditional organization of the last one hundred years—the skeleton or internal structure was a combination of rank and power. In the emerging organization, it has to be mutual understanding and responsibility.

This shift from hierarchy and power is related to the phenomenon of post-bureaucracy in which the specialized technocratic elites which used to control the formal structures of organizations and formal management education, is giving ground to emerging, often informal, communities and networks of knowledgeable practitioners. It is within such changing organizational contexts that twenty-first-century leaders will practise and refine their leadership skills, and that we, as management educators, will be tasked to produce future leaders and to understand their impact.

For management schools like ours at Lancaster, strong partnerships with organizations and engagement with their strategic development plans offer a partnership approach to leadership development in which business leaders, researchers, and teachers all work together in a concerted way. We are involved in running the *Centre for Excellence in Leadership,* which provides leaders and managers in educational institutions such as universities and colleges with development programmes and leadership research findings and we are rapidly developing this approach across both the public and private sectors.

Our work with individual leaders in the development of their interpersonal skills and abilities is set within broader complex interactions between specific leaders and their socially organized environment. We approach leadership as a social process that is engaged with the broader community in which it is situated and contextualized.

This is in contrast with the growing academic literature on leadership which has repeated many of the characteristics of the literature on management competencies, namely producing lists of 'excellent leadership qualities' and identifying the possible characteristics of 'charismatic leaders'.[1] The search for excellent or charismatic individual leaders resonates with the myths of heroic rugged individualism which traditional formal management education transmits. However, the turn to practice has shown how many apparently individual achievements are actually sustained by shifting communities of practice in which newcomers not only learn from old-timers but also invent and innovate and challenge traditional practices at speeds which traditional management hierarchies are ill-suited to keeping up with. Such rapidly shifting social networks and communities of practice are not led by individual technical experts, the heroic geniuses of the past, but are characterized by 'distributed leadership', a post-heroic form of leadership for an emergent post-bureaucratic world.

Conclusion

In our view, management education has suffered by being overly individualistic, abstract, analytical, and technocratic at the expense of developing the interpersonal, human, social, cultural, political, and ethical understandings relevant to the appliance of techniques in the practical, material, social, and moral world. Mintzberg, Grey, and Mitev and other critics, have a point here. The renaissance in leadership studies and leadership development, we believe is useful in exposing the actual complexity of the material social world in which managers move. Leaders are often singular but effective leaders mobilize complex social and material networks and leadership is distributed within such networks in ways which do not follow a neat hierarchical formal chain of command. More research is needed, and research should focus on particular contexts, specific sectors of business, with their own in-built, deeply structured moral–political dilemmas, which vary hugely (from say health and education institutions at one extreme to the energy and defence industry at the other).

In our view, leadership research needs to address the problems of leadership in context, examining the complex social, gendered, raced, ethical, and cultural political relations between leaders and led, and providing detailed insider-accounts of the work and practices of leading, following, and acting in practice. We believe that academics have a legitimate role in addressing such issues and nowhere more so than in business and management schools, which should not be confined to the simple role of technical training school in the absence of these concerns.

Note

1. We are indebted to David and Margaret Collinson for this observation.

References

Bougoyne, J. G. (1989). 'Creating the Managerial Portfolio: Building on Competency Approaches to Management Education'. *Management Education and Development*, 20, 1: 56–61.

Champy, J. (1995). *Reengineering Management: The Mandate for Leadership*. New York: HarperCollins.

Drucker, P. (1988). 'The coming of the new organization' *Harvard Business Review*, January-February.

Drucker, P. (1995). *Managing in Times of Great Change*. New York: Penguin Books.

Edvisson, L. and Malone, M. S. (1996). *Intellectual Capital*. New York: HarperCollins.

Goffe, R. and Jones, G. *The Character of a Corporation*. New York.

Grey, C. and Mitev, N. (1995). 'Management Education: A Polemic.' *Management Learning*, 26, 1: 73–90.

Fox, S. (1997). 'From Management Education and Development to the Study of Management Education.' In J. G. Burgoyne and M. Reynolds (eds.), *Management Learning: Integrating Perspectives in Theory and Practice*. London: Sage.

Fox, S., Dewhurst, F. B., Eyres, J., and Vickers, D. (2001). *The Nature and Quality of Management and Leadership in the Professions*. London: Council for Excellence in Management and Leadership.

Hayes, R. H. and Abernathy, W. J. (1980). 'Managing our Way to Economic Decline.' *Harvard Business Review*, July–August: 67–77.

Mintzberg, H. (1976). 'Planning on The Left side and Managing on The Right', *Harvard Business Review*, July/Aug: 49–58.

16

What will Tomorrow's Organization/ Company look like over the Next Couple of Decades?

Val Gooding

One thing that will remain constant is that business starts and ends with the customer, but exceeding customer expectations and keeping customers will become more challenging.

The successful companies will be those where strategy is based on change and continuous improvement. They will carry out constant research among their customers and act upon it. They will make change stimulating instead of something to resist. They will also put more trust in their employees to think on their feet and apply individual solutions.

The rate of change, however, is increasing because of a number of factors:

- The changing view of the business organization: is its primary role to generate profit in the interests of its shareholders; or has it more complex responsibilities to a host of 'stakeholders', including its employees, its customers, and the community?
- Increasing customer expectations.
- Increased regulation in many industries.
- Globalization brings more opportunities—and more competition.
- Demographics: The over sixties already outnumber the under sixteens and some say we will have to work into our seventies. Over the next ten years, ninety million of the population of Europe will be over the age of sixty. The 'grey' worker is becoming more important as baby-boomers age.
- Technology is affecting work patterns fundamentally. IT may encourage more people to stay at work beyond normal retirement age, and will offer more home-working opportunities.
- Continual improvements in technology and communications will call for non-stop innovation to retain competitive advantage. Capital investment will increase because resources will need constant updating.
- The internet will become the natural point of entry for many more customers and organizations will no longer have to be on a huge scale in order to access global connections.

- The concept of the corporate citizen will be much more powerful. Society will demand of all companies that they contribute to the communities where they do business.
- For the next generation, flexibility will be more important as more people will work in small companies—99 per cent of UK businesses in 2001 employed fewer than fifty people.

Competitive pressures will mean a greater emphasis than ever before on capturing competitive advantage. Focus on reducing costs will lead to greater outsourcing. There will be more SMEs as a proportion of total business enterprises, and the concept of a job or career for life fades further. Organizational structures will be less dependent on location, and more on fast and reliable communication between far-flung work units. More people will have no fixed office base, using hot-desking, the car, or the home, as alternatives. The average 'life-span' of companies will drop, as better data and communication encourages more start-ups but a more punishing environment for companies which no longer have a competitive edge. De-regulation and de-nationalization across more industries and markets will accelerate growth. Service sectors will continue to grow at the expense of heavy industry, putting more emphasis on the value of knowledge and intellectual property as opposed to physical labouring skills and heavy machinery. Loss of job security will be off-set by more freedom, more opportunities, and more flexibility to switch industries or countries in pursuit of a career.

But in my view, in the developed countries, there is one issue above all others that is putting, and will continue to put, pressure on managers to change their priorities and behaviour and that is the shortage of suitably qualified labour.

In the past, many businesses have responded to pressure from organized labour in how they conduct their employee relations.

In some companies, whole swathes of middle managers have devoted their entire careers to 'managing' the relations with trade unions. Traditional union power is waning, but in its place a much more complex challenge is emerging.

How to attract, retain, and motivate the best employees in an increasingly constrained labour market? In a market where, for the best people, the prospect of perfect job mobility means that, if their expectations are not met, they can leave and find new employment immediately.

In the health and care industry, where my own company, BUPA, operates, this challenge is already acute. There is a serious shortage of healthcare professionals in most Western nations. The future existence of health and care businesses is absolutely dependent on their ability to staff their facilities. Where are the doctors, nurses, carers, and managers of the twenty-first century going to come from? And if we have them, how do we keep them?

As employees change, asserting their bargaining power as a scarce resource, so the role and style of management will need to change too. The role of management and the job of managers is going to have to take more account of employees and their needs, and not simply their needs at work. In a tight labour market, employees can demand that attention is paid not just to their job and working conditions, but also to how that job fits in with their family and social life outside work. Employers may regard this as unreasonable, but at their peril: people will switch jobs to an employer who is more interested and sympathetic.

How will the Role of Management Change?

The key change in the role of management will be the need to respond positively to the changing demography of the workforce, and to the new power exerted by a scarce labour resource.

In some industries, the recruitment problems have been partially solved by exporting jobs, for example electronic processing or call centre work being undertaken in India. In other sectors, businesses have imported people—a process which has been going on for decades in the UK, but which is a growing trend in health and care, where our health services are now to a certain extent dependent on imported labour: doctors, nurses, carers, and other healthcare professionals.

Despite the necessity of using the import/export solutions for certain circumstances, most employers will continue to be faced with the challenge of recruiting, retaining, and motivating their workforce. Economists might argue that wages will be forced up in a constrained labour market, but in my experience, at the practical level, it's not always the highest paying employer who is the most successful in the long run. Of course, pay needs to be in the ball park of market rates for the sector, but managers will need to be much more ingenious at deploying other tools to get the best people.

Those managers who are cleverest at anticipating and responding to employee needs will be the winners. There are several factors at work here, and in our company the following are becoming more and more prevalent.

Work/Life Balance

More and more people are saying they want a balance between their working life and their home life. Young people entering the workforce want more of a rounded lifestyle than the generation that preceded them. They don't see a successful career as being the ultimate goal, and many people are now valuing time more highly than money. This has huge implications for managers. Flexible working, whether it be part-time, annualized hours, at home, term-time only, or other patterns, is becoming more common everywhere. Sabbatical leave, career breaks, longer parental leave, more holidays in lieu of a pay rise, all are becoming more common.

And while it may be essential to offer some element of flexible working in order to remain competitive in the recruitment market, there can be significant problems in achieving coverage of the workload, as well as fairness for all employees. One well-known airline found itself cancelling services this summer because it had offered too many part-time contracts to its cabin crew. And in our health sector, where care has to be delivered on Bank Holidays, at Christmas, and through the night, someone has to work those shifts.

Life is no longer simple for managers who have to respond to the demand for work/life balance, but who have to balance that demand with the needs of customers for reliable delivery of a service or product.

Communication/Involvement

Where once employees expected to be told what to do without too much explanation, now our twenty-first-century people expect to know the *why* as well as the *what* in the duties they perform. And, as in the education system and in family life, young people expect to be involved and consulted on decisions affecting their jobs. They are hungry for information to help them understand their roles better, and they want access to all levels within an organization. E-mail enables even the most junior employee to communicate directly with the Chief Executive—a genuine 'flattening' of the traditional hierarchy.

This need to communicate and involve has big implications for how managers spend their time. Being 'out there', alongside customers and employees, will be the only way to manage effectively. The days of being shut away in an office handling paperwork are over. And communication is becoming much more two-way. Managers who are always on 'broadcast' and never on 'receive' will fail. Listening is becoming an essential part of the skill set, and one which may take up more and more of a manager's time.

Personalization

In the same way as consumers expect personalized service, employees are expecting a more personal approach from their managers. Where once, people accepted being 'led', as one of a large body of people, all being treated the same, all directed in the same way, a model based on the military, now they expect to be treated as an individual. This means being interested in the lifestyle and external issues for employees, as well as their job or career-related needs. Again, a time-consuming task for managers, where the old expectation that people should not bring their problems to work is disappearing.

Job design and training will need to reflect the talents and qualifications of individuals, rather than the 'one size fits all' which prevails today. No longer will people accept being managed as one of a number. They will want and demand one-to-one relationships with managers, and will see this as a right. Opportunities for training and development will be actively sought, and the concept of life-long learning will distinguish the good organizations from the average. Personal growth, which is receiving more and more attention as an important part of people's lives, will need to be facilitated and delivered by managers in the workplace.

Incentives

Rewards and incentives will play a more important role in twenty-first-century management. The need for continuous improvement, the competition to meet customers' ever-increasing expectations, and the pressure to out-perform, will encourage a reward culture, in which individuals and teams are incentivized to succeed. Incentives can be 'fun' tokens, rather than necessarily financially based: a night out at the pizza restaurant, or an extra-special party at Christmas, have in my experience often been very effective as rewards or 'thank-yous'. Managing in a reward culture is more complex. Ensuring that the incentive system is fair, relevant, and motivational is a vitally important part of a manager's role. A failed incentive scheme is worse than no scheme at all.

Meaning

In our experience at BUPA, more and more employees are seeking something more than just earning a living when they go to work. Expectations of companies are changing. More new recruits are asking about our policies on social responsibility, on diversity, on ethics, and on the environment.

People want to identify with the values of their organization, and to feel proud of what it stands for. Equally, people want to feel that they and their organization are doing something worthwhile, something which gives a meaning to their job, a reason to get up and go to work every morning. And the organization must live up to the values and purpose it espouses, otherwise dissonance and cynicism creep in, and ultimately disillusioned people leave (or worse, they stay, under-perform, moan, and infect others!).

The need to do work which has meaning will become increasingly important in the affluent societies of the twenty-first century, and in my view it will be just as important for the most senior executives as it will be for their more junior colleagues. We are all becoming more choosy, as we can afford to be. So managing people well needs to include being able to articulate, and personify, the values and purpose of the organization. It is relatively straightforward for us here at BUPA. What we do is health and care, and our vision is encapsulated in eight words: 'Taking care of the lives in our hands'. It's our goal, and the 'lives in our hands' includes our employees, as well as customers and patients. We know that our people identify with this goal, and are proud of what they do to contribute to it. But even in organizations where the 'meaning' is harder to express, managers must distil the essence of their business and be able to explain it in a motivational way. It may be obvious, or obscure, but it is vital for attracting employees in the twenty-first-century.

A Healthy Workforce

The incidence of stress in the workplace is reaching epidemic proportions, and in the UK days lost to business through stress-related absence are second only to those related to back pain. As a company actively engaged in occupational health, BUPA works with employers to try and ensure that all reasonable steps are taken to avoid stress in the workplace, and to help employees when stress becomes too much to handle. Avoiding 'burn-out' is going to be critical for companies. Making the workplace professional and orderly yet friendly and caring is essential, and this delicate equilibrium needs constant attention if it is not to get out of kilter.

All of the above are about making your organization 'a good place to work'. In that context, the climate in an office or shop or hospital is critical in achieving the 'feel-good' atmosphere which encourages top performance. The way senior executives and managers behave, their openness, friendliness, optimism, and professionalism are in my opinion hugely under-estimated in creating the right culture in an organization. And this leads directly to the question of management style.

How will Management Style Change?

The 'command and control' culture is dying. In order to cope with the demands from employees, managers will need to be highly skilled communicators. Empathy and listening skills will be key. Sensitivity, a tolerant temperament, and excellent influencing skills will be more important than pure intelligence or even industry knowledge. The manager will become much more of a coach, positioned alongside rather than above his team, working with them, acknowledging their concerns, ideas, and aspirations. Being a great motivator will be important, as well as having the skills to improve the performance of those whose contribution is not up to scratch. Managers will be judged on their staff turnover as well as on their sales figures. All this will take up more time.

So do we need more managers? No, because the digital age means that many organizations have been able to flatten their management structures, as electronic reporting of business data eliminates layers of the hierarchy. However, we will need *better* managers, and will need to train and educate them differently. The personality profile of successful managers will change, emphasizing empathy and sensitivity in particular. Management training and education will need to focus much more on developing behavioural skills, and attempting through work experience attachments, case studies, and role plays to provide sufficient 'live' experience of challenging management problems. Managers will need to be more adept at handling ambiguity, and making trade-offs between competing stakeholder interests (for example, time off for employees versus next-day delivery for customers). Some of those who might traditionally have sought a management career may no longer be suitable candidates.

Business will continue to be a race, in which the fittest and leanest are winners and the weakest fall by the wayside. In the twenty-first century, the businesses with the best adapted and most highly evolved managers will win. The competition for the best people will be so intense, that no competent employee will have to put up with a sub-standard job or boss. Managing this shifting balance of power in a way which meets the needs of all stakeholders is one of the highest priorities for business in the twenty-first century.

Index